I CALL

TO

REMEMBRANCE

I CALL TO REMEMBRANCE

TOYO SUYEMOTO'S YEARS OF INTERNMENT

Edited by Susan B. Richardson

Rutgers University Press
NEW BRUNSWICK, NEW JERSEY, AND LONDON

Library of Congress Cataloging-in-Publication Data
Suyemoto, Toyo, 1916–2003.

I call to remembrance : Toyo Suyemoto's years of internment / edited by Susan B. Richardson.

p. cm.

Includes bibliographical references.

ISBN-13: 978-0-8135-4071-9 (hbk. : alk. paper)

ISBN-13: 978-8135-4072-6 (pbk. : alk. paper)

1. Suyemoto, Toyo, 1916–2003. 2. Central Utah Relocation Center. 3. Japanese Americans—Evacuation and relocation, 1942–1945. 4. World War, 1939–1945—Concentration camps—Utah—Topaz. 5. World War, 1939–1945—Personal narratives, American. 6. Japanese Americans—Biography. I. Richardson, Susan B., 1936– II. Title.

D769.8.A6S89 2007

940.53'1779245—dc22

[B] *2006032246*

A British Cataloging-in-Publication record for this book is available from the British Library

TEXT DESIGN AND COMPOSITION BY JENNY DOSSIN
Manufactured in the United States of America

For Toyo

I call to remembrance my song in the night;
I commune with mine own heart; and my spirit made diligent search.

Psalm 77:6

CONTENTS

EDITOR'S PREFACE

Preparing the manuscript of Toyo Suyemoto's camp memoir for publication has been a labor not just of love but of joy and dismay as well: joy that Toyo's unique poetic and prosaic responses to her World War II internment will now be accessible to readers; dismay at the facts of the incarceration. I discovered that with each new account I read of the unprecedented removal and incarceration of thousands of people and the more times I encountered the same detailed litany of their humiliation and suffering, my dismay intensified; familiarity did not provide numbing.

My editing task consisted primarily of merging and organizing the several versions Toyo had left of her memoir. One major editorial decision that I considered was the addition of a chapter on the Topaz Public Library, which was important to Toyo both in camp and afterward. Toyo had elsewhere written an account of the formation and use of the camp library, but it did not appear with the other memoir chapters in the loose-leaf notebook of work she had entrusted to me. Only later did I discover among her papers in the Special Collection at Ohio State a prospectus of chapters indicating she herself had planned a library chapter after all.

I made a few changes in the order of the chapters although I was careful to maintain the chronological flow of the narrative. I also eliminated the numerous repetitions that had crept into chapters written over a number of years, tightened some sentences and paragraphs, reined in the generous use of hyphens and commas, and occasionally substituted one word for another, choosing words that Toyo herself used. For example, in certain places I changed the word "center" to "camp" to make clear that the reference was to Topaz, not to an entity within the camp. Otherwise and in all, the memoir is Toyo's.

The terms *Nisei* and *Issei,* used throughout the memoir, quickly become recognizable, and they are italicized only on the first use. Other Japanese terms, used infrequently though repeated in some cases, are italicized throughout. When Toyo used a Japanese term or phrase, she glossed it in a following parenthesis; occasionally a gloss is repeated in a later chapter. For the ease of the reader, I have not eliminated these repetitions.

Toyo was primarily a poet, and she embedded numerous poems written during or about the internment in her memoir. I have included other poems, not limited to those from the camp experience, in my introduction, and I have added some poems between chapters in the memoir itself. These can be recognized as the editor's additions by the presence of a date at the end of the poem.

The pen-and-ink drawings come from the margins of the Topaz Public Library guest book, which now resides in the Suyemoto Special Collection at the Ohio State University Libraries in Columbus, Ohio. The drawings have not been published before, and efforts to attribute them to their artist have so far been unsuccessful. It is tempting to think they were done by Toyo's artist father, although there are reasons to doubt it and nothing solid to validate the idea.

There are numerous people who have contributed to this presentation of Toyo's work, and I am very grateful for their various kinds of help. My Otterbein College colleague and friend, English professor James R. Bailey, first introduced me to Toyo. Over the years, Jim shared concert and theater subscriptions with Toyo and so helped her fulfill a promise made to her son. In adopting a kind of familial role, he also periodically prodded, even chided Toyo to keep working on her memoir. Jim has been unstintingly supportive of this project and has provided wise suggestions, corrections, photos, and—as Toyo's executor—permission to use all of the material in the special library collection. For all of that, I give him my heartfelt thanks for making my job easier and the results better. Maureen H. Donovan, associate professor and Japanese studies librarian at the Ohio State University Libraries, has been extremely helpful in making available the materials in the Suyemoto Special Collection; it was she who first pointed out to me the library guest book with its pen-and-ink drawings of camp life. Karin Higa, senior curator of art and director of curatorial and exhibitions at the Japanese American National Museum, graciously gave her time in trying to identify the artist of the guest book drawings. I am abundantly appreciative also, for the guidance and helpful suggestions of Jane Beckwith of the Topaz Museum in Delta, Utah, and for her photograph of the shell brooch given to Toyo by her Issei student. Toyo's nephew, John Kidd, has generously tracked down and shared family photographs of Toyo and her son, Kay, for inclusion in the book, and I thank him very much for his gift of time and effort in unearthing the photo albums. Michael Tangeman, professor of Japanese at Denison University, kindly checked the accuracy of the translations for the numerous Japanese phrases and terms contained in the book. Working with editors at Rutgers University Press has been wonderfully instructive and thoroughly enjoyable, and I should like especially to thank Kendra Boileau and Nicole Manganaro for all their help and good advice in guiding the manuscript through its stages of publication. My thanks also go to freelance editor Karen Johnson, whose cheerful and meticulous attention to the manuscript amended my textual slips and oversights. Finally, thanks to Jenny Dossin whose design for the book would have delighted Toyo.

I am immensely grateful for the financial support that has come from the California Civil Liberties Public Education Program (CCLPEP). This program was created through legislation by the California legislature in 1998 with the goal to fund projects that will educate the public so that this regrettable episode in American history will not be forgotten. The CCLPEP grant has made possible the inclusion of the guest book drawings and work by other Topaz artists in the memoir. My particular appreciation goes to Elaine G. Yamaguchi, program director, and Trina Dangberg King, program associate for the CCLPEP, while Patrick Hayashi, a member of the CCLPEP advisory committee, has my special thanks for shepherding my application through the approval process. I am also enormously appreciative of the collegial encouragement from the English Department at Denison University and of the gracious help from Anneliese Davis, the department secretary, who always knew how to smooth my way.

Finally, as in all my life projects, my husband, Dominick Consolo, has been my mainstay, always providing, as needed, the appropriate support for each task at hand, whichever one was current of the many and varied kinds of professional and personal demands that were part of this joyful project. I thank him with all my heart.

NOTE ON THE DRAWINGS

Toyo Suyemoto was camp librarian at the Topaz Public Library during the final years of her internment, and the pen-and-ink drawings included in *I Call to Remembrance* come from the margins of a guest book for visitors to the library. The drawings, published here for the first time, are not signed, and efforts to identify the artist have so far been unsuccessful. The images provide a counterpoint narrative to that of the memoir, juxtaposing the artist's visual rendering of life in Topaz with Suyemoto's written account.

Like Toyo's prose, the spare line drawings carry an understated tone as they document common camp activities. Initial scenes show internees struggling with or searching for their baggage and watching their belongings being tossed unceremoniously into the back of a truck–a testament to the massive uprooting that has taken place. In other scenes, people are trying to settle into camp —planting trees, gathering coal for the barracks stoves, scrounging wood (probably to construct rough tables and stools for their unfurnished barracks rooms), hanging up laundry, and carrying trays of food from the mess-hall. Little children go to school; students go to the library. For pastime, people read books or papers, the Issei take their walking sticks into the desert, women knit or sew, and some internees tap at the typewriter–perhaps writing for the *Topaz Times*. Still, boredom characterizes life in camp, and in one scene we see a solitary man lying back amidst bottles strewn about the floor. Other drawings record the indignities of camp in a matter-of-fact manner similar to Toyo's descriptions of camp life: the crowded barracks, the assaults from ferocious dust storms, the need to lug pails and dirty clothing to the distant laundry room, as well as to don robes and *geta* (wooden clogs) and pack towels and toothbrushes for the bedtime trek to the communal latrine. Other depictions introduce a quiet humor in their critique of camp conditions: for example, there is a man shown eating (an apparently indigestible meal), then making tracks to the outhouse (a symbolic but not an authentic camp building); another drawing shows a couple who are sporting their newly-acquired and very much oversized government-issue coats. Certain other drawings even manage, in a few strokes, to illustrate the distinctions in life style between the Issei and Nisei generations that emerged and were exacerbated by the conditions of life in the camp.

The guest book is now part of the Toyo Suyemoto Special Collection in the Rare Books and Manuscripts Library of the Ohio State University Libraries. The publication of the drawings is made possible by a grant from the California Civil Liberties Public Education Program.

INTRODUCTION

Toyo Suyemoto—poet, librarian, Nisei internee #13423—frequently spoke to groups about her World War II removal from the West Coast and internment in Topaz, the Central Utah Relocation Center.[1] Despite her small stature and soft voice, she commanded a riveted attention from her listeners whether they were schoolchildren, college students, colleagues, or a community group. Toyo's report on her incarceration was forthright, yet remarkable for its absence of bitterness, its avoidance of accusation. While under no illusions about the losses she had suffered, most grievously the loss of her only son, she refused the role of victim and, instead, exemplified those characteristics modeled by her parents' Issei generation of *shikata ga nai* (acceptance of what must be) and *gaman* (calm endurance, perseverance in the face of adversity). Her manner disarmed and charmed her audiences; her message appalled them.

She began speaking about the camp experience in the early 1970s and, like others of her Nisei generation, took it as a personal duty to tell her story so that the calamitous injustice imposed on the Japanese community after Pearl Harbor—principally motivated, as the U.S. government finally acknowledged, by "racial prejudice, wartime hysteria, and a failure of political leadership"[2]—would not be repeated. Writer Yoshiko Uchida, one of Toyo's high school students in camp, expresses this sense of obligation in her novel, *Journey to Topaz:* "I hope by reading this book young people everywhere will realize what once took place in this country and will determine never to permit such a travesty of justice to occur again" (Uchida 1971, viii). *I Call to Remembrance* is Toyo Suyemoto's testimony to that experience and her commitment to that goal.

Toyo Suyemoto's Life

Toyo Suyemoto was born on January 14, 1916, in Oroville, California, and grew up in Sacramento's *Nihonmachi* (Japan town), where the Japanese language flourished and where stores sold Japanese remedies, Japanese cosmetics, and bamboo cutlery. Her father, Tsutomu Howard Suyemoto, had come to the United States as a teenager for his education shortly after the turn of the century, during the height of Japanese immigration, and her mother, Mitsu Hyakusoku Suyemoto, followed him after a long, ten-year engagement. Toyo was always quick to point out that her mother was not a picture bride and that she had become engaged to Tsutomu before he left Japan. Toyo was their first child, named after her two grandmothers, whose first names were Toshi and Yone. Toyo tells us that her mother gave her sisters Japanese names—Hisa, Mae, and Masa—while her father chose English names for the boys: William, Howard, Joe, Roy, and Lee (and Benjamin and Franklin for the twin boys who did not survive infancy).

Like many Issei, Toyo's parents believed education to be the key to full membership in American society, and they emphasized the importance of education to their children, providing them a home filled with books and art. Her father had earned degrees in mining engineering from the universities of Nevada and California, Berkeley, but unable, as a Japanese, to find a job in that field, he became an insurance salesman. Toyo writes that in the Japanese community "he also served as an interpreter for other Issei when they had to consult a doctor or a lawyer" (qtd. in Harth 2001, 24). Her artistic father enjoyed gardening and painting; when the family was uprooted from home to the camp, he found a place for his paints in the limited baggage allowed. Toyo's mother, from a samurai family, graduated from normal school, making her unusually well-educated for a woman of her time. She read widely in literature and philosophy, and out of what Toyo reported to be her phenomenal memory she would recite poetry and drama to her children. One time she surprised Toyo by reciting the whole of the "To be or not to be" soliloquy from *Hamlet* in Japanese. While her mother spoke limited English, she nonetheless completely understood her children—including their slang—and was never at a loss in directing her children's education.

Though her mother might refer to the children as her *yabanjin* (barbarians), both parents supported their Americanization. They sent the children to the farther Baptist church, rather than to the Buddhist temple across from their house, in order for them to receive the stricter discipline offered by the Baptists. Toyo liked to recall that her mother's diligence in getting them out of bed and ready to go Sunday mornings resulted in the children's perfect Sunday school attendance. Her father, insisting that they learn to speak English free of accent, declined to send them to Japanese school. Toyo regularly expressed her deep admiration for her parents—her gentle, artist father who showed her how to appreciate beauty in art and nature, and her strong, wise mother who guided their large family, first, through the struggles of life in prewar California and, thereafter, through the wrenching dislocation of the war years. She was Toyo's exemplar of *gaman,* the subject of numerous of her poems, and a strong figure in her memoir. Her mother's family crest was the butterfly, and Toyo identified herself with the butterfly, choosing note cards and jewelry with a butterfly motif and pointing out the cross-cultural nature of the butterfly, which signifies happiness in Asian art and resurrection in Western religion. From time to time, Toyo would lament her failure (as she perceived it) to match her mother's strength and wisdom. To her friends, however, Toyo was herself the model of an honorable, humane, and tough spirit who met more than her fair share of loss and grief with grace.

Toyo completed the two years at Sacramento Junior College in 1935, where English professor Richard Reeves encouraged her poetry writing. Then, as her siblings also were approaching college age, her father moved the family to Berkeley to facilitate their attendance at "his" university. Toyo graduated from the University of California, Berkeley, in 1937, with a major in English and Latin. She particularly noted the stimulating poetry writing course of Berkeley professor and poet Josephine Miles and remembered with pleasure her Chaucer class with the legendary Bertrand H. Bronson, whose encouragement of Toyo and her writing extended throughout the internment years and beyond. While she was in camp, he prompted her: "Keep your poetry blooming. Water it a little each day" (personal note to editor, June 3, 1993). She often mentioned her correspondence with him and the delight and difficulty associated with a letter that eventually came in the years after the war signed "Bertrand." Even with this permission, she initially found it difficult to use the familiar address for her esteemed Dr. Bronson.

During her years at junior college and university, Toyo became active in the West Coast circle of Nisei writers, regularly contributing poems and essays to the English sections of the vernacular newspapers and literary magazines of the Japanese community. After graduating from UC, Berkeley, Toyo took a job as a live-in housemaid and cook because, she reported, "only menial labor was open for Oriental grads" (conversation with the editor). In 1939, she began graduate work in English at Berkeley, then left her studies to marry Iwao Kawakami, a Nisei journalist and part of the West Coast literary circle. The couple moved to Oakland, California, and in October of 1941, their son, Kay, was born.

Pearl Harbor interrupted their lives and their marriage. In the uncertain and hostile climate that followed in the wake of the Japanese attack, Toyo wanted to rejoin her family in Berkeley, but her husband determined that he would move to San Francisco to be near his newspaper job. On Christmas Eve 1941, the couple agreed to separate. Toyo and baby Kay moved back to Berkeley and, in April 1942, they were evacuated together with her parents and siblings. The couple never reconciled their differences. During the three and a half years of their shared internment in Tanforan and Topaz, Iwao did not visit Toyo or their son, and they were divorced after the war.

As she tells us in her memoir, Toyo was one of the group of college graduates who organized the high school program in Tanforan. She taught English and Latin classes there and again in Topaz, where she also added adult classes in English as a second language for the Issei. At the end of 1943, when the stressful schedule of both day and evening classes began to affect her health, she transferred to working in the Topaz Public Library, an event that led directly to her choice of career.

As the war drew on, a policy of encouraged relocation out of the camp was instituted beginning in 1943 for those who could find a school or a job in the Midwest or East. Bill and Hisa were the first of their family to leave Topaz, he for school in Maryland, she for work in Chicago. Bill soon transferred to school in Cincinnati, and gradually Toyo's other siblings joined him there. Toyo herself decided to stay in camp along with her son, parents, and youngest brother, Lee, until the camp's closing in late October 1945. In the end, they too decided to relocate in Cincinnati rather than return to California because Toyo's mother was determined to keep the family together.

Once in Ohio, Toyo, as the eldest daughter, took on a major share of the household duties, cooking and cleaning for the large family. She noted ruefully that she would complete ironing her father's and brothers' shirts at the end of a week just in time to start over on the next week's batch. She sewed and mended for the family, reversing buttons and—a task she said she hated—patching overalls. To her household duties she soon added employment outside the home as librarian at the University of Cincinnati, first in the College of Nursing and Health, where she worked from 1946 to 1957, and then in the university's periodical room from 1957 to 1959. Later, she became assistant librarian at the Cincinnati Art Museum, where she worked until she returned to graduate school.

Her son, Kay, continued to suffer from severe asthma, the result of living in a contaminated horse stall at the Tanforan Race Track. Even though he never associated with horses, he developed a serious allergy to horse dander and, throughout his three and a half years of incarceration, battled repeated bouts of pneumonia and asthma. In August 1958 at age sixteen, while undergoing a new treatment for his condition, he slumped into a coma from which he never recovered. Out of this devastating loss of her bright, engaging son and companion, Toyo determined that she would fulfill the promises that Kay had exacted of her. Presciently, he had asked his mother to do three things if anything should happen to him: first, return to university for a library degree; second, continue her subscriptions to the symphony and theater, and invite a companion in his place; and, finally—an amazing request from a young son—be happy. As Toyo once wrote, Kay was "a lively and witty—and wise—lad who meant so much to me" (personal note to editor, August 2001). Her son's admonition, perhaps buttressed by the spirit of *gaman* instilled by her parents, seemed to support Toyo in her determination to maintain a positive and cheerful outlook on life.

Honoring Kay's first request, Toyo enrolled at the University of Michigan and completed a Master of Library Science in 1964. She had job offers from libraries in New York City and Toronto, but she decided to locate near her Cincinnati family and accepted a position in Columbus with the Ohio State University libraries. She ultimately became head librarian of the Social Work Library and assistant head of the Education/Psychology Library. As she had retained her married name, she became affectionately known as "Mrs. K." by her colleagues and students. She retired from Ohio State as associate professor emerita of the libraries in 1985. After a period of declining health, Toyo Suyemoto died in her home in Columbus on December 30, 2003.

Toyo Suyemoto, Poet

Toyo named herself poet. She wrote her first poems while still in grade school, and throughout her life she filled her poetry notebooks with completed poems. When as a child she became angry at one of her siblings or upset by some small occurrence, her mother would advise her, "Toyo, turn your tears into poems" (conversation with editor). Lawson Inada called her "our major Camp Poet and Nikkei Poet Laureate" (Inada 1995, 206). Speaking one time to a school group, she called herself "the Nisei Emily Dickinson" (Toyo was a guest speaker at Professor Richardson's Asian American Literature class, Denison University, spring 2000).

From the vantage of age fifty-seven, Toyo informs us that "the writing of poetry, which I began in the fifth grade, has been a primary interest all these years" (Suyemoto 1983, 73). Years earlier, at nineteen, she wrote an article titled "Sic Persona . . . Only a Very Few Could Understand the Workings of Her Lonely Heart . . . ," in which she describes (in third person) her beginnings as a poet: "All her nineteen years, she had been possessed with a sensitive, photographic memory, which proved rather trying at times, but not always." Her article continues:

> Her deep interest in literature led her to creative writing. When she was in the fifth grade she had first experimented in a jingling bit of verse on spring . . . just a gushing juvenile composition. Later in the ninth grade she ventured into verse for the second time, but not effectively. Then months passed, and she transferred to the senior high school, entering as a second-year student. It was during these sophomore semesters that changes took place to impress her writings forcibly . . . and she was but seventeen at this time. (Ellipses in the original, May 13, 1935, clipping from Toyo's scrapbook, newspaper not identified)

By the time Toyo was attending Sacramento Junior College, she had already become part of the energetic literary circle of West Coast Nisei writers who were publishing their work in the English sections of Japanese newspapers and magazines. From 1935 to 1941, Toyo contributed both poetry and prose to these vernacular publications. She wrote two weekly columns: "Potpourri" for the *Hokubei Asahi* of San Francisco and "Medley" for the *Seattle Courier.* During this prolific period, her poetry regularly appeared in various magazines and newspapers, including the *Kashu Mainichi* of Los Angeles; the *Japanese American News* of San Francisco; the *Great Northern Daily* of Seattle; and *Leaves,* a literary magazine in Los Angeles. Throughout 1940 and 1941, *Current Life,* the magazine for the American-born Japanese, edited by James M. Omura, also featured her poems. She published in numerous other American publications, but she was surprised to discover that several of her poems and an essay had also appeared in a bilingual collection of Nisei writings, *American Bungaku,* published in Tokyo in 1938.

The heady prewar literary environment on the West Coast is captured in the scrapbooks that Toyo compiled (and which miraculously survived the war): one scrapbook contains her own published poems and essays, another is filled with clippings of the work of her numerous fellow Nisei writers: Mary "Molly" Oyama, Chiye Mori, Tooru Kanazawa, James Omura, Tosuke Yamasaki, Larry Tajiri, Kay Nishida, Carl K. Sato, Yasuo Sasaki, Dave Tatsuno, and Welly Shibata, to name some of the most prominent. Young, many of them idealistic, these writers gathered to discuss literature and philosophy, corresponded with one another between meetings, published updates of one another's doings, and wrote critiques of one another's work. In print, they self-consciously debated the proper and future role of their generation, sometimes lamenting what they perceived to be Nisei failings. They looked forward to a flowering of the Nisei literati, to the first Nisei novel, and to their own maturity when their place in literature would be assured.

The scrapbook is filled with clippings from the vernacular press that make attributions to Toyo like "the leading Nisei poetess" ("Review of Nisei Literary Achievemens in 1934," *Hokubei Asahi,* January 1, 1935), a member of the "advance guard of nisei writers" (Larry Tajiri, "Our Literary Nisei," November 5, 1934), or "a rising Nisei literary luminary" ("Toyo Suyemoto, Tad Uyeno, Kaz Oka Visit World-Sun," December 21, 1935). The writer of the *Bay View* even judged her to be "the closest approach to genius among Nisei writers" (August 23, 1936.). An article on Toyo and her poetry by Yama Dorii in the *Japanese American News* begins with the headline "'Beginnings of a Song . . . .': Of Toyo Suyemoto, a Nisei Writer with the Gifts of the Muses . . . Who May Someday Mirror in Magic Poetry the Cry of the Nipponese in America" (ellipses in the original, *Japanese American News,* May 27, 1935). In another column, Jimmy Omura writes, "Invariably when nisei literature is discussed Toyo Suyemoto creeps into the picture. She shares with Chiye Mori the distinction of being the foremost second generation adventuress in verse" (October 25, 1934, clippings in Toyo's scrapbook).

In her own article, "'The Promise of an Early Dawn . . .': Vibrant and Laughing," Toyo addresses a much discussed topic, the role of the Nisei:

> Chiefly in creative writing, the Nisei have disclosed a flexible ability and style. He [*sic*] depends not on acquired Americanisms in thought and verbal

> expression, but on the clear-cut imagery and music directly from his Japanese inheritance of learning. The literature of the Nisei will win, no doubt, a commendable distinction, when the promise of the early dawn has been transmuted into afternoon splendor.
>
> Surely, someday, the difficulties of the Issei and the problems of the Nisei will be reflected in a long poem, a novel or a play. . . . The harvest of the second generation will restore to the first generation the assurance of a far-reaching Japanese-American era. (January 1, 1935, clipping in Toyo's scrapbook)

In their concern for the proper role of their generation, writers criticized what they saw as the Nisei lack of refinement. A July 22, 1935, essay about Nisei culture by "Mignon" contains the subtitles "Average Nisei Writers Are Egotists" and "Nisei Reads Just Frothy Books." And in his column "Drifts," Jimmie Omura wrote:

> One of the most interesting programs attended by this columnist was the Berkeley Fellowship meeting Sunday. Speakers emphasized the Nisei theme. Rather than feeding the audience a lot of blah-blah, . . . this stress upon problems closer to home came as a welcome message.
>
> Talks by John Nagahama, Masao Takeshita, Miss Toyo Suyemoto and "silver-toned" Dave Tatsuno touched upon the various phases of the second generation life. In a measure, there was something significant in each address. Back-slapping, which so often clutters Nisei talks, was missing. In its place there was the blunt crusade against the ills which face the Americans of Japanese ancestry. ("Cliques . . . A New Trend," September 24, 1935, clipping in Toyo's scrapbook)

In the aftermath of the Pearl Harbor attack, the Nisei literary community was scattered, their literary production abruptly suspended. The trauma (and logistics) of the mass removal of all Japanese Americans from the West Coast curtailed not only the publishing, but the very creation of new work by the Nisei writers. Toyo notes that "that spring" of 1942, amidst the traumatic evacuation of her family out of Berkeley to the Tanforan Race Track in San Bruno, California, "my dated poetry notebook shows an abrupt gap in my writing" (Suyemoto 1983, 75). And in the first chapter of her memoir describing the weeks after Pearl Harbor, she writes, "Poetry had been an integral part of me while I was in school, but for some time my writing had dwindled to nothing" ("Berkeley").

Nonetheless, shortly after their second uprooting in the fall of 1942 from the Tanforan center to the permanent camp in Topaz, Utah, camp writers and artists banded together to establish a literary magazine, *Trek*—one of the premier magazines produced in the camps—which provided a venue for poems, essays, stories, and drawings. At the urging of a friend, artist Miné Okubo, Toyo began to write for the magazine. She notes in her memoir, "[Miné's] prompting enabled me to keep writing poetry. The journal provided a needed medium for the creative writers in our camp" ("Into Another Year").

Indeed, poetry played an important role for Toyo as she struggled to survive the internment. The first chapter of the memoir includes several poems written in early 1942, when public opinion had turned ugly and government restrictions were being imposed; these poems, she writes, "expressed the uncertainty I felt" ("Berkeley"). In her preface, she tells us that her poems "written prior to evacuation and during internment were composed in intense reaction to the circumstances of the time"; and later in the memoir, after she has arrived in Topaz, she responds to her own distressed question, "How long are we to be here in this forsaken place?" by writing, "I could not openly speak of the pain I felt or ask the questions that assailed me, and poetry was my outlet" ("Settling In"). In the end, Toyo contributed poems (and an essay) to all three issues of *Trek* and to a final, fourth issue called *All Aboard.*

Not surprisingly, the internment experience profoundly affected the subject and tone of Toyo's poetry. After receiving the June 1943 copy of *Trek,* a friend in Berkeley commented on the change she detected in her writing, saying that the poems in *Trek* "seem a far cry from the way you wrote even two years ago, a kind of ferocity new to your mind" ("Weighed in the Balance"). *I Call to Remembrance* incorporates most of the poems that Toyo wrote during the internment years, including all of the poems published in the camp magazines; these poems exhibit a remarkable intensity of feeling paired with an economy of expression and an edge sharper than much of her earlier, more romantic poetry.

After the war, Toyo began again to publish her work in numerous journals and anthologies. Even before leaving Topaz, she submitted her work to the *Yale Review,* which accepted two poems for the winter 1946 issue. Other poems resulting from the evacuation experience appeared in *Common*

Ground in 1948 and in the anniversary anthology of the Writers League of Greater Cincinnati in 1960.

While in Cincinnati, she became active in the writing group of the American Association of University Women and, from 1951 to 1960, published her work in the group's magazine, the *Crealettre.* Also during this period, she earned admission to selective poetry workshops at the University of Cincinnati, one conducted by Randall Jarrell, another by Karl Shapiro. In graduate school at the University of Michigan during 1963 and 1964, Toyo gave poetry readings and published a series of poems in the 1964 issue of *Crux,* a literary magazine issued by the Ecumenical Campus Staff of the university.

After she settled in Columbus, Ohio, Toyo continued "to keep her poetry blooming." She published poems in numerous small journals as well as in such anthologies as the 1969 *Speaking for Ourselves: American Ethnic Writing,* the 1989 *Longman Anthology of World Literature by Women, 1875–1975,* and the 1996 *Quiet Fire: A Historical Anthology of Asian American Poetry, 1892–1970.*

In 1975, Toyo was honored at the first Asian American Writers Conference in Oakland, California, as one of Thirteen Pioneers to receive the Asian American Writers Award. In her absence, another honoree, Toshio Mori (the short-story writer and Toyo's fellow Topaz internee), accepted the award for her. In the 1990s, she contributed haiku to the fund-raising brochure for establishing the Topaz Museum at Delta, Utah. A 2004 public art installation celebrating poetry's "vibrant and varied presence" in Berkeley, California, included "In Topaz," one of her poems published in the camp magazine, *Trek.* Along with poems from many poets, including Shakespeare, Josephine Miles (Toyo's University of California professor), and Muriel Rukeyser (a poet much admired by Toyo), her poem appears on a sidewalk poetry panel on Berkeley's Addison Street. The poems are collected in *The Addison Street Anthology: Berkeley's Poetry Walk,* edited by Robert Hass and Jessica Fisher. In her later years, she compiled a lifetime collection of poems spanning the years from the 1930s to the 1990s in a manuscript (currently unpublished) entitled "How Small a Whisper."

Toyo Suyemoto's Poetry

Like other ethnic American writers, Toyo Suyemoto inhabited two cultures, and her writing was influenced by both her American experience and her Japanese heritage. Her mother was well versed in Japanese literature and wrote poetry herself. In Japan, Toyo's grandfather would compose a haiku and her mother would add two more lines to make a tanka. Through her mother, Toyo was exposed to classic haiku masters like Matsuo Bashō and Kobayashi Issa, and she often employed Japanese poetic forms, especially the haiku, in her work. She included numerous haiku, tanka, and senryu[3] in her collection "How Small a Whisper." As she writes, "I am always mindful of [my mother's] admonition to treat the haiku or tanka form with respect for their rigorous discipline. I do conform to the syllabic count of 5, 7, 5 for the haiku, and that of 5, 7, 5, 7, 7 for the tanka. According to her, I must set the premise of the poetic thought in the first line (the first five syllables) and add solidity, or descriptive strength, in the following lines, so that the meaning is extended, or defined, by the reader or listener" (Suyemoto 1983, 76). Elsewhere she writes, "In writing the *haiku* and the *tanka* in English, I find the forms demand a discipline at once acerbic and refreshing" (Suyemoto, "Sidelights").

Here are some examples of her poems in Japanese forms.

SENRYU
I drop the paper
I am reading, and see you
Gravely reading me!
(August 1940)

SENRYU
I explored his mind,—
A pleasant hallway that reached,
At last, a closed room.
(October 1940)

HAIKU
The bright moon followed,
But my shadow walked ahead:
I hurried between.
(October 1944)

TANKA
I cast the weighted
Meaning into the clear stream
But catch no response.
Should I flick the wand once more—
Or wait a little longer?
(May 1947)

The next two poems honor the poet's mother.

HAIKU
Crickets tolled the night
As her breath failed; their chiming
Still rings in my mind.

Death held one hand, I
Her other; then gently she
Drew her hand from mine.
(August 1951)

IKEBANA
Triangulated,
Dimensions of my world are
Heaven, man and earth.
(April 1953)

LAST ROSE
One last rose in bloom—
Strange how it brings all of June
Into this small room.
(N.d.)

HAIKU
How perfect the rose
Bowing in final, fragrant
Gesture to autumn.
(October 1959)

Tanka
Could words fall like snow,
Perfect in form and meaning,
My thought would whiten
In multiples of pure praise
The very air about you.
(January 1960)

Haiku
Love held too tightly
Smothers in the fisted hand—
Imprisoned firefly.
(February 1973)

Haiku
This spring moment time
Has placed in my hands is mine—
But not forever.
(March 1982)

Haiku
Soundlessly winds shake
The lilies-of-the-valley
And ring out their scent.
(April 1989)

Haiku
Mortality stares
At me steadily—I smile
And return that gaze.
(May 1993)

Perhaps the practice of writing haiku and tanka influenced her overall preference for the discipline of form in her poetry. She observes, "As much as I enjoy reading what is termed 'free verse,' I write consistently in form: the double quatrain usually, sonnet, rondeau, the haiku or tanka. Over the years I find that my lines have become more compressed, and I use not only a regular rhyme scheme, but also the dissonant rhyme" (Suyemoto 1983, 75). It is not surprising that she was drawn to poets, like Emily Dickinson and Sarah Teasdale, who employed these forms.

Nonetheless, while her Japanese heritage helped shape her subject as well as the form of her poetry, Suyemoto's language is English and her poetic sensibility is essentially American. Her poetry is rooted in her literary studies and nourished by her familiarity with American and British writers. She especially admired Sarah Teasdale, Edna St. Vincent Millay, and Christina Rossetti, and on a list of favored twentieth-century poets appear the names of Langston Hughes, Countee Cullen, Char Hansen, and Louise Bogan. Her primary muse, however, was Emily Dickinson: "Poetry is my observation of the world around me, and through it, I record my impressions. I read, and admire, many of the English and American poets, but it is Emily Dickinson who has had the greatest influence on me" (Suyemoto, "Sidelights").

The influence of Emily Dickinson manifests itself in Suyemoto's partiality to the quatrain and in her employment of near rhyme. More substantively, the poems of Dickinson, like the haiku encountered through her mother, presented Suyemoto with poetic models that combine a simple, compact form with a complex thought or a dense, multilayered impression; the poem places demands upon the reader to meet and match the impression or complete the thought. Some of her most successful poems exhibit this combination of compactness and richness. Here are some examples:

SAND

Time will flow from the scooping hand,
Like microscopic flakes of sand,
Dribbling from palm down to the ground,
Loss whispered in a hasty sound.

It will escape, though fisted tight,
And merge, as darkness blends with light
On edge of dawn, with grains I may
Have held, and spilled, thus yesterday.
(October 1946)

Egg and Stone

The egg, beside a stone,
Bears no comparison:
The wonderment of each
Is more than shape or touch.

The fragile shelters life,
The hard once grew a leaf,
Compelling mind to know
Far more than eyes can see.
    (August 1966)

Time Countermands

Time countermands
Mere nothingness,
For being lends
A simple grace.

Mortality
Bestows and hones
Awareness in
My very bones.
    (August 1979)

Foreshortened

Foreshortened time deludes
    As I have learned to see;
Perspective granted me
    Jests with eternity.

The last remaining strokes
    Of shadows and of light
No Piranesi now
    Could such stark lines repeat.
    (February 1993)

Suyemoto frequently employs the longer, though still disciplined, sonnet form. She chose the sonnet for a number of moving poems written in honor of a person, especially of her mother or her son, Kay. Here is a sonnet that commemorates Anne Frank and another for her son:

Anne Frank

She wept for naked children in the rain,
When dulled by loss, the adults could not weep;
She shivered with quick fear that made flesh creep,
As they marched past in school-room ranks again
To Auschwitz furnaces. Could she explain
How fire burns, or say how gray and deep
The ashes cool, long after nightmares sleep?
She blessed them with her tears and inward pain.

And in the end, when Belsen was a smell
To be endured in shocked intakes of breath,
Her face all eyes, her body wasted thin,
She knew compassion had no strength to tell
The dusk from dawn, and certitude of death
Embalmed the hope that living might have been.
(February 1958)

Birthday

Dear Kay, oh, this was such a day that you
Would glory in—the warm October sun
Bronzing to shiny patina the hue
Of leaves; defiantly the colors run
In spurts through fading flower-beds and blaze
Afresh, till very air can gleam in pure
Dimension, cleared of early drifting haze—
Autumn enchantment visible and sure.

This was a day your senses could acclaim,
When in reflective mood you would assert

This was the proper month to have been born.
Because you once had known and loved the same
Perfection of this season, I advert
To your wise counsel I am not to mourn.[4]
(October 1958)

Suyemoto was pleased by commentary from the British critic David Daiches that validated her reliance upon form. In 1960, Daiches wrote: "I am sure that you are right to employ a certain regularity of stanza: it clearly suits your talent, with its quiet precision and obvious gift for verbal and rhythmic discipline. . . . It is a pleasure to come across a talent both so controlled and so genuine, a use of language at once delicate and firm" (ellipsis in original, quoted in Suyemoto 1983, 75).

In spite of ample provocation for her to do otherwise (and in contrast, perhaps, to the work of some Sansei poets), a scant number of her poems take the racism she suffered as their subject. Very few poems make overt reference to prejudice or discrimination; some exceptions are "My Yellow Face," "Prejudice," and a poem included in her memoir, "Guilt by Heredity." Even the numerous poems that deal with dislocation and loss or, like "Hunted," with an implicit oppression characteristically treat the impact upon the poet, rather than the injustice of the treatment or the shame of the perpetrators.

Hunted

The hunted cannot plead:
Fear cramps the throat
And forces back the ache
To silenced note.

No sound can out to beg
Or bitterly accuse;
Cold tightens in the vein
And grips the pulse.

Only the hunted knows
The sense of ill
That paralyzes breath
And numbs the will.

I know: it was my voice
  That lost its sound,
Myself who bled and died,
  Run to the ground.
  (November 1946)

In commenting upon her mode of writing, Suyemoto revealed, "The late quiet hours of the night are, for me, the most conducive for reflective thinking and the writing of poetry. Although the poems are quickly written, they have actually gone through a long period of gestation, from the first impact of thought to the finished lines. The words shape themselves according to the image retained within the mind" (Suyemoto, "Sidelights").

The Memoir

Like her public talks, Toyo Suyemoto's memoir disarms with its matter-of-fact tone and a focus on the quotidian details of coping with life in the camp. In spite of the restrained tone, however, many details of camp existence must strike the reader as outrageous, an affront to reason and decency.

The fundamental paradox between the everyday, "normal" camp life created by the internees and the surrounding abnormality of the camp's very existence is subtly and heartbreakingly explored in "The Legend of Miss Sasagawara," a story by Suyemoto's fellow Nisei writer Hisaye Yamamoto. The portrait of the central character, a ballerina interned at the Poston, Arizona, camp, shows her gradual sinking into madness until at one point she is hospitalized at a mental facility outside of camp. The story is told from the point of view of two teenagers who think and act like any American teens of the 1940s, concerned with fitting in with their peers and dreaming of future husbands and living "happily ever after." They see Mari Sasagawara as dramatically larger than life, but also as an irritant that upsets conformity, and they more or less accept the community judgment that her behavior and she herself are crazy.

But Yamamoto's story provides a more complex consideration of madness. As in Topaz, in the context of the Arizona concentration camp, the so-called normal life of the teens takes place where people have been unceremoniously ripped from their homes and shunted into primitive, carelessly constructed, tar-papered barracks that neither provide privacy nor protect their residents from the besetting violent dust storms and extremes of temperature. The barracks, moreover, are hemmed in by an imprisoning barbed-wire fence and isolated by a vast, inhospitable desert. The reasons for their suffering these conditions are neither sensible nor benign. It is only later, from a perspective outside of the camp, that one of the teens begins to understand what the story has presented to the reader all along about where madness lies, about the anomaly of treating the abnormal as normal. The story suggests finally that Mari Sasagawara's "crazy" response—while taking its toll on the individual—may actually be more rational than accommodation to the absurdity of the incarceration.

I Call to Remembrance exhibits a similar, double-voiced complexity by which we are often lulled into taking the camp existence as a given. We attend to the interesting details of establishing schools, a library, and livable quarters and admire the often-ingenious survival techniques of camp residents. But the memoir also limns the portrait of a Miss Sasagawara–like figure: a block neighbor, Setsu, who flaunted an independence, or at least showed her impatience with what she apparently saw as the pettiness and hypocrisy of the camp's social protocol. Disdainful of the unstinting criticism of her conduct by others, Setsu refused to accept her situation as normal.

The memoir does not analyze the reasons for the incarceration nor rail at length against its base injustice. At one point, Suyemoto writes that she "railed against" the debilitating dust storms that plagued camp life by writing a poem—yet both comment and poem focus on the natural element, not on human oppression ("As 1942 Ended"). There are occasional, brief comments that register criticism or dismay, but these are almost invariably followed by admonitions to endure or adjust, or by expressions of hope for "the coming spring." For example, she writes: "Though we inveighed against our internment, or whatever disgruntled us at the moment, we were aware that beyond the daily routine of living, our functioning as a group of people depended on our own efforts. Indirectly, I learned from my own family and other evacuees to adapt to and accept the limitations of this four-cornered, mile-square world. . . . Annoyances continued to edge some days, but I could better understand now *shikata ga nai*" ("As 1942 Ended").

In her description of settling in to life in Topaz, she notes that "the only way to survive was to adjust to conditions in this war-created community" ("Settling In"). And much later, she considers the traumatic fallout from the loyalty registration and her own responses: "I mulled over the sequence of the drastic events as we tried to maintain normality as best we could. If I had not rescinded the qualifying clauses added to my reply on the loyalty question, I too might have been among those transferred to Tule Lake. . . . What good would protests have done? I found nothing consoling in the thought" ("In the Length of Days"). A poem ("My Thoughts Twist and Twist") follows this passage as once more Suyemoto turns to poetry as her outlet for expressing anxiety; still, the poem ends with a recollection of quince blossoms.

An occurrence at the Tanforan Assembly Center illustrates the cruel absurdity of the camp management. Suyemoto reports without commentary the order issued by camp administrators after internees had ingeniously erected windbreaks made of wooden stakes and discarded cardboard cartons to try to protect their barracks against the damp, chilling San Francisco Bay winds. The administrators ruled that the windbreaks had to be dismantled because "they made the camp look like a hobo jungle site." Who would notice the windbreaks and be offended is puzzling since visitors were not allowed farther into camp than the grandstand. The ludicrous hypocrisy of this order might be laughable if it were not literally creating a hardship for real people and philosophically placing more value on an image (itself puzzling, as even without the windbreak the barracks could hardly be considered upscale) than on people's welfare. But Suyemoto merely, and practically, concludes, "Without heating facilities in our rooms, we dressed as warmly as we could in the clothing we had brought with us" ("Tanforan Days").

In a rare instance, she admits to feeling anger when the gracious lady from Block 4 in Topaz collapsed in the women's latrine, yet she stifles her response: "Anger at the futility of the situation welled up in me even though I knew necessity compelled acceptance" ("Block 4-8-E"). Again, she ends with an expression of hope—for the woman's recovery (although subsequently the unfortunate woman died).

Throughout the memoir, there are instances where the intolerable reality complicates the bland, seemingly tolerant description. Suyemoto tells of her visit one night to the latrine when she was challenged by a watchtower guard. She was stopped by the glare of a spotlight and the noise of something whistling by her head. While not insisted upon, the oppressive and unjust humiliation of being the target of missile and spotlight during a routine visit to the inconvenient latrine must lodge in the reader's imagination ("Intake at Tanforan"). Also understated and even more alarming is the account of a distraught mother with a dangerously sick child trying to secure medical help. Again she declines to cry aloud; she writes only of an "inner turmoil," her "silent outcry" as she describes without histrionics her efforts to get help for her child. Nonetheless, the desperation of the situation, compounded by her powerlessness in the face of inadequate medical resources and impersonal bureaucratic delays, must shake the reader ("Kay's Illness").

In another place, there is a focus on the fact that hundreds of paper flowers crafted by the Issei women decorated the funeral of James Hatsuki Wakasa, shot by an overzealous guard on watchtower duty. But *after* the fact, beyond the explicit rendering of the tragedy of needless death, there comes a realization of the outrage of a situation that would spawn such an event and of the terror inflicted upon a people trapped defenseless behind barbed wire and vulnerable to a hostile and violent power ("Weighed in the Balance").

The memoir is characterized by this disconnect between the reality of the situation and Suyemoto's recounting of it. The descriptions of inconvenience (the long lines, the lack of privacy, the utilitarian food) or of restricted freedom (the barbed wire, the guard towers, the armed escorts) or even of rank prejudice (the difference between the Japanese and Caucasian salaries and quarters in camp, the hate-driven treatment suffered from outside townspeople, or the public vituperation from press and legislators) sound more like reports that inform than like jeremiads that protest. Nevertheless, the reader can hardly avoid registering the absurd travesty of the very enactment of internment—and then marveling at the memoir's quietly brave presentation of the experience.

Structure of the Memoir

I Call to Remembrance is a chronological account of the internment experience, a story that Suyemoto, in her dedication, states "must be told" so that those who do not yet know will come to know. In telling her story, Suyemoto employs several thematic threads that stitch together the narrative. She intended the memoir to honor the short life of her son, Kay, who "gave meaning to [her] life and [whose] spirit inspires this book" ("Author's Preface"), and the presence and growth of Kay unify and enliven her account. The early chapters report on his birth and his place in the family in Berkeley. Events recounted in other chapters occur, we are told, when Kay is five months old, or six months old, or two years old. We learn that he begins to crawl and then takes his first steps at Tanforan in the crowded horse stall, "scuff[ing] the toes of his little shoes on the rough flooring" ("Another Move"). We experience the train ride from California to Utah through Kay's eyes as he watches the towns, telephone poles, and grazing animals through the dusty train window, and we lament Kay's first uncelebrated birthday that occurs as the family is being herded into the new, permanent camp. Kay's bath, in the communal latrine building, becomes an important ritual for the family and a pleasant gathering spectacle for the block neighbors. Suyemoto states that she could gauge the passage of time by Kay's development "as he outgrew his shoes as fast as his infancy" ("In the Length of Days").

Kay's care occupied her attention, and his lively, innocent presence brightened the bleak situation for the whole family. A clouding element, however, was the continual, nagging concern about Kay's health. "Kay's Illness," a pivotal chapter located between the Tanforan and the Topaz chapters, recounts the aftermath of the cold the baby was suffering at the time of evacuation and the development of his life-threatening asthmatic condition. Thereafter, the narrative is fraught with reports of Kay's repeated asthma attacks and hospital stays, a history that had dire repercussions later. Kay's compromised health eventually cut short his life.

The memoir also traces the changing relationship between the Issei parents and their Nisei children. The prewar family pattern of authoritative father, deferential mother, and obedient children is disrupted by the camp experience. The parents' roles are stripped away; the family unit is submerged into the communal group; the family surname itself is replaced by a number. The memoir describes how communal places—latrines, laundries, recreational halls—supplant the private home for social gathering. Children find a new freedom from parental oversight and spend their time with friends, away from the barracks home. Mealtime in the mess hall at a picnic table cannot replicate the traditional family time: fathers might eat separately, and children usually preferred to eat with their peers. Suyemoto describes some Issei observing the Nisei jitterbug dance parties or student behavior in the classroom, shaking their heads, and muttering *rambo-na kodomoi* (unruly or rowdy children). Where before the parents made decisions for their children and taught them respectful behavior toward their elders, now the children began to assert a new independence. The Issei, barred from citizenship by American law, were periodically restricted as well from assuming leadership in the camp government. Handicapped by lack of English, they were forced to depend upon their Nisei children to deal with the Caucasian camp administration.

On the other hand, as the role of the Issei men diminished, Issei women took on an uncharacteristic, public role. Their traditional homemaking responsibilities, especially meal preparation, had been rendered irrelevant; and they had time available not only for such traditional activities as sewing, reading, and crafts, but for an activity counter to tradition—public organizing. At the time of the government's proposal for an all-Nisei fighting unit, the mothers gathered together in protest against what they considered a policy of discrimination against their draft-age sons, and they drew up position papers to present to the authorities. Issei men also objected to segregated units and called on the Nisei to oppose the policy, charging them with their earlier failure to assert their rights as citizens to defy the evacuation orders. Suyemoto reports, however, that the Nisei, whose views on the segregation issue generally differed from the Issei, "refrained from outright comments"; soon the majority of them stopped going to public meetings on the topic because "they saw the volunteer program as of no concern to the alien Japanese" ("Registration for Loyalty"). In the final chapter, Suyemoto summarizes the shift in the intergenerational relationship:

> During the three years we lived there, changes had occurred in the family structure. The second generation had turned away from the repressed, obedient behavior they had been taught and had become a more vocal and self-sufficient group. Even the girls were able to speak up during the relocation planning to say that they did not want to return to the West Coast after their friends had relocated to the Midwest or to eastern cities. Although the Nisei were still bound by filial ties to their parents, they wished to make decisions for themselves, particularly eldest sons in the armed service or in jobs outside, or college-age students facing the choice of a school. ("Tree of the People")

Grass

Another prominent theme permeating the memoir is that of grass and green growth.

A child said, *What is the grass?* fetching it to me with full hands;
How could I answer the child? I do not know what it is any more than he.
(Whitman 1973)

While Toyo Suyemoto deliberately invokes the spirit of Emily Dickinson in her poetry, a curious connection also reverberates between her memoir and the work of Walt Whitman, that other giant of nineteenth-century American poetry. The long line and sweep of subject and the exhaustive catalogues and declamatory expression of Whitman's poetry make a dramatic contrast with the concise, often elusive expression and compact form of the poetry of either Dickinson or Suyemoto. Yet *Leaves of Grass,* the title Whitman chose for his epic collection of poems celebrating the promise of a new kind of democratic, egalitarian, and inclusive nation, points to a correspondence between the (peculiarly American) iconography of grass and the very idea of America: The child asks his question in "Song of Myself," and the poet explores numerous possible answers about the meaning of grass, beginning with these.

I guess it must be the flag of my disposition, out of hopeful green stuff woven.

Or I guess it is the handkerchief of the Lord,
A scented gift and remembrancer designedly dropt,
Bearing the owner's name someway in the corners, that we may see and remark, and say *Whose?*

Or I guess the grass is itself a child, the produced babe of the vegetation.

Or I guess it is a uniform hieroglyphic,
And it means, Sprouting alike in broad zones and narrow zones,
Growing among black folks as among white,
Kanuck, Tuckahoe, Congressman, Cuff, I give them the same, I receive them the same.
(Whitman 1973, 33–34)

Grass—beautiful grass, hopeful grass, fertile grass—sprouts, in Whitman's image, throughout the nation, in all its zones, a hieroglyphic signifying an equality and inclusiveness for all races, regions, and classes of American people. Except grass did not sprout in Topaz, and in Topaz were thousands of Americans denied on the basis of race the equality, inclusion, freedom, and individuality supposed to be their birthright.

Suyemoto's *I Call to Remembrance* also links grass metaphorically with the American experience. Grass, notably the *absence* of grass and the *longing* for grass, constitutes a visual and tactile leitmotif in the memoir, delivering a message that contrasts with and qualifies the promise of the American experiment in Whitman's poem. The memoir provides a stark report on how democratic America failed an entire group of its citizens and how the American ideals of liberty, justice, and equality were betrayed.

References to grass and growing things occur throughout the memoir, and the included poems abound in images of plants and colorful flowers, trees and roots, spring and budding, as well as their opposite—arid, dusty, unyielding earth, a treeless and barren spring, the harsh, violent uprooting of live things. This organic imagery laces together the memoir's chapters, tracing the ironic contrast between the realities of camp life and the promise of America.

I Call to Remembrance opens, in the "Author's Preface," with an organic phrase, a reference to the widespread impact of the "drastic uprooting" of the Japanese. Grass as metaphor appears in the first chapter, describing the immediate aftermath of Pearl Harbor in a haiku Suyemoto wrote in March 1942 that "expressed the uncertainty [she] felt." Both chapter ("Berkeley") and poem end on the word "grass."

I cannot say it
In measured phrases, but I sense
Winds troubling the grass.

The war was, of course, a publicly troubling time for all Americans, but for the West Coast Japanese, trouble and uncertainty ruled their personal lives. As the family is evacuated from their home in Berkeley in April 1942, Suyemoto wonders: "Would we ever come back to this familiar street after the war? . . . These trees we saw now, the grass, the leafing hedge would be remembered when this confusing moment was past, and later more significantly perhaps" ("Morning of Departure"). Throughout the memoir, recollection of the time before evacuation tends to center on growing things. As their first spring in Topaz arrived, her mother and father wonder "what might now be sprouting and visible in the Berkeley yard." But, Suyemoto observes, their current reality entailed "nothing green and alive in the earth" ("Weighed in the Balance").

From their initial incarceration in the assembly center at the Tanforan Race Track in Bruno, California, the family and the other Bay area Japanese were transferred a few months later to their permanent camp. As she recalls their preparations for the move to Utah, Suyemoto comments: "As much as I hated the sight of the tall, enclosing fence topped by barbed wire and sentry-posts and the irritations of Tanforan, . . . we were still in our home state. The grass flourished abundantly in the center field of the race track; the eucalyptus trees swayed gracefully in the wind outside the forbidding fence; the trees within the camp were still green in the full growth of their leaves" ("Another Move"). But already, in the holding pen that was Tanforan, grass itself had become tainted, shown itself to be unnatural. First there was grass where it was not welcome, growing up between the unseasoned, gaping floor planks in their horse stall home so that, in addition to sweeping the floor, they "had to cut off the plumes of the fox-tails and the wild grass" ("Tanforan Days"). Later, Suyemoto turns this into a poem:

TANFORAN ASSEMBLY CENTER

The grass grew through the floor
   Between uneven planks
   In sparsely ordered ranks
Up to the thin, warped door,

And yet could not creep out—
   I too heard the calls
   Of spring outside the walls
As winds tapped from without.
   (February 1948)

Grass, like the people trapped behind "the thin, warped door," was growing where it did not belong. Furthermore, "grass grew within [the] enclosed section of the racetrack, and when some of the Issei recognized edible plants, they gathered them to augment what was being served in the mess halls. But a warning was issued by the hospital about bacterial spores on the plants that might be injurious to human health." So the very grass that should nourish the spirit was toxic to human life in this place of imprisonment.

When the evacuees transferred to Topaz, they found no trees, no shrubs or flowers, no grass. "Here," Toyo writes, "was not a single blade of grass or even a stunted bush. The landscape was a complete change from anything previously known" ("Entry into Topaz"). There was only an alkali dust that covered their persons and their barrack homes with a white powder that battered and blinded them when whipped into a fury by the incessant winds or that turned with the rain into a sucking mud. In addition, she writes, "Because there were no trees in our camp, we saw no birds. Daylight came without the twitter of city sparrows, the cooing of pigeons, or the occasional crowing of a pet rooster. This was a wasteland that overawed such remembered sounds" ("Settling In"). This "complete change of landscape" is not a fair or interesting exchange, but stark deprivation, challenging—overawing even—one's memory of normality.

In recognition of the deprivation, camp authorities brought in trees and shrubs in a landscaping attempt, but many of the trees died in the hostile environment,[5] and the scope of the planting was curtailed. "Original plans for Topaz called for a program for landscaping the blocks. Each residential block was to be provided with a small park with trees, shrubbery and lawns in the open space beside the recreational hall barracks. But the parks never materialized. The open space in our block remained a dry sandlot where my brothers sometimes played baseball with their friends" ("As 1942 Ended").

Although the residents created small miracles in coaxing gardens out of the earth in front of their barracks—Suyemoto's father nursed a bulb sent by a friend from outside into a thrilling flower—in camp was no grass, no expanse of lawn, that iconic, necessary component of the American dream house. Further, the absence of grass was absolute for the young Americans born in camp or brought to camp as infants. With no experience of grass, they had no knowledge of even its possibility.

Bill Hosokawa relates an experience with grass in his memoir, *Out of the Frying Pan,* that spurred him to hurry his family's relocation out of the Heart Mountain internment camp. One day, Hosokawa took his three-year-old son with him on an errand to nearby Cody, Wyoming. The boy had spent more than half of his young life in the camp, and Hosokawa writes:

> As we walked, he carefully avoided the lawns. I watched curiously until he pointed to the grass and asked what it was. "It's grass," I said. "You can walk on it. Take off your shoes and socks and try it." Cautiously, he tested the grass with his bare toes, feeling the soft coolness. Then he pushed himself out like a swimmer entering water. "It's grass, Daddy," he exulted. "You can walk on it! It feels good!" I started to laugh but was choked by a surge of anger. "No matter what the government thinks of me," I muttered, "it has no right to deny my son the pleasure of walking on grass any day he wants." (Hosokawa 1998, 56–57)

Suyemoto relates a similar experience when her already four-year-old son, Kay, first encountered grass after they arrived in Cincinnati from Topaz. Kay was entranced by the strangeness and the beauty of the grass. "Nice, nice," he told his mother as he bent over and tentatively touched the grass. "It's nice!" She does not include this anecdote in her memoir, but the importance, the beauty, the aliveness—the *necessity* of grass informs her simple, yet packed poem "In Topaz." Written in November 1942, the poem ends with the hope that grass will triumph, that it will "come to life, / Outwitting barren ground!" ("As 1942 Ended").

Out of her characteristically optimistic bent, Suyemoto's answer seems to be "yes," grass will outwit the barren ground, and the interned people will outwit deprivation and injustice. She describes how the library outwitted the absence of evergreen trees at Christmas time by making a kind of mobile in the size and shape of a conifer with graduated wood wheels, dry willow branches, and green crepe paper. This Christmas tree was decorated with colorful paper and fabric and suspended from the ceiling, and "whenever the doors opened, [the mobile Christmas tree] swayed and turned gently, delighting everyone who came to the library" ("Topaz Public Library").

Suyemoto concludes her memoir on a note of hope. In the final chapter, called "Tree of the People (Topaz Community)," she explicitly employs an organic metaphor that likens the experience of the internees to the real trees brought to the Topaz site. She extends the metaphor to the official "Shield of Topaz," a stylized, tree-shaped drawing that symbolized the camp community through a graphic representation of the camp population by age groups. Although elsewhere there is emphasis on how few transplanted trees took root, here Suyemoto focuses on the positive, on those that did survive, even though "many" may actually represent a small proportion of the trees planted. "When Topaz was planted in the wasteland, there were no natural trees to be seen. Into the arid barrenness, hardy trees and growing saplings were brought in from outside the fence and planted in the blocks. With buckets of water and constant care from the interned people who longed to see green growth, many took root although buffeted by the sweeping dust storms, the snows and ice of winter. Like the trees, the people uprooted from the West Coast grew into a community and survived" ("Tree of the People"). Finally, Suyemoto appends a poem beyond the last chapter, "Spring's Return." It declares that "nothing can break me now" and echoes her mother's often repeated adage that there will always be another spring for the willing heart. When Toyo used to protest to her mother that it wouldn't be the same spring, her mother would respond, no, not the same spring, but another spring.

Thus, Suyemoto begins and ends her memoir with an image of uprootedness to encapsulate the violent disruption and damage to living things, the threat to life itself that was the sorry experience of the World War II internment of the West Coast Japanese, immigrant and citizen alike. Yet she ends also with a notion of community and a positive anticipation of the future. Despite everything, her indomitable spirit embraces acceptance and hope.

Grass
It was there all the time, you know,
Hidden beneath impassive snow—
The strong aliveness of the grass,
Invisible, but there, below

The trampled white, streaked muddy-dark,
So mind could not relate or mark
The unseen from the seen, until
The first few blades showed green and stark.
(February 1961)

Notes

1. *Nisei* refers to second-generation Japanese Americans born in the United States. *Issei* refers to first-generation, immigrant Japanese who were denied American citizenship until after World War II. The *Kibei* were born in the United States but educated in Japan.
2. This phrase concludes the second paragraph of the Civil Liberties Act of 1988, Public Law No. 100-383, August 10, 1988, enacted by the U.S. Congress and signed into law by President Ronald Reagan.
3. The *senryu* is a humorous or satiric poem dealing with human affairs, usually written as a haiku.
4. Toyo's son was born October 13, 1941, and he died August 7, 1958. Shortly before his death, knowing his health was precarious, he admonished his mother "to be happy."
5. Leonard J. Arrington reports (in *The Price of Prejudice*) that 75 large trees, 7,500 small trees, and 10,000 cuttings of shrubs were obtained from Utah State Agricultural College, but that "nearly all the trees and shrubbery died; the alkaline soil, heat, and wind foiled efforts to get grass and flowers to grow" (Arrington 1997, 24–25).

I CALL

TO

REMEMBRANCE

Kay Kawakami, June 1958. Photo courtesy of John H. Kidd.

For Kay

This day, my son, is the fifteenth anniversary date since you were hospitalized in a coma from which you never awakened. Much has happened in the intervening years, the good and the bad, rewarding and disappointing, the joyous and the sad, woven into a texture of living that was denied to you. I only wish that I could share, as we once did, these moments to remember.

The task that I now have before me is the story of the internment years, which began before you were able to comprehend what loss of freedom and rights meant. Because your health and the length of your life were affected by your early years in an internment camp, the story must be told—for those who will wonder what happened to the Japanese Americans on the West Coast after Pearl Harbor.

July 25, 1971

AUTHOR'S PREFACE

Between those segments of time that we call pre– and post–World War II is a sharply delineated period of three and a half years which my family experienced as displaced persons in an internment camp. We were among the 120,000 of Japanese ancestry removed en masse for reason of "military necessity" from the coastal states of California, Washington, and Oregon and confined in guarded camps by the government of the United States.

My narrative of this removal of the Japanese from the West Coast is strictly personal. Political, economic, and racist motives for this forced exodus have been explicated by scholars in substantial reports and documents, but I am convinced that the impact of the drastic uprooting on so many can only be related by those who were uprooted.

What happened in that period from the early spring of 1942 through the late autumn of 1945, brief enough in retrospect but long in living then, I now recall from writings of my own at that time, in prose and poetry, as well as mementos and camp publications. The period spanned the infancy of my son and distorted what might have been his healthful development; the experience eventually canceled his short life. So for his sake, and for those who should know that detention camps did exist in this country, I write this testament.

My account relates the events of the evacuation from the day when my family first learned of our departure date from Berkeley to the assembly center, the Tanforan Race Track in San Bruno, California, through the years in the Central Utah Relocation Center. In the Utah camp, which we called Topaz, we lived as communal units rather than as individual families. From the beginning of the internment, we were identified by family numbers instead of our surnames.

Existence in the Utah camp reflected the fact that this settlement of 8,000 Japanese was composed of people alike in physical features, but very different in temperament, attitudes, and background. They were human beings who endured and accepted and adjusted to the tremendous change the war between the United States and Japan brought about. I shared their experiences. I have used fictional Japanese names when I could not recall the actual so that I could tell of the unusual qualities that these people possessed.

In *The Life of Poetry,* Muriel Rukeyser speaks of "the many songs we do not know: miners' songs of the past, the songs of the Chinese workmen on the western railways, the poems of the Nisei camps, the lost songs of the slave underground" (Rukeyser 1949, 102). The poems I wrote prior to evacuation and during internment were composed in intense reaction to the circumstances of the time, and they are incorporated in the following chapters.

During the war years, friends outside and within the camps helped me bear the unexpected, the tragic, and the happier moments, and I am grateful to them and to my family who gave me strength. My son, Kay, whom I lost two months before his seventeenth birthday, gave meaning to my life and his spirit inspires this book.

CAMP MEMORIES

I have dredged up
Hard fragments lost
I thought, in years
Of whirlwind dust.

Exposed to light,
Silently rough
And broken shards
Confront belief.
(N.d.)

1

BERKELEY

We will need to remember then
    How sunlight burnished to a flare
The arch of bridge across the wide
    Gold-spattered bay,

How sound from the city below
    Crept softly up the hill to where
We were and faded into dusk
    Along with day.

Berkeley, encircled by rounded hills and sloping down towards the San Francisco Bay, has the self-assured air of a college town, unlike Sacramento, the state capital, which retains a sturdy relationship to the farmlands. To us from the flat valley region, the view of the bay and the hills was refreshing. The summer was free of the clinging humidity that we had known before. Even the cool fog that rolled in from the bay and lifted in the morning seemed different from the penetratingly chill tule fog that hugged the ground in Sacramento during the winter months in the valley.

Our rented house in Berkeley had more space than our previous home although we seemed to fill the rooms as soon as we were settled. There were no tall trees in the front and back yards, but many plants—rose bushes, syringa, fuchsia, japonica, and perennials—for Father to tend. Mother still had her sweet peas in the spring, roses in the summer, and, later in the year, her cosmos, asters, and dahlias. Once, as she was transplanting small plants from the fence to the side of the house, she came to me with a plant cupped in her hands and held it out towards me. I saw an open blossom, small buds, and delicate leaves, supported by matted roots in the ball of dirt. She bent her head over what she held, then looking up at me, she exclaimed, "See, here is all of life."

By the time the family had moved to Berkeley, I (the eldest) was graduated from the University of California with majors in English and Latin. My brothers and sisters advanced through their school grades, and the older of them followed me to the same university. Bill and Hisa majored in bacteriology, Mae in hospital dietetics, and Roy in physical chemistry. Howard and Masa were in high school, and Joe and Lee in junior high school.

Life in Berkeley was a placid flow of school years though Mother and Father struggled to keep us fed and clothed. As in Sacramento, friends stopped in often and would be invited to stay for dinner. Father had nailed in all the leaves to the dining table since we needed an enlarged table to seat all of us. There were times when Mother had to set another small table in the living room for our friends, rather than crowd them into the circle around the family table.

Two years after graduation, I returned to the university to do graduate work in English, but I left, with studies towards a master's degree unfinished, to marry a Nisei newspaperman from San Francisco. We lived in Oakland, but adjacent Berkeley could be easily reached by a streetcar, and I could visit my family whenever I wished. By the autumn of 1941, I was expecting a child, and Mother prepared me for the advent with rigorous advice about enduring pain without any outcries. She had welcomed each of her children with hand-made garments that were simple for dressing a newborn. Now she made little kimonos of soft materials for her first grandchild. My son was born in October, and she named him Kay.

My husband worked for a Japanese newspaper in San Francisco and commuted across the San Francisco Bay each day. At home I cared for Kay and marveled at the miracle of his being. On the morning of December 7, I turned on the radio to catch the early broadcast before I picked up the baby out of his crib for his first morning feeding. The news that the harried announcer was presenting at that hour was unbelievable and horrible. He was describing the attack of Japanese planes on Pearl Harbor, the naval station on the island of Oahu in Hawaii. How could it be? It was beyond comprehension. In my mind, I was shouting, "Why? Why?"

When the broadcast ended, and the announcer had finished with the local news, I sat still, stunned, with Kay held in my arms and my thoughts in a turmoil. We were Japanese too. What would happen to us? I learned soon enough.

The neighbors upstairs, who had been on speaking terms and who also had a young boy just beginning to walk, now turned a cold shoulder and passed by unseeingly. That evening I could not buy a quart of milk at the grocery store nearby, where I had been shopping for months. Since I was no longer welcome there, I now had to go for blocks to an open market where farmers sold their produce from stalls. I began dreading to walk that distance because I felt accused by the eyes of every passerby.

At the open market some of the farmers would not sell to me. The only stall-owner there who greeted me warmly—and how pleasant I found her smile—was an elderly Italian woman, a wiry wisp, with a sweet face seamed by living, wise eyes that looked directly into mine, and work-strong hands. Inquiring about the *bambino,* she would weigh out the vegetables and fruits I selected, would name a price for each, and, before handing me my purchases, would add another handful to the paper sacks. She must have understood more about the aftermath of Pearl Harbor than she could say, and she would try to reassure me with a compassionate glance, "You no hafta pay now." But I did.

My youngest sister, Masa, who had liked little babies from the time she was in kindergarten, came to visit us whenever she could, and from her I gathered how concerned Mother and Father were. They reported regularly at the first of every year to register as aliens, and though they had been in this country for a long time and had never returned to Japan, they, like all of the Issei, were ineligible for citizenship. Mother had kept in touch with her family with infrequent letters, but as time passed, she lost her mother and brothers without ever seeing them again. There were certain memorial days when the scent of incense and flowers lent a lingering fragrance to the house, and on those days she seemed somewhat remote from us.

In the weeks after the calamity of Pearl Harbor, whenever I had occasion to visit Mother in Berkeley so she could see Kay, I could sense that she was troubled. She kept reminding us that no matter what happened to her and Father, we were to remember that we were citizen-born and that our loyalty belonged to this country. We had been hearing that the Federal Bureau of Investigation was interrogating Japanese families, making numerous sudden arrests, and taking the Issei away on the slightest suspicion, and Mother was afraid that this might happen to us. About this time, my brother Roy enlisted in the United States Army.

Poetry had been an integral part of me while I was in school, but for some time my writing had dwindled to nothing. In the mild California weather, the japonica, or flowering quince, had started to bloom in December, and the scarlet flowers graced the bushes before the leaves appeared. In my mind, even as a child, I had equated the blossoming of the japonica with the promise of spring. But now, with the declaration of war, I was not sure what the coming spring portended. So two weeks after Pearl Harbor, I wrote in haiku:

Beyond mind's torment,
Reach out and grasp a sprig of
The flowering quince.

This was self-admonishment not to forget what Mother often said, that spring would always return, fresh and timely, to the waiting heart. But the immediate situation of uncertainty and fear held me bound in chilling doubts.

The Japanese "problem" had been under the jurisdiction of the Department of Justice, but now the control was transferred to the War Department. On December 11, the Western Defense Command was established, the Pacific coast became a theater of war, and General John L. DeWitt was named the military commander. We were uncomfortably aware that the public temper had turned spiteful, as commentators, newspaper columnists, and politicians grew vehement. They vituperatively hinted that the Japanese living on the West Coast were committing acts of sabotage, that we were too dangerous to be allowed to live along the coastline, even that we should be deported. It is ironical to recall that at this same time my brother Roy was in boot camp and that he was nicknamed Sabotage by his fellow soldiers, and later Private Snafumoto, a play on our family surname, Suyemoto. Like the rest of us children, Roy had never studied Japanese in a language school, so he could not qualify for special service. Consequently, he was stationed in the States while he was in the army.

Since my husband worked for a bilingual newspaper, he was more informed than I about the progress of war. He predicted that the Japanese could be deported, or else detained where we would be closely watched. The thought alarmed me, as I could not imagine American citizens being exiled to a strange country, or being imprisoned without cause. We began considering what we should do in case this drastic removal happened.

He did not have the attachment to his family that I had to mine probably because he had lost his mother when a young boy. As we discussed what to do, I felt that we should move to Berkeley, but he preferred to stay in San

Francisco, a city he knew well. He was as determined in his desire as I was confirmed in mine to return to Berkeley. So it was that we separated on Christmas Eve 1941, and Kay and I went to live with my own family throughout the subsequent years of his infancy and adolescence.

From January 1942 on, feeling against the Japanese gained momentum and became abrasive. The distinction between alien parents and citizen children was no longer significant. We were all classed together as being related to the enemy by reason of heredity. Yet of all the thousands of Japanese on the Pacific coast, two-thirds of us were citizens by birth.

Then on February 11, President Roosevelt instructed the War Department to prepare for a wholesale evacuation of the West Coast Japanese. And on February 19, the President signed Executive Order 9066, authorizing the War Department to establish military areas in Washington, Oregon, California, and a portion of Arizona, and to exclude any or all persons of Japanese ancestry from them. This order applied only to the West Coast, and General DeWitt was given the responsibility of implementing the restriction.

By then, the flowering peach trees along the Berkeley streets were a mass of delicate pinks. And in mid-February I wrote in my notebook:

> The soft scent of peach
> Follows after in the rain—
> My heart is shaken.
>
> Look at these petals
> I gathered from the peach tree,
> Few moments of spring.
>
> I grasp selfishly
> At these delicate moments
> Against later loss.

At the same time, I wrote for my son, when he was exactly five months old:

> PROMISE
>
> Here is the seed nurtured
>   Through a long winter spell,

Sprung freshly to the warmth
  Of sun from its dark shell.

A promise yet, will mine
  Flower, fulfill its leaf
And bud, and thus annul
  Remembered frost and grief?

In March, many Japanese had moved voluntarily, at great sacrifice and expense, away from the coastline and reestablished themselves in hopes of escaping the evacuation. But in the end they too were included in the mass removal. We ourselves could not have moved voluntarily because most of us were intent on finishing out the school year, and Bill was teaching bacteriology at the university. During this month, the Wartime Civil Control Administration (WCCA) was formed as the operating agency of the Western Defense Command to carry out the process of removal, with Colonel Karl Bendetsen as director. Then on March 18, President Roosevelt created the War Relocation Authority.

On March 24, Public Proclamation No. 3 imposed a curfew on the Japanese, and we had to be indoors, off the streets, between the hours of 8:00 p.m. and 6:00 a.m. Violation of this regulation meant fines and imprisonment. If I were invited out to dinner by non-Japanese friends, I sometimes needed an escort home. At this time, civil control stations were established in designated areas by the WCCA. One member of each family was then asked to report to one of these stations and register for the entire family. People without families registered individually.

The turn of events pointed to a forced removal, and apprehensively we began to prepare for the moving. Because most of us were still attending school during the day, the burden of the early sorting and packing was left to Mother and Father. One weekend, Father and I packed all of our books and had them stored with a Caucasian acquaintance. Much remained to dispose of, but once the book shelves were bare and we began discarding our belongings, we realized with sudden intensity the finality of the moving, the fact that we might never be permitted to return.

These brief haiku that I wrote that month expressed the uncertainty I felt:

Will it be simple
To uproot the clinging heart
And toss it aside?

Let us turn away—
Darkness falls even as we
Contemplate the day.

I cannot say it
In measured phrases, but I sense
Winds troubling the grass.

2

APRIL 1942

The breath of flowering peach along the quiet streets of Berkeley ushered in the uneasy spring of 1942. Certain natural events like the punctuality of the changing seasons disregard the way people treat one another, and they enchant the observer with the perfection of the moment. So the wisteria bloomed again and purpled the exterior of an old church near the campus, and the new grass turned the winter-drab ground to a brisk green.

Morning in our household began with clatter, the sounds of a large family waking, one by one. There was a steady procession to the bathroom, then assembly around the breakfast table, and a gradual diminishing of voices as my brothers and sisters departed for school. The hiatus, after the dishes were washed and put away, for me meant a quick run down the stairs to the backyard. The multi-colored sweet peas were climbing higher on the strings that Father had staked from the soil to the top of the fence. The japonica no longer had its early flame-bright brilliance, but its leaves were glossy. And the April sunlight was sweet as the scent of the white syringa.

Mother would join me later to commune with plants in her own way. Her slender graceful fingers would gently guide a tendril of the sweet pea to curl more securely around a taut string. She would stand back a pace and absorb in a glance the riotous colors. That strong face, expressive in its reserve, contained unspoken joy. This particular day of spring she wanted my six-month-old son to share in the loveliness, so she went back into the house and returned with him in her arms. She had wrapped him in a worn, heavy sweater of hers against the coolness of the air. She walked slowly along the fence as she told him in Japanese what was in bloom, and his eyes followed her pointing finger. Today, instead of a red- or plum-tinted sweet pea blossom, she gave him a sprig of syringa to hold before she took him in for his midmorning nap.

This morning was not unlike the others that our family had experienced in this rented house. Except for my youngest brother, Lee, coming home at noon for lunch, there was little interruption while Kay was asleep, and Mother and I had time to talk. There was a restfulness within its walls. After lunch, Mother went down to the basement to finish washing the clothes that she had put to soak earlier, and I, upstairs in the kitchen, could hear faintly her scrubbing on the washboard.

Suddenly the telephone rang repeatedly, insistently. I answered. Bill was calling from the university, where he was a teaching assistant in the bacteriology department. He was brusque; "Ask Mom to come to the phone right away." I dashed down to the basement to summon Mother. She turned from the washing with a questioning look. Wiping soapy hands on her apron, she followed me upstairs and went to the telephone.

The conversation on her side consisted of a series of *Hai* (yes), and one word in Japanese, meaning "tomorrow," as a question. When finally she turned away, I asked, "Why did Bill call? It's just around two o'clock, so he must still be in lab."

Mother replied, "We are to leave Berkeley tomorrow morning early. The large families are being moved out first. Bill will be home as soon as he finishes teaching this afternoon."

The dismay I had seen on Mother's face, as she listened to Bill, must have been reflected in mine. There was no hesitancy in her firmly set mouth, in the gravely serious eyes, and no tears. She had too much to plan, to discard, before we had to leave Berkeley. And I thought of other times when calamities had struck that she met in just this way—pushing into place a lock of gray hair over her ear, exhibiting a decisiveness that revealed the inward direction of her mind, giving a lift of the shoulder. The hand that brushed her face, however, could not erase her concern.

I recalled the earlier hours of the morning, the beds made, the clothes picked up, even the familiarity of the patterned wall paper. My eyes viewed the pattern, diamond-shapes and lines that flowed together. Now, at once, the pattern was not to be. But I could not stand there, musing, with Mother urging, "We have things to do before tomorrow morning."

Since Bill had told Mother that he could not leave the university until later in the afternoon, he had delegated errands to me. I was to go to the Wartime Civil Control Administration station, which for us was Pilgrim Hall of the First Congregational Church, to register for the family and obtain identification tags for our baggage and our persons. Walking up Shattuck Avenue, I wondered where our family would be sent and whether I would ever walk this same street again.

At the Civil Control station, there were other Japanese people waiting silently with a stodgy, patient air. To the Caucasian official who eventually called me to the desk, I explained that my son had a slight cold and asked whether departure could be postponed for a few days. She listened attentively, but could not give me an immediate answer. She went into another office to consult a supervisor about my request and returned to inform me that my parents and brothers and sisters would have to leave as scheduled, but that I could remain behind with my baby and depart the following week with another contingent.

The thought of staying alone in the house with Kay after the other family members were gone was too forbidding for me to adopt this plan. At the registration, the Japanese people were being assigned family numbers by which they would be known throughout internment rather than by their individual surnames. If I remained behind as I had requested, there was the possibility that I would not be included in my parents' family number, but would be assigned a separate identification. This might mean other living quarters, and with the days ahead so vague, I could not face the added uncertainty. So I decided to leave with my family and registered Kay and myself under the family number of 13423.

Very few of our Caucasian friends knew that we would be moving so soon. So before returning home, I stopped at a former classmate's home to let him know that we had to leave the next morning. He was aghast that we had so little time to prepare for the trip. He promised to come with his wife that evening to say farewell. Long a friend of the family, his chief concern was for Mother, whom he regarded with deep affection.

When I reached home, Mother was directing each brother and sister as they arrived from school to sort and pack for the departure. Packing our clothes was simplified by the fact that we were restricted to essential personal effects that we could carry ourselves. Mother advised us to select some warm garments since we did not know where we were being sent. To dispose of a favorite blouse, or shirt, or sweater, was a wrench, and a lively discussion accompanied the selections. My brothers brought large cartons into the bedrooms, and we put clothing we could not take into them. They filled rapidly.

The packing was interrupted at intervals, as strangers began coming to the door to inquire whether we had anything for sale. The door had been left unlocked, and they walked in unannounced and strolled curiously through our rooms. They watched us as we sorted out clothes. Mother, despite her politeness, was irked by their staring and incessant questions. Finally, in order to be rid of one persistent onlooker, she priced the dining table, chairs, and kitchen stove for the inclusive sum of five dollars. She needed to get on with her work.

Father felt that we had been wise to pack the books the previous week for storage. When we learned that the army would store household items of a certain size at risk, we tagged some of the larger pieces of furniture The oversize wardrobe in my sisters' bedroom with doors that never closed completely was one item tagged, but we joked about the army storing something as awkward as that. Besides the wardrobe, we also tagged the library table that my sister Hisa liked to use for studying.

I called the offices of the Salvation Army and the Goodwill Industries about the quantity of clean clothing that we could contribute. Since it was now late in the afternoon and arrangements could not be made for picking up the cartons that day, I said that I would leave the basement door at the side of the house unbarred for pickup the next day. Mother, methodical in the packing of the cartons as she was about our suitcases, placed tissue papers between various garments. My brothers carried the cartons, as each was packed to the brim, down to the basement and stacked them in even rows.

Mother was just beginning to cook supper, planning at the same time what could be eaten picnic-fashion the following day, when I suddenly remembered that I had left the all-important tags at the friend's home I had visited in the afternoon. I hurried to his home, as I had to be back before the curfew hour. Our friend's wife had returned from work by then so, to safeguard me, they decided to escort me home. We paced down the street, where I had sped by earlier in the day, in silence.

As we passed a drugstore, she suggested that she provide a supply of disposable diapers and liners for Kay. Within the drugstore, I stood between my tall friends as other customers in the store directed cool, unsmiling glances at us. Thinking of the younger ones in our family, Joe bought favorite flavors of ice cream for them. It was past the curfew hour when we arrived at our house, so I was thankful that my friends had accompanied me home.

Mother's dinner was good, and the ice cream was delicious, but somehow that evening I felt an odd bolus obstructing my throat. A subdued group sat around the dinner table, and the change from the morning hubbub was noticeable, like an unprecedented drop in temperature on a stormy day. Leave-taking had an indescribable sense of finality, as good-byes were repeated with our friends, and hands clung to convey what words could not say.

After the younger ones had gone to bed, Mother, Father, Bill, and I stayed up to continue with our chores. Mother had kept letters from her relatives in Japan whom she had not seen since she left home in 1915 and never returned to visit. That night Bill made a bonfire in the backyard and burned these letters, to which were added kindling, scraps of clothing, the debris of school papers, the clutter of family living. The Brownie box camera that we had forgotten to turn in to the police was smashed with Father's axe, and it was tossed into the fire. All night long the bonfire burned, consuming once significant possessions.

Father cleaned the basement. He regretfully gathered up his gardening tools and put them together against one wall. As I watched him do this, the bright hours of the morning when I had enjoyed his garden seemed sharper in my mind. He had packed his artist's brushes, canvas boards, and oil paints so, perhaps, he would later be able to produce the colors of his plants in his paintings, but he would not be able to reproduce the scents or the textures of fine-grained flower petals.

I did a last minute laundry of baby garments. Since our clothes line was strung near the bonfire that Bill was tending, they dried quickly in the night air. But days later, in the assembly center, I was to remark on the smoky smell of Kay's little clothes. Long after midnight, Mother suggested that I try to sleep for a while. The house no longer seemed the haven it had been; a strangeness had seeped through the rooms. I stopped by Kay's crib. He was sound asleep, a small hand fisted near his face. I drew the blanket closer around his shoulder, and I soberly wondered what he would remember years later of this process of evacuation.

This spring was no sign
Of faith, but a brave promise
Of blind believing.

(December 1941)

3

MORNING OF DEPARTURE

The following morning when I awakened, rubbing sleep from my eyes, the early light was creeping in through the window and wiping the grayness from the bedroom walls. I glanced at the tall, brown-painted wardrobe in the corner of the room, with one door slightly ajar as usual. Drowsiness vanished completely as I recalled immediately what this particular morning impended. I would not have to push against that wardrobe door again before Mother reminded me, as it now stood empty. *Empty*—the word caught in my thought, like a dry, useless leaf stuck on the prong of a rake. I sat up.

Our home, rented for so many years, would be empty too in a few more hours. Its rooms would no longer contain the laughter, often irrepressible, the irritations, the togetherness of a growing family. The house was still quiet so I knew my brothers in the adjoining room were sleeping yet. I looked down over my shoulder at my sister beside me with her relaxed hand out upon the covers. Then I heard water running from the kitchen tap, and the odd squeak of metal as it was shut off. Mother was starting to make coffee for our last breakfast in this house.

I slipped out of bed, pushed my feet into thonged slippers, and re-pinned my straggly hair. Putting on clothes had a peculiar newness this morning. There was no decision to make as to what to wear since I had laid out the night before the suit and blouse that could not have been packed into the filled suitcase anyway.

Evacuation, up till now, had been merely a printed word that appeared in public notices and newspapers, but at this moment it was a coldness seeping into mind and body. The preparations for this day had begun two months ago, slow, tedious, shifting from day to day, as we learned we were an unwanted people in the state.

The winds of hate and unrest had gained in momentum. Since that ominous Sunday in December, I had observed changes in the attitudes of acquaintances who used to visit, the troubled feelings of all those I knew, the shop clerks who would not wait on me, the customers who would edge away from me when I stood at counters in stores, the passers-by on the street who would look at my Japanese face with animosity in their glance. It would not have mattered, even had they known, that I had a brother serving in the army. The storm was sweeping us away, but I had not foreseen the uprooting would be so soon.

Mother called to me from the kitchen, "You had better get up. It will be time to leave. Wake your sister up too." I leaned down, and putting my hands flat on the bed, I shook it vigorously. Waking, she protested the roughness, "Go away, will you?"

I said, "It's time you were up. We have to have the bedding rolled up, you know."

So she sat up and yawned, "You're dressed already? The boys—." She did not have to finish her query.

The boys were indeed up, and we could hear scuffling in the next room. Then we heard Mother going into the front room, and now laughter overlaid the noise. The bathroom was the next stop for their quickened movements. Our brothers were of junior and senior high school age, and they had worked as a team in running errands, packing, and lugging the large boxes of clothing we had to leave behind up and down the basement stairs.

I remembered momentarily their pranks, the boyish antics in this house—playing knights with wooden swords, one of my brothers wearing my fur-collared winter coat for a cloak on a sticky summer day. One evening, two of the youngest boys had latched the doors leading into the bathroom to sail their toy boats while taking a bath. They would not come out despite Mother's appeals, and they continued to splash and have fun. She finally had Bill rout them out by propping a ladder outside the house under the window and shouting at them that they had best finish their bath. They had their quiet times, too, when they would be studying or reading together.

My little son was awake now and wanted to be included in the morning activities. I changed him, washed his face and hands, and dressed him for departure. I made sure that the disposable diapers were at hand in his bag and would not be forgotten. As I held him, my brothers and sisters talked to him about leaving, but how could the baby know where we were going, or understand the uncertainty of the days ahead?

Breakfast was a somber occasion, but hurried, as there were still the final packing and chores to do. How bare the house seemed, even though we were leaving behind furniture, book shelves, stripped beds, kitchen equipment. In spite of the army's offer to store furniture, we had not received enough tags to put on what we wanted to keep.

After breakfast, Father spread out on the living room floor the large pieces of canvas I had pieced together to roll up the bedding. I had bought yards of canvas and cut them the length of bed sheets and stitched two pieces together to serve as wrappings. I had embroidered the family surname on each square of canvas, and on a duffle bag into which I stuffed diapers and baby clothes. Father placed blankets, sheets, and pillows from each bed on the canvas and expertly rolled up the bedding, tied each bundle with a rope in a certain way so that it could be hoisted easily. The boys helped carry the bedding rolls and suitcases out onto the front porch.

The fog had lifted early, and the spring sunlight glowed on the pink and purple bells of the fuchsia beside the steps and heightened the green of the hedge that enclosed the front yard. I stood a minute on the porch and pictured Father tending his plants with such care. I thought to myself, "This will be the last time that I shall see this garden, the last time that I shall be walking down these worn steps."

I moved forward, as my family members were already going down the wooden steps. Mother, I noticed, went down slowly, one hand on the banister. I took another backward look and saw Father lock the front door and drop the key into the tin mailbox. We would never need that key again, and the mailbox, the house itself, would no longer be identified with our family.

As I reached the sidewalk, I felt that I was but one of many other exiles in war-torn countries who were evicted from their homes with whatever belongings they could manage to carry. All of them, including my own family, had been caught in the flood tide and swept away. I bent my head quickly for an instant, as my eyes stung. I could not grieve now, when Mother especially would not express her misgivings in tears.

I realized that a pattern of living was being altered, and that an unprecedented process of transplanting was taking place by government order. We were being uprooted by formidable elements, and the future could not be foreseen. Where we would eventually settle, no one knew.

Our young Caucasian neighbor, Frank Closson, drove his car to the curb in front of the house and waved to us. He had offered yesterday to drive us to the Civil Control station to spare us the long walk with our luggage. He said little, after greeting us, as he piled the luggage into the car. Because of our numbers, he had to make two trips.

As we drove up the familiar streets that I had walked so often on the way to the university, I could see trees and bushes in bloom, a bright spring in contrast to the drabness of our spirits. I kept asking myself: What kind of accommodations would we have? What kind of Japanese people would we encounter, since most of our friends had been Caucasian? Would we have medical care in camp, now that my son had a cold? What about schooling that had been disrupted for the young people? What would happen to us after the war, and where would we fit in, once we were released from custody?

Similar thoughts kept recurring in repetitive fashion as I held Kay, unaware of his part in this upheaval. He was simply content to be in my arms. Mother looked tired, having stayed up all night after sending me to bed, and she was silent, but her eyes seemed to be saying farewell to the neighborhood. Was she thinking of her often-repeated assurance: spring comes back to the waiting heart. Inwardly I cried, "When?"

When we reached the Civil Control station in the church, we found the entire city block, and the church itself, surrounded by armed military guard. A soldier stood guard at the door, bayonet drawn, and he looked unsmilingly at the hodgepodge of Japanese people and baggage, though he seemed to sense the admiring glance of little boys. When we got out of the car, Frank reached out for my brothers' hands and shook them quickly, as he mumbled, "So long—good luck!" Father gave him a small envelope containing money and said, "Thank you very much." Frank nodded several times before he turned to go back to his car. My brothers kept looking after him until he had driven out of sight.

Baggage was piled up on the sidewalk the full length of the city block. Greyhound buses waited along the curb. We went into the reception room of the church. Caucasian church women had prepared tea and coffee and arranged plates of sandwiches, but no one seemed hungry, except the very young.

Most of the Japanese sat in family groups, much like ours, with suitcases beside the chairs. Children of school age were chatting animatedly, but their Issei parents looked on with dignified resignation. A yielding patience lay curved in their folded hands, but bewilderment shadowed their faces. The adolescents, free of school, seemed to take the departure as the beginning of a new adventure. Some of the parents conversed softly about something that had been forgotten in the rush of packing, or of their children, or about interrupted schooling. Whenever I caught the glance of an Issei, he would smile at Kay and bow politely, yet there was restraint and worry in the smile.

I helped Mother to a chair. She and Father bowed to the others seated nearby in customary greeting. An elderly man, sitting hunched beside his wife, looked up hearing Mother's chair scrape the floor. He smiled wearily, and I recognized a shopkeeper I had seen often. He seemed to have lost life itself. Father sat near, talking of the weather to a young couple with a baby. I watched their baby reaching for his mother's hat, and I smiled at this. The young mother saw my quick smile and remarked to me, "He doesn't know what is happening." So he did not; neither did my own child.

I motioned to my sister Hisa, and we drifted over to a double door that opened out on a lawn, trim and green. The sidewalk that stretched beyond the lawn was the way we had often walked to the university. I caught her elbow, "Remember?" And she nodded.

Everything that we had once known was now packed away in the mind. To recall was to shake out memories that had to be put away instantly. We barely talked, but our thoughts must have run in parallel grooves. Would we ever come back to this familiar street after the war? We could not say. Hadn't Mother said that he who speaks certainly of tomorrow, unpredictable as it was, makes the devil laugh? These trees we saw now, the grass, the leafing hedge would be remembered when this confusing moment was past, and later more significantly perhaps.

We were summoned to board the buses. So a hubbub arose, a stirring to gather belongings, anxious voices of parents starting a roll call of their children. The people were divided into assigned groups, and bus drivers consulted leaders of the groups. As group numbers were called, the people lined up to board the buses. Military police opened the bus doors, and we stepped up as family numbers were called. The luggage was loaded onto a moving van that was to accompany the entourage. Hisa saw to it that Mother was seated by the window. Mother smiled when I turned around from my seat in front to ask how she was. I glanced back at the church, stolid in the midmorning sunlight, the sentry by the door, curious spectators, and friends waving at us, and I said inwardly, "Goodbye, goodbye."

Our bus was soon filled to capacity, all good Nip-faces, I thought irrelevantly, and the bus started to move. A high school girl was singing a rally song. To my ears it sounded like a comic dirge. The bus rolled down streets we knew, and the young people called out the street names as though on a sightseeing tour. We saw for the last time the houses we had walked past during the years we had lived in Berkeley. The young voices grew quiet as we went past their own neighborhoods. They spoke regretfully of school and friends they were leaving behind, but the Issei did not say anything as they watched the moving landscape. They were more acutely aware of the sudden exile. Their children babbled on in lively English without yet comprehending the loss of status in the country of their birth.

The bus swung out into a wide lane on the outskirts of Berkeley, along the east side of the bay, crossed the long span of the bridge, and then into the fog-bound city across the bay. The bus passed sparsely populated districts, but people on the streets stared at all the Japanese on the bus. The bus slid smoothly along the highway after traversing San Francisco until it came to San Bruno. It was noon when the passengers sighted the Tanforan Race Track, now appropriated as our assembly center. The sun was warm, the bus ride was concluded, and the passengers were restless.

PORTRAIT
(Mother 1888–1950)

She came attired in silk,
A stranger to this land
Where welcome was a stare
And unresponding hand.

As years passed drudgery
Became her daily wear,
Her smile a shy attempt
To speak, yet could not dare.

But dignity she kept
Seemed rich and splendid when
The child she once had been
Recalled lost spring again.
(January 1987)

FOR FATHER
(1887–1959)

You taught me scents in air
And magic of colors
Your garden held, where grew
A multitude of flowers.

You saw the subtle grace
In shadows of the vine
Sun-patterned on the wall,
And made that wonder mine.

Your patience coaxed the roots
To live and sustain growth—
And too the child who watched
Love blossom in the earth.
(April 4, 1996)

4

GROWING UP IN NIHONMACHI

Growing up in my family world, located in a *Nihonmachi* (Japanese town), of central California, was not entirely bliss, yet not a hardship either. I was secure in the circle composed of my father, my mother, myself, and my eight younger brothers and sisters. When very young, I did not think it strange that our family celebrated both Christmas, with tingling anticipation before its advent, and the more ritualistic Japanese New Year's Day; both a firecrackery Fourth of July and *Hina-matsuri,* the Dolls' Festival for Girls, on March 3rd; Easter and Thanksgiving along with *Tango-no-sekku,* the Boys' Festival, on May 5th. Belonging to a racial minority on the West Coast was not as earth-shaking in my childhood as it was to be in a much later time.

As a small child, I somehow sensed that Father and Mother were more liberal in their thinking and training of us than other Japanese parents I was acquainted with in our community. I thought so, even when I felt that certain of their views about my conduct and behavior were restrictive and truly old-world Japanese. The generation gap between them (the first generation Issei*)* and us (the second-generation Nisei) was bridged by their tolerance, if not total understanding, of the American ways that we children absorbed. I was not fully to comprehend the inner strength of my mother and the artistic sensitivity of my father until I was older. Not until then would I realize how much they had given of themselves that I might be myself.

Of course, in grammar school, as I chummed, quarreled, sided with children of other nationalities—Chinese, Black, Mexican, Italian, and White—I learned that this country was often called "the melting pot." But I also discovered that the differences of ethnicity were never completely melted down and that skin color, distinct racial features, and the way we lived created significant differences. The very fact of our being born American was generally qualified by the biological adjective of "Japanese"; we were the Japanese Americans.

In Sacramento, as I was growing up, a large section of the city towards the river was predominantly Japanese. There along familiar streets were boarding houses for the migrant laborers and fruit pickers who followed the crops up and down the state at harvesting times; private homes; the drug stores where we could get Japanese patent remedies as well as legitimate prescriptions; hardware stores that stocked Japanese cutlery, honing stones, and bamboo utensils along with U.S.-made tools; dry goods shops that carried Japanese cosmetics as well as American fabrics and notions; fish markets where we could buy fresh sea bass or tuna to be thinly sliced for *sashimi* for dinner; Japanese restaurants that were small, neighborhood eating places; and even a hospital named after the owner's daughter and staffed entirely by Japanese professionals. In this section also lived clusters of other ethnic families but the Japanese were in the majority. Our home was often the gathering point for the children of other races, who were always welcomed by our parents.

The Japanese language was heard every day on the streets and at home. We were taught to bow politely to our elders whether we knew them by name or not and to give the proper forms of greetings. The varying dialects of the Japanese language used by the Issei told of their regional origins in Japan. Mother could imitate some of the phrases and transliterate them into the more conventional Japanese that we understood. Many of my Japanese friends came from families engaged in small businesses or farming.

However, my parents' background differed significantly from most of the Issei. Mother was not a picture-bride as a number of other mothers were, for she had become acquainted with Father in Japan through her brothers who had attended school together, and she and Father became engaged before he left Japan. She was descended from a Samurai family and had received an education unusual for women of her day—completing normal school, roughly equivalent to an American teachers' college of today. Before coming to this country to marry Father, she taught school.

My father did not migrate to the United States as a laborer, but as a student. He had completed high school in Japan, but on arrival in California, via Vancouver, he enrolled in high school again to learn the English language. Years later, when I was studying Sir Walter Scott's *Lady of the Lake* in secondary school, Father picked up my book to browse through it and expressed a strong distaste for that particular work even though he did reread *Ivanhoe* from time to time. Later I understood why when I saw his copy of

Lady of the Lake with interlinear translations of the poetic lines written in Japanese in his fine hand. It was interesting for me to learn that Sacramento's Sutter Junior High School, where I attended, had once been my father's high school.

Father continued his schooling at great self-sacrifice, and he majored in mining engineering at the University of Nevada. He later transferred to the University of California at Berkeley to further his studies in the same field. He and Mother corresponded during the ten years of engagement that they were apart. One time, after he had first encountered cotton candy at a fair, he packed and sent her a large box to share it with her. She was puzzled of course to open a large carton to find a handful of pink sugar grains rattling around the bottom of the box. When Mother came at last to this country as a Japanese-language teacher, she and Father were married in California.

The girls in our family were given Japanese names—Toyo, Hisa, Mae, and Masa—but the boys were given American names by Father—William, Roy, Howard, Joe, and Lee. Father was so interested in American history that he named our twin brothers, who died when babies, Benjamin and Franklin, and the youngest in our family was named after another American historical figure whom Father admired immensely: Robert E. Lee. In a Japanese family, preference is generally given to sons over daughters, and this was partly true in ours because Bill was the *chonan,* the eldest son and heir, although by birth rank, I was the first of the children. However, in educating us, our parents made no distinction between their daughters and sons.

As taught, we children paid deference to Father in his position of control and authority, but secretly we felt that Mother, with her insight and imperturbable logic, was more than his alter ego. They both stressed education, appreciation of beauty, hard work, respect for age, and responsibility to the family and one's own self. They provided an extensive collection of books for us, and time to read, and they often shared in our games. I am still mindful of two Japanese words that I heard spoken frequently: *giri,* meaning "moral obligation," and *on,* meaning "duty"; fulfilling these two terms, when our desires ran counter to them, at times caused rebellious feelings and protests.

Our gentle, courteous mother could be firm, unshakably so when she had to be, but she must have despaired sometimes about teaching us ideal behavior and manners. Occasionally she would refer to us wryly as *yabanjin*—her "barbarians." One morning when I was in a hurry to leave for school, she taught me an effective lesson. If I missed the first bus, I would miss the right transfer that would take me to the junior college in time for my eight o'clock class. I had gulped down my breakfast of coffee and toast, picked up the pile of books and notebook, rushed through the hallway, kicked the door open and was almost out the front door, when I heard Mother call after me in an unmistakable, not-to-be-questioned tone of voice, "Will you please come back here?" I answered, "Oh, Mom, I'll miss that bus!" She repeated, without raising her voice, "Will you please come back here?" So I reluctantly walked back to her, standing at the kitchen entrance, and when I faced her, she looked straight into my eyes and said, "Now you may go, but when you reach the front door, open it with your hand, not your foot, and before the door closes, catch it with the same hand so that it does not slam." I missed the first bus that morning, to be sure. Since she had a great sense of humor, I do not doubt that she smiled to herself that day!

Growing up in a family like ours meant learning to make ourselves understood bilingually. Our parents expected us children to speak correct Japanese and English. Father said Mother was the one truly fluent in literary Japanese. Although Father was fluent in English, he and Mother spoke to each other in Japanese, and Mother spoke Japanese to us, with only a smattering of English words. However, she understood far more of our English and slang than she would admit. Father spoke English to us because of expediency, and if we had anything vital to relay to Mother beyond the scope of our limited Japanese, he would translate for us. But generally, the children chattered in English, spiced with current slang, and we conversed with our parents in a strange mixture of the two languages.

Sometimes we found it convenient to have Mother go to the door to deal with a salesman. She would bow so politely and then say with much dignity, "No spik English." She and the salesman would bow to each other and part in a cordial fashion. We who were hidden beyond the door would giggle and commend Mother afterwards with "That was fine, Mom!"

Both our parents enjoyed reading, and so did we. Our Japanese schoolmates considered it rather unusual that we had an English set of encyclopedias, the entire Harvard Classics, dictionaries, reference books, novels, and a collection of children's books of poetry and prose. At Christmas, we were presented with toys and games that we had to share with one another, but the books given were our very own. Mother read extensively in translation, and it was she who familiarized me with the names of Nietzsche, Schopenhauer, Debussy, Chopin, Beethoven, Bach, Shakespeare, and others. She amazed me one day while I was still in junior high school when she asked me whether I had read Shakespeare's *Hamlet* and a certain speech of his that began, "To be, or not to be." She then proceeded to recite in Japanese, very beautifully, the whole soliloquy.

Father read in both Japanese and English, and he would discuss news of interest with us. He would rummage in a second-hand book store on his way home from work and bring back copies of the National Geographic magazine or, for me especially, books of poetry, some of which I still have. At the end of the week, he always picked up the latest issue of the *Saturday Evening Post* and a bag of old-fashioned chocolate drops, and whoever of the children met him first at the door was handed the magazine. The candy was distributed after supper. At times, he was practically mobbed at the door.

A hobby that Father cultivated was his painting in oils, and this he maintained from as long as I can remember until his death, when unfinished canvases spoke mutely of his interest in art. The Crocker Art Gallery was but a few blocks from our home, and I would be so pleased if, on an afternoon he was staying home, he would ask me to go along to the museum. I would skip beside him as I hung onto his hand since, for a short man, he took long, even-paced strides. At the museum, I would follow him quietly, as he wandered through the galleries and noted how a cloud formation was painted, what tints indicated a hillside in bloom, what colors stretched out the shadow of a mountain.

Another pleasure of his was the gardens in the front and back yards of our house. He never worked as a gardener for a living, but he spent hours in developing his chrysanthemums, sometimes grafting plants as he had learned to do from a friend, and babying the growing things tenderly. Because Mother enjoyed the splashy colors of the sweet peas (although she considered large zinnias rather garish), every spring one portion of the backyard fence was covered with sweet pea vines. He also grew some vegetables to add to the family meals.

In Japanese culture, the woman is generally self-effacing and humble before her husband, but Mother, despite her innate grace and conformity to tradition, was not that meek. She could be blunt and outspoken with us when need be, and even with Father. She was not easily swayed by the arguments of her barbarians although she listened to us. There were times when we called her the Court of Last Appeal, and she would smile back at us and say, "That's all right; Mama right."

Yet she did conform to custom in her way. One spring morning, when Father was busily transplanting her favorite beds of flowers from the backyard to the front, she stood inside the screen door at the front entrance to watch him. I overheard her say to herself, "Oh, that impossible man!" So I asked, "Why don't you go and tell him to stop what he is doing, Mom?" She demurred, "I couldn't!" so I volunteered, "You want me to go and tell him?" She looked aghast at me, "Oh, no, you mustn't."

The Japanese and American holidays that our parents observed for us were exciting and colorful. On March 3rd, Dolls' Festival, Mother would make a step arrangement in Father's office room, with the cherished Japanese dolls at the top and our everyday dolls on the bottom. She would let us invite our little girl friends over with their dolls and would serve us dainty Japanese confections that Father would purchase at a Japanese shop. And on May 5th, Boys' Day, Father would erect a tall bamboo fishing pole reaching near the top of the cherry tree in the backyard and attach five large paper carp, which gulped in the air and fluttered high, one for each of his sons. The carp represented courage and perseverance in the face of difficulties as the fish fought upstream. Not many Japanese families knew what a turkey dinner was when I was a child, but our family also celebrated Thanksgiving Day with turkey and trimmings. Of all the holidays, Christmas and New Year's were the most pleasurable and exciting for us.

Most of the Japanese in our community made much more of the New Year's holiday than of Christmas since they were Buddhists, and it is the holiday most traditionally observed by all Japanese. Days in advance, Mother would have us help in the overall housecleaning, and she would start preparing foods that were special to the occasion. What was most meaningful to me at New Year's was the customary Japanese decoration she would tie on the two posts on our front porch, an arrangement of pine, bamboo, and flowering plum called *sho-chiku-bai.* The pine signified longevity, the bamboo rectitude, and the flowering plum fragrance and grace.

As more New Years came and passed, we grew and adventured beyond the immediate family world, and we explored a more heterogeneous existence under the influence of schools and teachers and friends of different races. Eventually, as the older of us reached college age, Mother and Father decided to move from Sacramento to Berkeley, probably because Father had attended the University of California decades before. There was no well-defined Japanese community in Berkeley, and since housing restrictions existed against nonwhites, Father rented a house many blocks away from the university campus. Here the family lived until the spring of 1942, when the consequences of Pearl Harbor focused on us and others of our race on the West Coast, targets of anti-Japanese hatred.

NIHŌNMACHI
(Japanese town, Sacramento)

Where houses breathed at night
  And gardens smiled by day,
The Japanese of this town
  Lived daily history

War later changed. Here once
  These people sang their past
And danced new dreams, but now
  Familiar ways are lost.

The town died, not by bombs,
  But by the wrecking ball.
No trace remains, no flower
  To grace a window sill.

Instead tall stark structures
  Tower, like cenotaphs,
Built on the settled dust
  Of obliterated lives.
  (September 1989)

5

INTAKE AT TANFORAN

A large, imposing grandstand loomed before us when the buses finally halted. At the racetrack gates there were armed soldiers to remind the Japanese evacuees that this was their entrance into protective custody. There were earlier arrivals standing and watching inside the fence, strangers peering out at strangers who were to live together in confined quarters. Caucasians working inside the center paused, too, for a hasty glance at the busloads. A guard came to check the passenger list with each driver, and the evacuees had to wait in the bus until we were given permission to get off.

We were herded into the racetrack grounds, families huddled in bewildered groups and then led to the side of the grandstand. My son in my arms looked about at the strange surroundings with a child's steady stare. The young people were quiet now, finding no tongue for their uncomfortable feelings as they looked around at the high, barbed-wire barricade, the sentry-boxes situated at intervals along the fence. Their faces spoke their reaction.

We filed along in a line, carrying our suitcases and bundles. I stayed beside my mother, and together with my father, sisters and brothers, and young son, we moved slowly in line, the sun bearing down warmly on us. Removing coats and jackets meant more to carry, so we kept them on. The inauguration of waiting in queues took place on this morning, and thereafter this waiting became a camp ritual.

The men and boys were separated from the women at the far end of the line. We were all searched rapidly for concealed weapons. The men and boys were subjected to a more thorough search, as Caucasian hands frisked them, feeling quickly over their clothes, especially pockets. I saw a pocket knife removed from Father's pocket. I felt hands pass over my body, and I recoiled inwardly, but kept my face averted from that of the inspector. I watched Mother submit to the inspection with calm dignity. I linked my arm through hers afterwards and whispered, "Mom, that was terrible!" And there was my sister Hisa, looking angry, but restraining her tongue.

Other Japanese who had been admitted to the assembly center before us came to welcome the newcomers in the intake line. Some of them spoke encouragingly, and others commented that this unpleasantness would soon be over as we filed past them into the cubby-holes under the grandstand. A medical officer looked down our throats and at the vaccination scars on our arms. When this cursory examination was finished, we were called to a picnic-type table with a Masonite surface. Here were seated several evacuees serving as clerks, and we registered under our family identification number, 13423, which supplanted our surname for the duration of our internment.

When one of the clerks learned that I had a different surname from that of my father and that my husband, from whom I had separated in December, was registered as being in camp, the official tried to assign me his identification number. I protested strongly, and for a few moments I was afraid that my remonstrance would be of no avail, but my family supported me in my argument. Assuming my husband's identification number would have meant living with him and his father in his barracks, apart from my own family. Fortunately, I was granted reluctant permission to remain under my father's identification number.

Young boys acting as guides were standing by, and one of them offered to take us to the rooms assigned to us. He led us from the grandstand, and we trudged behind him down a dirt road, around the far bend of the racetrack to the corner of the assembly center. As we walked along, we passed barn-like buildings where bales of hay were stored. Some of the bales had been broken open, and there were piles of hay here and there. Some Japanese people inside were bending over the piles with what appeared to be muslin sacks. The guide informed us that they were making their own mattresses for the army cots.

We passed other buildings which were stables, and finally the guide stopped to point out one, and said, "There it is!" It was another stable, which we were to call home for six months. When we walked in out of the bright sunlight, our eyes had to adjust to our first view of the interior of the stable. By leaving the door open, we could see more clearly what the place looked like. There was no furniture except folded army cots propped against the dismal and uninviting walls.

Our living quarters had once housed race horses, and now human beings. The size of our family had been of concern to the housing staff because, with twelve of us, we had to have two stalls assigned for our use. The original stalls had been extended with wooden partitions so that there were two rooms, with the swinging half-doors serving as dividers. The ceiling sloped from the back room to the front, and below the rafters an open space stretched the entire length of the stable. The rear room showed distinct evidences of the former tenants, with deep, rough hoof-marks imprinted on the walls, bits of hay right-angled stiffly in the cracks, nails jutting out at random, all whitewashed in slap-dash manner and somehow incongruous to our sight. Cheap mahogany-red linoleum covered the unscrubbed boards in the back room, and on damp days, so frequent in the Bay region, a rank, pervasive odor hung in the air. My son, who developed allergies during the internment period, retained even in his teen-age a positive four-plus reaction to horse dander even though he had never come in contact with a horse.

We soon met our neighbors, a family from San Francisco on one side and another from Berkeley on the other. They informed us as to when meals were served, where the latrines were, where hot water was available when it ran out in the washroom closest to our barracks, and what could be bought at the meagerly stocked canteen.

At first, until the assembly center was filled, we all ate in the common dining room on the ground floor (on the actual dirt) of the huge grandstand. Since it was now noon, we hurried to the grandstand and found a mass of people inching along in double lines towards the doors. When we finally reached the serving counter and picked up plates, we saw that there were particles of food clinging to them. We wiped these off with tissues that we had in our pockets before being served. That first meal consisted of red beans cooked simply with salt, boiled potatoes, unpeeled and looking suspiciously unscrubbed, plain white bread, and tea the color of the bean liquid. That evening we had another almost identical supper, so my brother Bill joshingly remarked that the only difference he could see was the color of the beans—white navy beans.

The expansive space under the grandstand had been filled with picnic tables with attached, backless benches. Every table was crowded. We sat at one near the dishwashing section of the mess hall. I watched young men on kitchen duty sweeping off uneaten food from the plates with their hands into slop cans, stacking the dishes in a square wire basket and sloshing them through soapy water and then into rinse water, and placing them on shelves to dry. No wonder there were scraps of food still clinging to the hastily washed dishes. We thereafter made sure that we carried cleansing tissues before entering the dining room.

There was no meat in Tanforan until the twelfth day, no milk for anyone over five years old, and no butter for anyone. Beverages consisted of coffee for breakfast, cocoa made with water for lunch, and tea for dinner. Eventually the center was divided into districts, and more mess halls were built to accommodate each area. A greater variety of food supplies was provided as the center became more settled, so meals were better balanced and more palatable. Some of the cooks made salted vegetable relishes that the Japanese eat as pickles. Usually a dish of these pickles would be set on each table, but unless we were early in line for a meal, that dish would be empty by the time we sat down at the table because the first arrivals would help themselves to all the pickles.

The assembly center was far from completed when we arrived. Carpenters were still building barracks in the center field of the racetrack. Additional washrooms, shower stalls, and laundry buildings were being constructed throughout the center.

Since we had no furniture except army cots, we salvaged scrap lumber, and Father made three stools to sit on and a makeshift table. None of the stools were of the same height and obviously not intended to be used at the table, but they did serve the purpose. Mother was glad to have the stools since she had insisted while we were growing up that beds were not chairs. More enterprising evacuees made off with whole planks from the piles that the carpenters needed for the buildings in the center field of the racetrack. As furniture was made and added to the bareness of the horse stalls, the residents began to adjust to their confinement.

During the first month, typhoid and smallpox injections were given to each evacuee, without yea or nay. My sister Hisa, a medical technologist, helped the doctors and nurses in administering these injections. The residents lined up outside the hospital after camp-wide notice for these injections, and as they filed past, they were asked a few questions for medical records. On the morning that I went, I dressed my son in a white infant's dress and bonnet. Carried in my arms, he was interested in seeing so many strange faces around him, and he responded with an answering smile when bystanders would speak to him. He was glad to see his aunt Hisa, but looked a little hurt when she applied the needle to his arm. Because people thought he was a girl, I soon took off his bonnet, and this pleased him.

The hospital at this time was not yet fully equipped, nor was the dispensary stocked with necessities. During the first ten days, there was only one doctor, Dr. Fujita, on duty. The hospital building itself was not a stable, but a newly built barracks with long rooms for wards. It was situated at the farthermost end of the racetrack oval so that from our end of the camp, we had a long, dusty walk, even if we cut across the racetrack rather than going around the oval.

Grass grew within this enclosed section of the racetrack, and when some of the Issei recognized edible plants, they gathered them to augment what was being served in the mess halls. But a warning was issued by the hospital about bacterial spores on the plants that might be injurious to human health.

Here again in the assembly center, curfew was imposed as it had been in civilian life just before the evacuation. Roll call was held every day at 6:45 a.m. and 6:45 p.m. Each barracks had a house captain who made the rounds to check on us. At times, little children made his checking a chore by visiting playmates in and out of the stables. Day and night, Caucasian camp police walked their beat throughout the center on the lookout for contraband. One evening, when one of them peered in our door and saw Mother reading a Japanese book, he took it from her. She gave it up without protest, though her eyes held a sharp glint. A few days later the book was returned to her without explanation or comment by the police; it was her copy of the Bible translated into Japanese.

Civil liberties were at a minimum. The entire center was closely guarded: watch towers manned by armed sentries surrounded the area, and searchlights played around the boundaries at night. One night about 2 a.m., I awakened to go to the latrine located around the corner of our stable. I put on a bathrobe and wooden clogs and stepped outside onto the porch-like walk, with several steps leading down to the ground, that had just recently been added to the front of the stable. I thought I heard a voice call "Halt," but did not realize the command was for me. I took a few steps forward, my clogs clattering on the porch. I heard a swift, whistling sound pass over my head. I stopped in fright. Then a searchlight was swung around, and I was caught in its glare. I stiffened, though I thought I could hear my own heartbeat. The sentry must have thought twice then because the searchlight moved away in an arc against the darkness. And I scurried off, my heart pounding, my legs shaky, on my necessary errand.

From the beginning of our internment, we were introduced to and trained in communal living. Since the partitions between the rooms did not reach the roof, a comment spoken in an ordinary tone of voice was audible from one end of the stable to the other. Private remarks not intended for a neighborly audience had to be whispered softly in each other's ears. The bathroom situation also posed the problem of no privacy. As there was no running water in the stall, we had to go to a communal latrine. So we learned to bathe in groups, eat in groups, carry on life's activities in groups.

EVACUEES

The exiles cannot choose domain
Where hostile eyes forbid the way
And voices ask suspiciously
Whether they go or stay.

The whole wide earth has room enough,
And yet their land denies them space
To wander in, or even rest.
For them there is no place.

The wind reechoes taunts and jeers;
The sun withdraws; the atmosphere
Grows chill with apprehension yet.
Why should they merit fear?

War-refugees in their own country,
Where can they travel now and put
Aside their doubts; what barren stones
Shelter surviving root?

(September 1945)

6

TANFORAN DAYS

There was no refuting the fact that we were no longer free, but shadowed by suspicion. The barbed wire fences and the sentry towers around our enclosure testified to our detention. As the days and weeks merged into routine, a pattern evolved from the daily rising, eating, sleeping, and enduring the inconveniences of our stable-room existence in the Tanforan Assembly Center. Little by little we adapted to the restriction of our narrow living quarters.

At times, we envied what the neighbors from San Francisco at the far end of the barracks had as furnishings which made their rooms more home-like: scatter rugs, pictures on the walls, Japanese objects of art, chairs, good bedding. They had had sufficient warning of the evacuation and so had been able to bring supplies and possessions of their own. Their rooms looked luxurious in sharp contrast to ours so sparsely furnished with the army cots and the mismatched stools made of scrap lumber. We had taken the evacuation orders literally and brought only the necessities specified by army orders.

The first month passed with us getting used to waking to windowless space in the back stall. Instead of seeing the soft green, geometric-designed wallpaper of the Berkeley bedroom, we now saw wooden walls with stiffened horsehair and uneven wisps of straw protruding from layers of whitewash and smelling of a strong animal odor. At least, we could tell ourselves, we were better off than other people residing along the center edge of the racetrack. There, the horse stalls had been built right on the ground and were infested by strange insects, as well as rats and mice.

Because we were among the first arrivals at Tanforan and there were many more to come, we sometimes went to the intake gate to see the newcomers being brought in, looking bedraggled and bewildered, with their odd-sized baggage and young children. If we saw friends among the newly arrived, we would yell greetings at them and give them our barracks address. After they were processed as we had been, we occasionally helped them prepare their mattresses. Not all the residents received mattresses like ours, filled with cotton batting. Later arrivals received cases made from firmly woven ticking, and they had to go to one of the barns and fill them with straw before using them as mattresses. I wondered how the elderly must have found it difficult to sleep on this makeshift bedding and adapt to the ugliness of the bare horse stalls.

We heard that by the end of the month, most of the state of California had been cleared of Japanese inhabitants. Throughout the spring of 1942, the Japanese were removed from their homes in the cities, towns, and farmlands and herded into the assembly centers contrived from racetracks and state fair grounds. Not only California, but Oregon and Washington shifted the Japanese out into similar, hastily devised centers. And the majority of evacuated Japanese were persons born in this country.

The building of barracks continued even as the Japanese were continually arriving in batches from the Bay Area districts. By the end of May there were more than a hundred new buildings in our assembly center. The new barracks, constructed at the far end of the race track oval and in the center field, looked cleaner and roomier than our horse-stalls. Superficial though this distinction seems, these new dwellings differentiated the people assigned to them as being more privileged in the assembly center society. These later arrivals had been forewarned by friends who had preceded them about the lack of many necessities in camp, and they came better prepared with belongings to cope with this new way of living. In our case, Father had to order some carpentry tools by mail, a washtub for my baby, laundry pails, and an old-fashioned metal washboard for scrubbing clothes.

The wide dirt road around the racetrack was the main thoroughfare for the entire community. From morning till night, the evacuees strolled around it, sometimes for exercise, and mainly because there was nothing better to do than go for *sampo* (a long walk). The trucks would rumble by jerkily as they hit the ruts in the road, and we would step aside until they passed and then resume walking through the dust that the trucks kicked up. On rainy days, the road and other paths became a sticky slough. I kept an old pair of shoes outside the door for slogging through the mud, and a laundry pail of water, hiked from the nearest shower building, for washing off our feet before we reentered our rooms.

In time, a veranda was added to the front of our barracks, and it ran along the entire length of our building with several steps at each end down to the ground. As the days grew warmer and the horse smells became more noticeable indoors, the veranda served as an outdoor living room for reading newspapers or chatting with neighbors. Now that they did not have to spend their time in housecleaning, or marketing and preparing family meals, the women took up embroidery and knitting. I learned to knit socks from a young neighbor, a high school student, who was very patient in repeating instructions about turning the heel.

At the grandstand, the camp's internal police force used the clubhouse for headquarters. The first deck of the grandstand became the recreation room where we were permitted to receive visitors from home after they had applied for passes. The visiting hours were limited to two hours midmorning and three hours in the afternoon, and passes had to be obtained beforehand. They could not leave the grandstand to visit in our barracks, and children under sixteen years of age who came to visit were not allowed to enter Tanforan. On one occasion when my youngest brother Lee's Caucasian classmate, Dudley, came to Tanforan with his parents, he could not come into the assembly center, but had to stand outside by the tall wire fence to talk with Lee. I met Dudley's parents, Mr. and Mrs. Knapp, on the first deck, and from that level of the grandstand, I could point out the different areas of the camp and verbally describe the interior of our horse stalls. Because the uncompleted camp lacked so much in physical comfort, the administrative officials did not want outsiders to take home eyewitness accounts of the crude camp.

Dudley's mother saved the comic sections from the city newspapers for my younger brothers, and she would sometimes bring us fruits and vegetables from her garden. Once when she brought fresh tomatoes, the military guard at the gate checked her package and informed her that vegetables were no longer permissible as a gift. She argued that by definition tomatoes were fruits, but the guard in his role as inspector was not convinced and, much to her dismay, he confiscated the tomatoes. The next time she came, she put tomatoes of even size into a mailing tube capped with metal, and whatever reason she gave for the contents, the tomatoes did come into our hands and were enjoyed by our family.

The front rooms of our barracks, which had been added on to the original horse stalls, were of unseasoned lumber. With the warmer weather, the boards dried out and shrank. Gaps developed in the walls, and the floor boards became spaced an inch apart. Then grass grew up between the floor planks, and we had to cut off the plumes of the fox-tails and the wild grass.

I had to dispense with wearing narrow heels, and when I swept the floor, I had no need of a dustpan. By the time I swept the entire length of the room, the dirt was swept, not under a rug, but under the floor itself. On cool days, the draft of fresh air came up through the floor. Our door did not close tightly, but then it had no lock. As the door seasoned, knotholes fell out of the wood, providing greater ventilation. When camp friends came to visit, they did not have to knock since they could peer through a knothole and see who among us was home.

Father saved one of the knothole pieces that had fallen out. He cut off one side of the small piece so it would stand on a flat surface. He sanded and smoothed the flat sides. For a few days I watched him pick it up in his hands and run his fingers over the wood. Then he opened his oil painting box, took out tubes of paint, and settled at the small table made from scrap lumber. He painted miniatures on both sides of the knothole. On one side, he painted the view of the South San Francisco hill that we could see from our door and the nearby nine-foot-high green wooden fence and the sentry tower. On the reverse side, he painted a view of our end of the barracks building.

There was no protection from the damp, chill winds that blew in from the bay. Some residents erected stakes in the ground in front of their barracks and ingeniously interwove the sides of large paper cartons to make improvised windbreaks. But an order was eventually issued by the camp administrators that they be dismantled and destroyed because, according to the order, they made the camp look like a hobo jungle site. Without heating facilities in our rooms, we dressed as warmly as we could in the clothing we had brought with us.

A number of the horse stalls, particularly those built close to the ground, were condemned by the San Mateo County Health staff members as unsuitable housing. Nothing was done, however, to move the residents in them to better, more comfortable quarters. About four hundred single men who were not assigned rooms in the stables lived in dormitory quarters in the grandstand. The huge room had army cots lined along the long walls as in a hospital ward, with less than two feet between each bed. The bachelors had to share the minutiae of crowded living, although a few, inclined to more privacy, hung blankets around their beds as partitions. A small group of women had been situated in another dormitory space in the grandstand, but later they were permitted to share rooms with friends and families willing to accommodate them.

Privacy was lacking, not only for the bachelors, but for everyone in the center. The barracks had been built to army specifications of a type intended as temporary dwellings for young soldiers. Conveniences were not included. They definitely were not constructed for use as family units, or for the elderly, or the very young. Here at Tanforan, barracks had no running water, no washbasins or other bathroom facilities. The latrine building we had access to was located around the distant end of the barracks. Even the latrine building had no washbasins, but only a long trough with water spigots jutting out from the wall. We stood on the dirt floor to scrub our faces and brush our teeth.

The toilets did not always function. In the women's unit, a half-partition separated pairs of toilets. Rather ingenious methods were devised by the older women to shield themselves when they had to use them. At times, I was amused to hear their polite conversation as they sat on the toilets. The rest rooms in the grandstand afforded more privacy since they were enclosed, but were too far to be convenient, a distance of numerous city blocks from our end of the camp.

There were a few shower stalls, without doors, at one end of the latrine room. We were fortunate if we could shower early in the evening. Chance dictated whether other residents had the same idea at the same time to bathe, or whether there was enough hot water in our latrine or in another nearby latrine building. If the supply of hot water had been depleted in our section, then we would have to hike some distance to another latrine building. As cohesive cluster-groups formed in each area of the center, we discovered that unless we had friends in the neighboring area, we were not welcome in our forays for hot water. It was then a matter of deciding to shower despite uncordial stares or simply forgoing the shower.

The Issei hesitated to use the showers which had no curtains or screens. The Issei women were accustomed to taking baths, and they brought buckets or small washtubs to bathe in. Shallow chlorine footbaths were made at the entrance of shower rooms in some of the buildings, but I was amused to see people sidestep the footbath and edge along the rim to enter the shower stalls.

One evening, in the women's unit of our latrine building, I was startled to see an old man sitting calmly in a large tin tub placed in a shower stall while his withered wife knelt beside him to scrub his back. Other women, coming in their robes with towels and soap dishes, were as surprised as I was. They would look at each other questioningly, but to each one the elderly wife would bow and apologetically explain that her husband was totally blind and needed her help. She finished bathing him with tender care and led him home to his barracks before she returned to bathe herself.

The laundry buildings were scattered throughout the camp. Each of these buildings had three rooms: a large room where double-sectioned tubs stood in rows, the ironing room, and the drying room where clotheslines were strung out. We hung our hand-washed laundry in the drying room, but from time to time a sheet or pillowcase, socks or a child's undergarment would disappear, items that were not readily replaceable. The problem in the laundry was the same as in the latrine building: lack of hot water. Some days I had to hike to another laundry for a bucket of hot water to wash baby clothes. Shortly before we were moved out of Tanforan, a camp crew put up community clotheslines in front of the barracks.

After the evacuees had settled in the center, a canteen was established under the grandstand, but its stock was small with little variety. The supply of daily newspapers it provided was limited, and often there would be a long line of people waiting to buy just a bar of soap or a tube of toothpaste. I learned to stand in line along with the others, and waiting became expected, even habitual. We stood in line at the post office, at the pay station, at the canteen, in the laundry for a turn at the washtubs, at the hospital for clinic service, at the mess hall. And wherever we waited, we had to identify ourselves by our family identification number.

Entertainment such as concerts, dramatic presentations, or motion pictures was not to be had in the earlier days at Tanforan. As camp life became better organized, however, talented, trained residents combined efforts to present song concerts and dance recitals. The singers sang not only Japanese melodies, but also American tunes currently popular. Eventually, motion pictures were provided weekly at the grandstand, and the moviegoers would bring blankets to sit on picnic-fashion. Those who owned folding campstools had to sit at the back of the room. The waiting line would commence to form soon after supper even though it would still be broad daylight. As they waited for the dusk to come, the people would chat, play cards, knit, or read until it was dark enough for the motion picture to be shown. No tickets had to be purchased—the mess-hall identification cards served as passes—and only time had to be expended.

At Tanforan, the residents became interested in a governing body composed of their own people, and they initiated a movement for self-government. They organized a campaign with slogans and rallies to elect an official

Center Advisory Council. The election gave the first generation evacuees their first chance to vote along with their citizen children. But army orders later limited the holding of offices and the voting to citizens only. Then in August, an army order dissolved all the assembly center self-government bodies.

We learned that there were demands for evacuee labor by sugar beet growers and that the Western Defense Command would permit Japanese labor if proper arrangements were made with the growers, government officials, and the War Relocation Authority. After a series of meetings in April 1942, an agreement was reached so that by the end of the year, evacuees were able to find temporary outside agricultural work.

Internees tried to make Tanforan a more habitable place during their stay although we knew that we would be moved to a more permanent camp. I saw small garden patches started in front of the barracks and carefully tended, with water carted in buckets. The gardeners compared observations on the growth of their plants and advised each other. The flowers and vegetables that sprang up reminded us of home.

To beautify the place that had never been meant for a human community, a group of landscape architects decided to create an artificial pond in the center field. Trees and shrubs were transported and transplanted around its edge. The gardeners worked with their own equipment to make a small aquatic park with a rustic bridge, promenade, and islands. The result was a spot of loveliness, touched by sun and rain, in a place that was so different from where we had come.

7

TANFORAN HIGH SCHOOL

As soon as the prospect of evacuation became imminent, some of the public schools in California accelerated the teaching of their Japanese pupils to enable them to receive full credit for the spring term; others were not that concerned, and the children had to repeat the unfinished requirements later.

For the young people who had grown up in closely-knit families and with school companions of other nationalities, camp life stripped away all that was familiar and orderly. Thrust so abruptly into a commune, they soon discovered that being in camp meant sudden freedom from parental authority and the regularity of school, so a few did take advantage of their new liberty. But the majority found idleness tedious and without purpose, and they often talked about the schools they had left.

The need for the stabilizing influence of schools was recognized by a group of recent graduates from the universities in the Bay Area. After an exchange of suggestions, I and the other graduates met to discuss the possibility of establishing a high school in the assembly center with a standard high school program. Although we were untrained and inexperienced, we proposed teaching the subjects we had majored in, which included mathematics, history, public speaking, home economics, and English. Since English was one of my majors, I agreed to teach the English course. Soon afterward, plans were made also for a junior high school. The program for both schools followed the core curriculum of the California education system.

Notices about the opening of a high school were posted in the mess halls and around the camp on poles and fences. To the amazement of the volunteer evacuee teachers, five hundred high school students registered for classes on the first day even though we could not assure them that our courses could be accredited.

The conditions under which our high school classes were taught were unlike anything experienced in former schools. The one place with enough room for our classes was the grandstand, and so the large open area inside the grandstand, where betting windows lined one wall, became the school, with no partitions between the classes. Instead of desks, our students sat at mess hall tables, and those who faced forward on one side of the tables balanced their notebooks on their knees. We had no textbooks so teaching had to rely on lectures. In my English classes, I had to outtalk the civics instructor to my left, the mathematics teacher to my right, and the public-speaking lecturer straight ahead of me. The students were often noisy, and those on the outer fringe of my class at times seemed more attentive to what was being taught in an adjoining class than in our own.

The teaching staff of five women and seven men was composed of graduates from the University of California, except for three who were graduates of Stanford University, California's rival institution—the principal, Henry Tani, and the two mathematics instructors, brothers Hiro and Iwao Bando. When our efforts to establish a school became known, outside schools began to send in discarded textbooks, and these were gladly received and used. We teachers wrote our own lesson plans, outlines, and assignments, and handed out duplicated lavender print copies to our students. Announcements of class schedules and memos from the principal's office also came as lavender copies.

The teenage students attended regularly and seemed to appreciate the opportunity to continue schooling and to fill the daytime hours with learning activities. Card games, checkers, chess, guessing games, and talk-sessions that seemed to go on interminably must have begun to pall. Otherwise, there was little for them to do but to wonder how long they would remain isolated in camp.

Disciplinary problems occurred as in any school, and, unlike their parents, the students were outspoken. Generally, a mild reprimand in class would suffice to tone down the exuberance of young spirits, but occasionally this was not enough. In one class, I had a handful in four rowdy boys whose ringleader was a tall boy with an affable personality and a friendly grin. Whatever Tony did, whether it was to annoy the teacher or fellow students, the other three imitated.

One morning when my patience had been stretched visibly thin, I called upon Tony, who was, as I had expected, unprepared to recite. He remained standing, with a half-smile on his face. I rapidly called upon each of his comrades, none of whom had prepared that day's lesson. Looking at each of them in turn, I calmly informed them that I was dismissing them from my class for the remainder of the term. I asked them to leave immediately. Tony, caught off balance, asked, "Right now?"

I nodded emphatically. Slowly he turned to his friends who sat beside him and said, "Come on, guys. She means out!" The class was quiet and more attentive through the rest of the class period.

Afterwards, there were mornings when I would see Tony sauntering between classes or standing at a distance to observe the class from which he had been dismissed. If I happened to glance in his direction, he would raise a hand in quick salutation. If I were reading a literary selection to the class, he would edge closer to listen.

My third-period English class, held before the lunch hour, was small with all girls, including my youngest sister, Masa. I was surprised one day to look up from my reading to see Tony seated in the back row, with the girls tittering among themselves and whispering. He sat up straight, ignored the giggling, made no attempt to be annoying, and listened well. After class he approached me and remarked, "I thought I'd come and visit you, Teach. I miss my class." Thereafter, whenever he felt that he wanted to be among school friends, or to chat with me, he would join this third-period class.

To carry on as normally as possible, the teaching staff planned weekly assemblies outside on the seats of the grandstand, looking out over the racetrack. The principal arranged to borrow a public address system from the camp administrators. The first assembly was a matter of great excitement among the teachers and the students even before it convened.

When the assembly was announced for that May morning, voices buzzed throughout the unpartitioned length of the grandstand school. At the time for assembly, the students filed out and climbed onto the seats in one section of the grandstand. We teachers seated ourselves on the bottom row. I looked up at the high school students, dark-eyed, dark-haired, outwardly oriental, but American in manners and youthful demeanor. There they were, with their notebooks, jostling against each other, chattering, laughing, pushing closer to make room in the same row for their classmates.

The midmorning sun lent a freshness to the green grass in the oval of the racetrack. There were adult evacuees, mostly Issei, walking leisurely around the racetrack, and they glanced up as they heard the hubbub on the seats above them. They probably wondered why the student body was gathered outside on the tier of seats instead of being indoors in classes. Anything out of the ordinary created diversion and interest. Because it was our first assembly and the teachers were uncertain as to the audience response, an odd solemnity invested the occasion as the principal stepped to the microphone and began speaking.

One of the teachers, George Aki, who was a minister, gave a brief invocation. Announcements by the principal followed, and then came the introduction of the teaching staff. As the teachers were introduced, each one stood up and remained standing. The University of California graduates were called upon first, then those from Stanford. As the first Stanford graduate was named and stood up, unexpected applause and cheering broke out from the student body. The uproar continued as the second Stanford graduate was called and as the third person from Stanford, the principal, named himself. The two universities had a long rivalry, especially during the football season, and their encounter on the football field each year was always spoken of as the "big game." In this instance, the Stanford graduates were in the minority, compared to the Californians, so the students, American-fashion, rooted enthusiastically for the underdog.

The minister sitting beside me turned his head to smile at me as the applause subsided. The students then settled down for the rest of the program. When the principal was ready to dismiss the assembly, he asked the student body to rise and come down quietly from the grandstand seats and return to their classes.

The students stood up almost as one—an interesting assortment of young faces, smiling, serious, glum, indifferent, acquiescent. The passers-by below the grandstand had paused to look up at us, and the spring sunlight shone on their heads. From where they were standing, the students could see over the racetrack towards green-painted fences with the sentry-boxes, the telephone poles outside the boundary of the camp, and the roofs of San Bruno beyond.

Then they began to sing. Who hummed the first note? Who nudged the other to continue singing as the first words started? But the melody and words of "God Bless America" floated out into the air, over the heads of the teachers who had turned around to observe these uprooted ones, over the people down below who had stopped to watch and listen, and across the racetrack. It was a moving benediction. The minister turned to me again, this time with tears in his eyes, and he muttered, "Blessed kids!"

8

KAY'S ILLNESS

Day in, day out, thoughts
Are woven into time's fabric
I finger with grief.

Here, the harassed mind
Pauses to cry out, at last:
I can bear no more.

During the hours I taught at the grandstand high school, Mother took care of Kay. I returned at recess and at noon to breast-feed him and to have lunch with the family in the mess hall before going back for the afternoon meetings. When he napped, Mother sat beside the cot and watched over him because I had had to leave his crib behind at evacuation.

Kay had been a healthy, contented baby, but the mild cold he had caught before we left Berkeley lingered on at Tanforan. His chest began to sound raspy, and when I bathed him, Mother would urge me to hurry, her eyes observant and concerned. I worried too, as he weakened. The chill at night, rushing up through the gaps in the floor, and the damp smell of the horse stall did not help his difficult breathing. His infection became far more serious than the early stages of his cold.

When a baby becomes ill and is but seven months old, he has no way of indicating his discomfort or verbalizing his discomfort or state of feeling except through vexed restiveness and disturbed crying. As he became obviously more ill, I began to realize that his infection had become very serious.

Fever burned in his weakened body so warmly that I could feel it through his clothing and mine as I held him in my arms. His face began to lose its roundness. His soft, smooth cheeks turned dry, and patches of skin on his face scaled off. He had lately begun to eat solid foods along with being breast-fed, but now he could not retain anything in his stomach, not even milk. He did try to eat, when coaxed, but as soon as he took something, all that he had ingested would be spewed out in a volatile vomiting. He became listless and limp, his cheeks hollow, his eyes sunken into their sockets. His eyes would trace the movements of his grandparents or an uncle or aunt in the room, and he would respond in some way when they spoke to him or took turns carrying him. But the once happy baby began to resemble a wizened mockery of a starving old man.

Through my sister Hisa, a medical technologist at the center hospital, I knew that the infirmary was not yet staffed except for a graduate nurse, nor equipped to admit patients. The dispensary was not yet stocked with proper medications. But I heard that a young woman doctor, Dr. Fujita, had come into camp. So after several days of trying to make Kay comfortable, I decided that I had to have the doctor see him. I walked from our barracks, located in one corner of the camp at a distance from the race track itself, to the far end of the oval where the hospital stood.

The doctor was not at the hospital, and I presumed that she was out on house visits. I stopped in at the medical laboratory where my sister's co-worker was arranging newly received supplies on the shelves, and she referred me to the graduate nurse on duty who, as it turned out, was someone I knew from Berkeley. The nurse listened sympathetically to my description of Kay's condition and suggested that I bring him to the hospital or have the doctor make a house call.

The nurse conveyed the message, and shortly after I had returned to the barracks, the doctor did come to see Kay. Dr. Fujita, an attractive, crisp woman with a professional dignity, listened to Kay's chest with her stethoscope, took his temperature, and ran a sensitive finger over his peeling face. She said that he had become severely dehydrated from the fever. She did not prescribe any medicine because she had none with her, and there was no antibiotic in the dispensary. She recommended that he be given liquids as often as possible to counteract the dehydration and that he also be sponged off with tepid water to cool his skin. Then she asked me to report to her if his condition did not improve.

Our neighbors from San Francisco, the Sakais, worried about him almost as much as my own family. During the day, Mrs. Sakai would run in to see how he was, and her facial expression showed how upset she was that more could not be done to alleviate his illness. The day after Dr. Fujita's visit, she came, visibly excited, to our door to announce that her own, long-time family doctor, Dr. Kitagawa, had just arrived in camp with a new group of evacuees. She hurried away. She had taken it upon herself to go and find him. She returned to our barracks with the doctor himself, a short, brisk man who was somehow reassuring as he lifted Kay gently off the bed. He talked in a quiet, fatherly manner and elicited a wan smile.

Then he, like Dr. Fujita, proceeded to examine Kay thoroughly. He asked how long he had been ill, and everyone in the room offered bits of information. Mother was able to tell him in detail because the Issei doctor could converse with her in Japanese. He shook his head and spoke seriously with her. Then he turned to me and said in English, "I am afraid that your son is very sick. I suspect pneumonia, and he should be in an oxygen tent right now. Will you bring him to the hospital as soon as you can? And I'll see what I can do."

He talked to Mother and Mrs. Sakai for a few minutes longer and left our barracks. The two women looked at each other and then at Kay in my arms, their anxiety and pity so evident on their faces. As I looked down at him, tears flowed invisibly over stony thoughts, and my stomach churned in spasms. Mrs. Sakai murmured, "*Yoru samui kara, ne*" (It is so cold at night).

Kay's respiratory infection had predisposed him to pneumococci, and the walls of the barracks, whitewashed and hoof-marked, had been no protection against the chill climate of the Bay region. His breathing sounded difficult and raspy, and his projectile vomiting was still continuing. His fits of crying sounded shrill and pathetic to my ears and were exhausting to that little body.

Mother took him from my arms, as I now had to get a basin of water to wash him and make him ready for the trip to the hospital. She would not countenance a full bath, especially when I had to take him clear across the lengthy oval of the race track. So I freshened and dressed him. His legs looked so wasted as I changed his diaper that I put several layers of clothes on him and wrapped him well in a baby blanket.

The walk to the hospital seemed unending as the wind blew up the dust from the racetrack. I decided to cut across the inside field, but I kept stumbling on the uneven, grass-matted ground. I pulled the blanket over Kay's face to protect him against the wind and dust as he lay passive in my arms. I was met at the hospital by the same nurse I had spoken to before. Somehow she had managed to locate a bassinet; she put Kay to bed and propped him up on a pillow to ease his labored breathing. As she tucked a small sheet around him, she exclaimed, "Just look at his lips! He is cyanotic and needs oxygen!" She straightened up and asked me to bring a supply of diapers, undershirts, and nightclothes for him.

Going back across the racetrack, without Kay, is a blurred memory. I somehow recall noting the slant of sunlight on the grass, the heads of weeds nodding in the wind, the evacuees promenading around the oval—and none of them aware of my inner turmoil, the silent outcry against the conditions of this camp into which we were herded. Back at the horse stall, I soberly gathered together the baby garments, and Mother helped me fold them. I forgot about food and so missed eating lunch at the mess hall. It was late in the afternoon as I plodded back to the hospital when I recalled not eating. My mind turned over and over the words of the doctor and the nurse.

I learned afterwards that Dr. Kitagawa had gone to the administrators and the army officials to plead that my son be admitted to an outside hospital immediately for the treatment he needed. He had brought in a scant supply of a sulfa compound in his medical bag, and this he had used for Kay as soon as he was at the camp hospital. After I brought his clothes there, I stood beside the bassinet. Kay's eyes were closed, and momentarily I thought that he was dead. But as I watched, I could see the faint rise and fall of his chest. His lips were now a peculiar shade of blue. He looked emaciated and ashen, so unlike the robust, laughing child of a few weeks earlier.

Toward supper time, the nurse said that Dr. Kitagawa had finally been able to arrange to have Kay accepted as a patient at the San Mateo Hospital, miles from the camp, since he direly needed oxygen. I waited in the hopes that I could accompany my son to that hospital, but I was informed that I could not go with him although a nurse would be permitted to carry him there in the ambulance. The ambulance from the outside arrived at the camp hospital, but the nurse with Kay in her arms and I waited and waited for what seemed an interminable time. Then the reason for the delay appeared before us. The ambulance had to be escorted to the outside hospital by an army jeep carrying armed soldiers.

This time, the return to the barracks as dusk closed in was even more bleak. The silence in our rooms was palpable that evening, as we missed Kay's presence. His being had become the focal point of our activities, and even the routine of his evening bath in the washtub, with buckets of hot water hauled from the latrine, had been an event in our day. Children from neighboring stalls would gather around to observe him in the tub, and Kay enjoyed the attention he received from his playmates and their parents who sometimes came with them.

Days passed, and there was no word as to how Kay was getting along in the San Mateo Hospital. The Japanese doctors could not telephone out to inquire for me, and there seemed to be no way of finding out. Then an acquaintance suggested that I write to the head nurse in charge of the pediatric floor and enclose self-addressed postcards. I did just that and enclosed seven self-addressed, stamped cards. I received two back the first week. The head nurse, to whom I was grateful, noted on the first postcard that Kay was in an oxygen tent and receiving intensive care, and on the second, briefly, that he was improving.

Then again days passed without a word. By this time, I was having a problem with engorged breasts so I expressed the milk into a basin and pitched it out on the grass. The neighbor women commented on the waste. Somehow, teaching in the high school kept me preoccupied with the daily routine of class assignments, papers to correct, tests to administer to my students. But at night, as I lay awake, I could visualize a pediatric ward with numerous cribs, sick children, doctors and nurses on their rounds, and one strange, oriental baby in that room. During the second week of Kay's stay at the outside hospital, there came another postcard, stating that he had had a relapse and needed further care.

The camp residents who knew about Kay's illness would come to visit and console me by telling me that if he were dying, or dead, I would have been notified, and that as long as I did not receive such final news, I should keep hoping. And I did hope and pray that he was receiving good care, as the postcards seemed to indicate. After two weeks, the camp hospital was informed that Kay could be discharged. I could not ask to go to the San Mateo Hospital. This time, Dr. Teshima, a newcomer in camp, was permitted to go outside to bring Kay home.

When we heard that Kay was coming back, all my family stayed in the barracks. Not much was said, but the anticipation of seeing him again was manifest. The neighbors gathered on the porch to wait, and the children outside soon signaled by their excitement that the doctor, coming the long walk from the camp hospital, was now nearing our barracks. Dr. Teshima, a young, well-groomed man, entered our room with Kay, still pale and lean, in his arms. As I reached out, the doctor, smiling understandingly, handed my son to me. Kay looked around the circle of faces slowly, then at his grandmother and up at me, and a bright, thin smile broke out on his face, as though to acknowledge the fact that he was now back among his own.

Dr. Teshima recommended that I submit a requisition for a kerosene heater and said that the camp hospital would approve the request. The kerosene heater was eventually installed in the outer room, and a young boy would, from time to time, bring a fresh supply of the fuel. The heater did make a difference in the comfort of the room on those days when we needed the heat. I resumed breast-feeding, and Kay began to mend. His face recovered a certain fullness. I soon learned that other mothers in our barracks who depended on bottle formula for their babies needed the heater even more than we did. Some of them had electric plates for heating baby bottles, but so often a fuse would be blown at an inconvenient time that they would come to our room to ask that the heater be lighted. Then there would be half a dozen small pots on the heater with baby feedings warming in them.

The relief of having my son back with us did not banish the peculiar stomach ache that had plagued me from the time he went to the hospital. I did not tell the family about the pain though Mother seemed to know that I was bothered by an unaccountable stiffness in my back. I felt particularly affected one morning, but I managed to teach through the first two periods. When the third-period class (in which my sister Masa was enrolled) assembled, I decided to read to the students rather than give them what I had prepared for that day. The pain in my midriff became more acute as the hour wore on. At length the class ended, and my reading was finished. As I began to make the assignment for the next class meeting, the air suddenly seemed stifling and dark, and I fainted.

When I became conscious and looked up, there stood over me Henry Tani, the principal, my sister, and her classmates. The students had rushed to his office-cubicle in the grandstand and summoned him. Henry helped me walk back to the barracks. Subsequently, I went to see Dr. Kondo, who had just joined the hospital staff, and he diagnosed ulcers. He made arrangements for me to go to the same San Mateo Hospital to have an upper gastrointestinal series of fluoroscopy done.

The morning that I had to go to the outside hospital, the ambulance called for me, but this time there was no armed escort. When the Caucasian ambulance driver saw that I was the only patient, and not an immobile, sickly one at that, he invited me to climb up into the cab and ride beside him. He asked about the camp on our way to San Mateo, and as I described its features, he kept shaking his head incredulously. Outside the boundaries of the assembly center, we rode by stores and houses, and passed automobiles and people who would not have given a second thought to the interned Japanese. For my amusement, the driver decided to turn on the siren and whizz down the streets. He grinned at me as the ambulance took the center of the road, and cars slowed and moved towards the curb. Little did those in the cars know that it was for my sake that they had to move over to let the ambulance pass.

After the report of the fluoroscopy was sent to Dr. Kondo, I was put on a strict regimen and special ulcer diet, which meant that I had to go to the camp hospital for carefully weighed, specified foods. Eventually, I was able to take a tray and bring back the food to eat with Kay. My sister Mae was one of the hospital dietitians, so she made sure that I ate what was prescribed. But to this day I have no fondness for ground liver, strained carrots, or strained spinach. Jello was the only thing on the diet that I could like. Nevertheless, I had to comply with the doctor's orders for several months.

INTERMENT

All that was mortal of my son
　Is crypted in the brain,
More comprehensive than the womb
　In circumscribed domain.

His seasons, eager in the growth
　That summered into death,
Now shade him where mnemonic nerves
　Toll over him my breath.
　(November 1958)

HOKKU

His shoji opened
To the quiet garden where
Spring is forever.
　(November 1958)

Suyemoto family, *from the left:* William (Bill), Mother (Mitsu Hyakusoku Suyemoto), Mae, Hisa, Father (Tsutomu Howard Suyemoto) with Roy on his lap, Toyo. Sacramento, California, circa 1923. Photo courtesy of James R. Bailey.

William (Bill), Hisa, and Toyo Suyemoto. Sacramento, California, circa 1922. Photo courtesy of James R. Bailey.

Left: Toyo Suyemoto. Elk Grove, California, 1938. Photo courtesy of John H. Kidd.

Above: Toyo's mother (Mitsu Hyakusoku Suyemoto) with her grandson, Kay Kawakami, five months old. Berkeley, California, April 1942. Photo courtesy of John H. Kidd.

Left: Toyo Suyemoto (Kawakami) and son Kay Kawakami, five months old. Berkeley, California, April 1942. Photo courtesy of John H. Kidd.

Toyo Suyemoto (Kawakami) and son Kay Kawakami, two years old. Topaz, Utah, 1943. Photo courtesy of John H. Kidd.

Toyo Suyemoto (Kawakami). Columbus, Ohio, circa 1974. Photo courtesy of the Ohio State University Archive.

Toyo Suyemoto (Kawakami) at the monument at Topaz, March 1983. Photo courtesy Sandra C. Taylor.

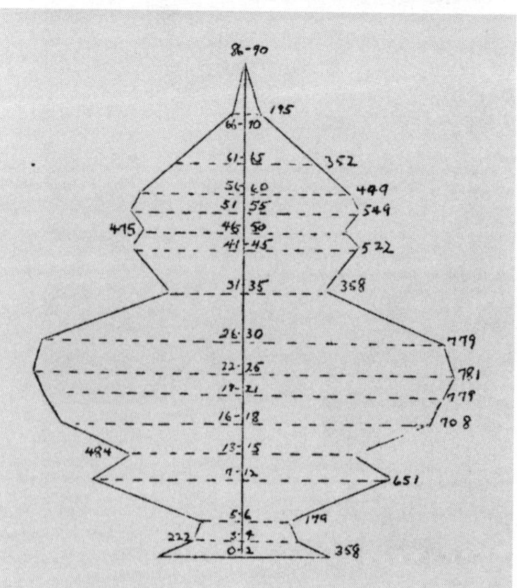

Official Topaz Shield, January 1943. From "Welcome to Topaz" Bulletin of the Central Utah Relocation Center, Project Reports Division, Historical Section, September 1943.

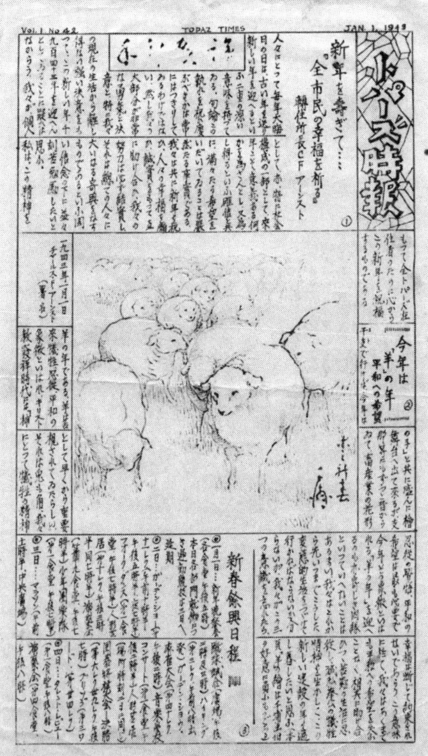

Vol. 1 No. 42 TOPAZ TIMES JAN. 1, 1943

トパーズ時報

新年を壽ぎて…
全市民の幸福を祈る

今年は羊の年
平和への希望

新春餘興日程

Drawing of sheep by Chiura Obata. *Topaz Times,* January 1, 1943.

Drawing of bath scene by Miné Okubo. Cover of *Trek* 1, no. 3, June 1943.

9

ANOTHER MOVE

Rumors began to trickle through the assembly center early in August that we would be moved to a more permanent camp—a relocation center in Utah which would be much larger than our current arrangement. We heard that ten relocation camps were being established under the War Relocation Authority, which in March had superseded the Wartime Civil Control Administration.

The thought of leaving California without prospect of return wrenched my mind. The Japanese idea of *furusato* (one's native place), the sense of belonging to a place where I had been born, schooled, and grown up, was not mere nostalgia, but an indefinable attachment to place. The younger people looked forward to departing from the home state with a more adventuresome spirit. Or was it adolescent bravado? For they too had misgivings about their ability to return to familiar places after release from internment.

The dubiousness of what was to come, the inevitable change, weighed upon us all, as we speculated about where we would be transferred. We had become accustomed, after a fashion, to Tanforan, and I reflected that when necessary, human beings can adapt to loss and discomfort. Japanese *gaman* was perhaps the key: enduring whatever happened, as the first-generation Japanese had done when they came to this country as strangers and met with discrimination and scorn because of their oriental faces and customs.

Summer was passing, and the warmth of days was bearable because we were still located in the Bay region, where the fog and the ocean breezes tempered the air. What gratified me most then was the fact that Kay was recovering rapidly from his illness. He was beginning to crawl, and he scuffed the toes of his little shoes on the rough flooring of our horse stall. His delight could not be contained in being able to transport himself around our crowded stall by standing up and hanging onto the edge of the cots with his funny, humping hips in play—and his baby sounds bubbling from him. His very being, and our concern for him, eased the passage of time and the inconveniences in these temporary quarters.

The seasons in our part of California were never extreme, and we had not known snow in quantity. In my growing up in the Sacramento valley, I had seen but two or three light snowfalls, a thick layer of sparkling whiteness that would quickly vanish after daybreak.

What I remembered of snow came from a time when I was no more than five years old. I had been put to bed in the evening at the regular time, so when my father came long after midnight to rouse me from sleep and whispered, "I want to show you something outside," I knew it was something unusual. He wrapped me in several layers of heavy sweaters and carried me out to the back porch, with Mother following us. He pointed to the white flakes drifting soundlessly in the darkness and to the cherry tree. I was wide awake now as I gazed at the cherry tree, which had strangely blossomed in feathery white. I heard Mother cautioning him not to let me get chilled, so he pulled the sweaters more tightly around me. There was a stillness in the air, and I stared at this marvel falling from the sky. Finally Mother said that I should be taken back to bed again. The next morning, as soon as I was dressed, I dashed out to the back porch, but there was just a trace of the snow on the boughs of the cherry tree and a few fast-melting clumps on some plants. But I always remembered the magical impression of the first snow.

Where we were going now was a vague surmise. We had no firsthand knowledge of the territory or the climate, although Father hinted that because of the altitude the winters would be colder and longer. As much as I hated the sight of the tall, enclosing fence topped by barbed wire and sentry-posts and the irritations of Tanforan, I had become used to the flow of days, the teaching of the high school students, and the congenial association with fellow teachers and neighbors. Though we still complained about the food—the sameness of menus and insufficient servings—and the distance to the latrine or laundry, we were still in our home state. The grass flourished abundantly in the center field of the race track; the eucalyptus trees swayed gracefully in the wind outside the forbidding fence; the trees within the camp were still green in the full growth of their leaves. Overhead I could hear the drone of airplanes, the P-38's, the sound of which even Kay had learned to recognize. Conjecture did not have the hard, precise outline of reality.

Bulletins began to appear on how to prepare for the next move, but no one knew until the end of the month when the relocation process would start. Once again we were faced with the chore of consolidating our meager possessions, deciding what to discard, saving whatever cartons and boxes we could obtain, and salvaging odd pieces of lumber for crates. Father took over the task of making the crates. This time, however, there was not much to dispose of, or to pack, as there had been for the initial move from our house in Berkeley. Two days before departure all belongings had to be packed and tagged, ready for inspection, so our sorting and selecting what we would need up to the last minute had to be meticulously planned.

By then, Kay had started to take his first steps. My sister Masa would encourage him by holding out her arms as she knelt on the floor before him. He would rise from a crawling position to stand unsteadily and totter forward to her. After a few steps he would sit down abruptly on his diapered bottom, then try again. I watched them as they repeated their actions. His joy in learning to walk was contagious as he persisted in his attempts. When he reached the safety of Masa's arms, his laughter announced his accomplishment.

After moving dates were scheduled, the first people to leave for the Utah location formed an advance work group of 220 volunteers to prepare for the induction of those to follow. Among the volunteers was my brother Bill, who joined the sanitary engineering crew because of his bacteriological training. On Tuesday, September 15, 1942, soon after the advance group had gone, the major transfer of people from Tanforan began under the charge of Lieutenant James H. Waddell, U.S. Army. Gradually the assembly center was emptied of its inhabitants, as group after group was moved out. Each night, until Tuesday, September 22, contingents of 500 people at a time, carrying pillows, cans with potted flowers, and household goods, boarded the train for the trip to the Utah settlement on the plains of Abraham, until 4,400 people were removed inland. Some 3,500 people remaining in Tanforan were transferred later. Our family left Tanforan towards the end of the transfer, in late September. We later heard that the last group had a miserable trip to Utah because they had all dined in the same mess hall where food contamination caused severe diarrhea for the residents.

Because our barracks in the far corner of the assembly center were near the departure gate, where the barbed wire fence had been snipped and rolled back to allow access to the railroad tracks just outside, our stable roof provided an excellent vantage point for seeing people off. Friends and residents from all areas of the race track came to see their acquaintances leaving for

Utah. The more agile climbed up the fence of the porch and clambered onto the roof with hand-drawn signs and banners, some with the message, "Bon voyage—see you soon!" The people departing, carrying their string-tied bundles, waved back at us and smiled at the enthusiastic send-off.

Shortly after Bill had left, as Mother and I were packing, I was listening to the morning news audible from our neighbor's radio. I paused suddenly when I heard: "A Jap spy has been caught in U.S. uniform and is in police custody in Oakland." Then the announcer gave the name of my brother Roy, who was then stationed at Fort Warren, Wyoming. I turned to Mother and exclaimed, "Mom, Roy is in Oakland right now and held by the police." She looked up from folding clothes, and said with a troubled note in her voice, "Go and get today's newspapers." So I rushed out to the canteen to buy newspapers from San Francisco and the East Bay. There in headlines was the news of Roy's arrest. According to the news account, he had returned to California on a furlough in order to see us. He was sent back to Fort Warren after his status was cleared, although we did not know what had happened until he wrote to us. He wrote that he had not been informed that the West Coast was off limits even to Japanese American soldiers, and that he missed the family.

When our group left Tanforan, Kay and I were assigned to a Pullman car and the others of my family rode in a coach for the three-day journey to Utah. The train we boarded was an antiquated one, creaking wearily and musty like a closed-up room. Kay and I traveled comfortably enough, but Mother had a bad time the entire trip. The movement of the train rocking from side to side, the jolting stops, the noise jangled on her, and disturbed other older people as well. She missed all the meals on the trip. My youngest brother, Lee, became ill, but even he fared much better than Mother. Citrus fruit was provided on the trains, so rather than going to the dining car, many of the old people satisfied themselves with the fruit.

The trip was a novel experience to Kay. He had never seen a real train before, and he watched intently out the dusty window as we went past towns, telephone poles, and open countryside. Curfew was observed on the train at sundown, so shades had to be pulled down. There was little to be seen at night, but when news ran through the train that we were leaving the arid reaches of Nevada and passing through Salt Lake City, shades were lifted an inch or two so we could peer out at the white expanse of the salt lake. Comments were made that it would be easy for a beginner to learn swimming in that lake, but with moonlight on the surface of the water, we saw what resembled a rippled desert.

After miles of sagebrush and rolling tumbleweeds, we finally reached the state of Utah on October 3 and arrived at the small sprawling town of Delta, about seventeen miles from our destination. Delta, to the east of the permanent camp, had about one thousand inhabitants, and this town, the only railroad center in the region, became the nearest approach to the outside world.

In Delta, we changed to buses under military guard, and thus we traveled the last lap of our journey from California. On our way to the camp site, we saw farms under cultivation not far from the town. Grazing farm animals caught Kay's attention, and I pointed them out and named them. Before, he had seen them only in picture books. "Big" was his comment. However, as the buses sped along the road, the landscape reverted once more to greasewood, tumbleweed, and swirls of dust.

RARE SNOW

Father said snow fell from the skies
    (In Sacramento?—No!)
Just as quiet petals
    Drift from the cherry tree.

He spoke of long, white roads he walked
    As boy in old Japan,
Later, in Canada,
    Of deep mounds he had seen.

A fine tale for a child, I thought,
    Who never knew by touch
How cold that whiteness was
    Beyond belief or reach.

Till one night late, he wakened me.
    Held in his arms, I saw
At last (I was but five)
    The marvel of rare snow.
    (May 10, 1989)

10

ENTRY INTO TOPAZ

The permanent camp in west central Utah, where we were interned for three years, was located in the Sevier Desert, once a lake bed and now a forsaken, isolated area consisting of about 17,500 acres in Millard County. Mountain ranges stood far away in the distance to the west, and one prominent peak, Mt. Topaz, gave the camp its commonly used name. Topaz was the result of public domain: tracts of land that had reverted to local authority for nonpayment of loans and several parcels purchased from private individuals. Ground had been broken for the camp on July 15, 1942, and on September 8, the military police arrived and were stationed in housing built for them in the corner of the camp. But Topaz actually came into existence on September 11, 1942, with the arrival of the advance group of Tanforan volunteers that included my brother Bill. Suddenly, with the induction of the San Francisco Bay Japanese, Topaz became the fifth largest city of the state of Utah, about 140 miles by rail southwest of Salt Lake City.

I had had no distinct concept of how the Central Utah Relocation Project would appear, but I had not expected such a desolate place, hemmed in by barbed wire and the elements. Despite the degradation of being penned in horse-stalls, Tanforan was still California. There we had viewed the grass and trees, as well as the gardens that the evacuees themselves had planted. Here was not a single blade of grass or even a stunted bush. The landscape was a complete change from anything previously known. The name bestowed by white explorers in 1776 was apt: Valle Solado, or Valley of Salt.

As far as eyes could see, the camp stretched out on the flat, dry, grassless plain, with rows and rows of low, black tar-papered barracks, burrowed into the ground. The entire panorama was depressing. The surrounding barbed wire fence with sentry-posts located at regular intervals around the site was reminiscent of Tanforan. But there the resemblance ended. Boundaries of this camp were identified with red warning signs posted one hundred yards apart, and these signs displayed copies of Proclamation 8 in both English and Japanese, forbidding egress.

The relocation project was a mile square in area and marked off into forty-two city-size blocks, of which thirty-four were used as residential quarters. Every block was identical, with twelve barracks for housing, six lined up on each side of the block, with an alleyway between these two rows. The alley contained lengthwise the mess hall and the combined laundry-latrine building. Each block had the capacity to house 250 to 300 persons.

As our bus entered Topaz, the unvoiced, shocked dismay on the faces of passengers was eloquent. Even the lowly dandelion, the bane of neat lawns, would have been a welcome sight here. Momentarily there flashed in my mind Father's garden in Berkeley and its profuse array of colors. Here was unspeakable dreariness and gray, stifling dust everywhere. When our bus halted at the main gate near the administrative section of the camp, we picked up our belongings, and I straightened my son's clothes. We stepped down from the bus and sank ankle-deep into the powder silt. The sun, untamed by clouds, beat on us relentlessly, and the heat made us uncomfortable. Tiny beads of perspiration glistened on Kay's button nose. He squirmed in my arms and kept turning his head from side to side to stare at the new surroundings and at the people who had traveled with us.

As soon as Kay saw his uncle Bill, deeply tanned and hair cropped close, waiting at the gate, he began to stretch forward and wave. For a child, this dismal environment did not seem to matter as long as he was circled by those who loved him. Bill walked up to us, reached out to Kay, and took him from my arms. He inquired about the train ride and showed concern for Mother, who looked so weary.

A small band of young Boy Scouts were assembled as a welcoming committee. They tooted vigorously on their brass instruments and blared out melodies we knew into the desert air. But when they began to play the familiar tune of the University of California, "Hail to California," I wanted to hide my face and weep for what could never be again. But not before all those people. Instead, I blinked the dust from eyes. A banner the Boy Scouts held aloft in greeting read: "Welcome to Topaz, the Jewel of the Desert."

In the intake procedure at the mess halls, residents were routinely processed, given identification cards, and assigned to their barracks. These identification cards were issued to everyone six years of age and older. We walked then, with Bill in the lead still carrying Kay, to our barracks in Block 4 in the first row of seven blocks fronting the warehouses, the administration buildings, the military police encampment, and the hospital. We were assigned to this block because Bill, Hisa, and Mae all needed to be near the hospital.

The barracks were a great improvement over the Tanforan horse stalls, although they had been built by the army according to designs for military housing for single soldiers, not for families. Each barracks was partitioned into six variously sized rooms, with the smallest rooms at the ends, about twenty by ten feet, intended for couples, and the larger, middle rooms for family groups. Because of the number in our family, we were once more given two rooms, in the middle, each about twenty by twenty-five feet. In order to go from one room to the other, we had to go outside the building and enter the other room by another door. My brothers decided to be together in one room, and the rest of us—Mother and Father, my sisters, Kay and I—took the other.

The rooms that we walked into, with unfinished walls and ceiling, were devoid of furniture. The place smelled clean as we inspected the rooms assigned to us, but the floor and the windowsills were covered with a two-inch layer of fine dust, and the floor was imprinted with a pattern of insect tracks. The exposed pine two-by-fours supporting the walls gave a rustic appearance to the stark rooms, but emphasized the condition under which we were to exist while interned. No running water or bathroom facilities were furnished in these rooms, although a cast-iron, pot-bellied space heater stood in the corner of each room. Later, sheetrock walls finished the rooms.

The new quarters provided more ample space, but we had no furniture until Father once again made makeshift stools and a table from scrap lumber. Also, for the sake of convenience, Father cut out an entrance through the intervening wall and hung curtains there. We appreciated this easier access when the cold weather came, but my brothers, in the second room, declared it an invasion of privacy.

Before we could bring our suitcases indoors, we had to shovel out the dust and sweep and mop the floor. That night eleven army cots were delivered to our rooms, but with just two mattresses. We lined up the cots against the walls as on a hospital ward and made makeshift beds, with one mattress for Mother and the other for Kay. The large pieces of canvas used for the blanket rolls were placed on the cots to protect ourselves against the draft. We used our coats and sweaters as temporary mattresses.

We discovered that first night that since Topaz was 4,650 feet above the sea level, temperatures could plummet drastically. We were cold all night long, especially when the padding we slept on shifted and bunched as we turned over. Within a few days, more mattresses and two army blankets for each cot were delivered to our door. We made up the other beds more adequately, and we were able to sleep more comfortably. I contrived a double bed for Kay and myself by placing two cots together. This was a precautionary measure as I missed the safety of his crib with its side rails, which had to be abandoned when we left Berkeley.

The morning after our arrival in Topaz brought the full realization that we were here to stay for the duration of the war. From the uncurtained, sliding window at my shoulder height, I could see the barracks ahead, identical in structure and appearance to our own. Though not visible from the window, off in the distance was the hospital and beyond that the military police compound. The patch of sky and the view itself seemed peaceful enough with the sunlight stretching across the ground, the wind holding its breath, and a quiet as yet unawakened by human sounds. At the same time, the stillness seemed immense and overwhelming.

At night the darkness engulfed the camp with the same sense of immeasurable space, so far from the lights of a city and the rumble of traffic on streets. The sky was studded with stars, unobscured by any tall buildings, so that I felt that if I stretched my hand upwards, I could almost touch them. That impression held in a poem I wrote:

Stand Back, Space

Stand back, space: I must lean
  Against your stars,
Be done with men's strange words
  And alien stares.

Sky, grant me room enough
  For me to breathe.
I must reach farther than time
  To catch my breath.

This was the permanent camp, and here we would remain until the government which had condemned us decided to release us. The camps were generally referred to as relocation centers, although in a press conference the same month we were inducted into Topaz, President Roosevelt himself called them concentration camps.

A sonnet of mine later described the impact that the first sight of our austere barracks had upon me:

Barracks Home

This is our barracks, squatting on the ground,
Tar-papered shack, partitioned into rooms
By sheetrock walls, transmitting every sound
Of neighbors' gossip or the sweep of brooms.
The open door welcomes the refugees,
And now at last there is no need to roam
Afar: here space enlarges memories
Beyond the bounds of camp and this new home.

The floor is carpeted with dust, wind-borne
Dry alkali patterned by insect feet.
What peace can such a place as this impart?
We can but sense, bewildered and forlorn,
That time, disrupted by the war from neat
Routines, must now adjust within the heart.

Another mode of living, another span of time, began with our entry into the permanent camp.

11

SETTLING IN

The first week in Topaz was a series of adjustments—becoming acquainted with new neighbors, coping with the weather, following mess hall schedules, resigning ourselves to the inconvenient location of the laundry and the latrine. Inwardly, we appreciated the fact that we were no longer in flimsy horse stalls, but at the same time, we realized how deep was the feeling of isolation. This separation from our home state and the outside world was difficult for most of us. We kept talking about remembered places in Berkeley and of friends there who still wrote to us. Struck by the barrenness of the place, we spoke wishfully about California; we experienced *natsukashi-mi,* the Japanese term for this emotional state of yearning, of longing.

The regimented existence in Tanforan had oriented us to communal living. Here, too, during this autumn season we arose early for the 7:30 a.m. breakfast (in the winter and spring, breakfast would be served at 8:00 a.m., and in the summer at 7:00 a.m.). We reported to the mess hall for lunch and dinner at the specified times with our identification cards in hand. The physical chore of settling in to the new center gradually lessened the abrasive shock of being moved again. The only way to survive was to adjust to conditions in this war-created community.

In conversation and demeanor, the Issei seemed far more patient than the Nisei. Our own parents as well as others of their generation had learned under duress to bear the unbearable. Now they feared that their hopes for their children were stunted by the restrictions of evacuation and internment. Still they clung to the views and values they had absorbed in their childhood. The Nisei, however, were not as attached to Japanese traditions, and in an atmosphere of divided feelings, we questioned our country, ourselves, and the reason for our internment.

The belief in life that Mother had, no matter what struggles were exacted of her, was strong even now. She still asserted, "Spring returns to the waiting heart." I had heard her repeat this phrase so often that the previous year I wrote the following haiku for her:

You embody spring,
For in your spirit April
Found a dwelling place.

And I followed this with another poem for her:

RENEWAL

Heart must keep faith with spring
  And not deny the grass
By soon remembering
  How swiftly it must pass.

This is the season when
  The full flowering peach
Brings back a loveliness
  Within the spirit's reach.

However, in camp in early October, the dream of spring was incongruous. We learned that the Tanforan Assembly Center was about to close, and on October 14th, the last group of 300 people from Tanforan arrived in Topaz. We also learned that in addition to our Utah camp, there were nine other relocation centers. Among them were Manzanar, the first camp, in southern California; Tule Lake, the largest, in the northern part of the state; Poston and Gila River in Arizona; Amache in Colorado; Heart Mountain in Wyoming; Minidoka in Idaho; and Rohwer and Jerome in Arkansas. All of them, like ours, were situated in remote places. Were they as desolate as ours, without familiar vegetation? Because there were no trees in our camp, we saw no birds. Daylight came without the twitter of city sparrows, the cooing of pigeons, or the occasional crowing of a pet rooster. This was a wasteland that overawed such remembered sounds. The little creatures that could exist in this dry countryside were only the scorpions, bats, and prairie dogs.

The sudden changes of temperature during the day at this high altitude caused frequent comparisons. The morning chill was sharper than the coolness of a California dawn. But in the afternoon, as the sun rose and it became hotter, the heat made some of the Issei women wear straw hats or carry umbrellas for shade.

The unexplored ruggedness of the country stretched into the distance, beyond the barbed wire boundary, toward the mountains miles away. Wherever I stood outside the barracks, nothing obscured the view. The sunsets, I discovered, were an amazing spectacle of flamboyant reds and oranges that faded slowly in intensity to the opalescent apple-green of twilight. At night my son, as entranced as I, soon learned to say "moon" when he saw the golden sphere suspended in the darkness, or "star" when the sky glimmered overhead.

Most of the Topaz population came from the San Francisco Bay area. As I came to know the residents, I began to perceive how diversified Block 4 was, from the professional careerist to the day laborer, from the aged to the very young. This diversity was true of the entire camp populace. Brought together because of race, complete homogeneity was neither noticeable nor possible. Among us were distinct variations and stratifications, in educational background, occupation, and family status. In particular, the generational difference between the Issei and Nisei affected their attitudes towards each other.

Formerly, in the Japanese community where we grew up, the family had been the identifying unit. Whenever we were introduced to others, we would give our surname and often even state the prefecture in Japan that Mother and Father came from. Now, in Topaz, the block was the unit to which we belonged. In exchanging greetings with someone from another location within the camp, we usually mentioned the block where we lived. The family entity we had known before the war had become decentralized. Now, even the family surname had been replaced by the identification number.

Where before the home had contained the family, knit closely by kinship and tradition, in camp the circle was dissolved. Mothers no longer had to market and cook; the mess halls substituted for them, and the children did not have to return home for their meals. I remembered the lively dinner hours in our Berkeley home, sitting at the large table and vying with one another to tell Mother and Father what had happened during the day. Here, for many, the barracks were simply a place to sleep. In the mess hall, families might sit near one another but often not at the same table. I noticed that small families with young children usually stayed at a single table, but if the children were of school age, the family disbanded. The young people liked to sit with friends or would sit with the mother if the father decided to eat with acquaintances at some other table.

The first week in Topaz, the meals were monotonous with little variety. For some days, no fresh greens or vegetables were served, so we appreciated the first spoonful serving of spinach. Later more provisions were brought into camp, but the meals had a certain sameness and certainly were not what we used to have. Food became and continued to be a favorite topic of conversation throughout our years in camp. Without a kitchen in our barracks, there was no way to prepare the special dishes that Mother had indulged us in or the desserts that Father and I used to bake. I had to obtain a hospital permit to get extra milk for Kay since milk was limited to the very young, invalids, and the aged. The so-called baby food available consisted of scrambled eggs or the peas and carrots cooked and served daily in the mess hall. Without a refrigerator, I improvised a cooler by filling a container partway with water and wrapping strips of cloth around the milk bottle to keep the milk from souring through evaporation.

The mess hall was as large as the laundry-latrine building. Both were tarpapered on the outside like the barracks, but barn-like on the inside, rough frame structures with open rafters. The cooking area and the serving counter, a stretch of Masonite, were at one end of the mess hall. The cooks and waitresses were from our own block. With few exceptions, the Issei cooks were inexperienced and unacquainted with American ways of preparing food. We had no menus, but ate what was served, although steamed rice was taken for granted as a staple. One day for lunch, however, beef kidneys were boiled with chunks of cabbage, and as the odor spread outside, those of us in line looked at one another and asked, "What is that?" Not even the very hungry boys would try this combination. Noses wrinkled and sniffed; this was one time when the servings on our plates remained untouched and uneaten and were scraped into the refuse pail under one end of the counter.

In the evening, the women in the block who had electric hotplates and could prepare extra food in their rooms carried buckets or dishpans filled with their pots, plates, and eating utensils to the laundry to wash in the two laundry tubs reserved for dishwashing. Like a village gathering around the town well, they flocked to wait their turn and gossip. Other women scrubbed clothes, and young mothers bathed little children in the farther laundry tubs. Without washing machines, women, including Mother and me, did the laundry by soaping, pounding, and kneading on metal or glass washboards. We rinsed and wrung out the wash, including sheets, with a dexterous twist of the wrists. We hung the laundry on rope clotheslines strung through half of the huge laundry room. And, as in Tanforan, once in a while I would find that an undergarment or a sheet had disappeared from our wash on the line.

To save steps, Mother kept one bucket aside just for drinking water. One of us was assigned the task of bringing back water each evening. Mother would cover this bucket with a clean towel, and we could dip the water out for drinking. The walk back and forth to the laundry-latrine building was pleasant enough during warmer weather, but in the late fall and winter months when the snow piled high against the front door, the necessary trips outdoors were a great bother. I could not sally out in just a cotton robe and a pair of wooden clogs, but had to dress completely against the cold weather. The latrine was far for the baby, so when Kay grew out of diapers, I purchased a toilet-chair by mail order for him to use in our room.

The women's side of the latrine was segmented into two compartments. One long room had wash basins lined up along the wall, and towards the back, a double-faced row of toilet stalls. The other room was cut up into doorless bath and shower cubicles. The lack of privacy still troubled us. Father said that even among the men, doors to the toilet cubicles were much desired. I often saw an elderly woman lugging a floorboard from a shower stall to prop up in front of her while she sat on the toilet.

The shower stalls had none of the tiled elegance pictured in decorating magazines but were primitive and solely functional, the concrete floor sloping to a drain with footboards out of wooden slats. If I wanted to shower, I had to ask Masa or a friend to take the opposite stall in order to minimize the embarrassment of public bathing. The girls tried to shield themselves by draping bathrobes over the supporting frame. For some of us, the showerheads were too high, so besides wet hems on our robes, we also finished with dripping hair. At least, thanks to Father, the furnace man for Block 4, we had ample hot water—an improvement from Tanforan.

I thought it was safer to bathe my young child in a regular bath tub and take a bath with him at the same time. After supper, I would gather the towels, his nightclothes, a soap box, and Kay himself, and set out for the latrine. The three bath stalls were partitioned, but like the showers had no curtains or doors. Kay liked his evening bath. His childish prattle and the noisy splashing as he played in the water would attract an audience. It was disconcerting at times to look up while washing him and see several Issei women standing in the doorway and observing us. They would nod and talk to him: "Kay-*chan*, you are having so much fun." Unabashed, he would stand up and answer them. I would attempt to chat politely and at the same time try to cover myself with a skimpy washcloth. Just as the case back in our own rooms where walls were thin and doors had no locks, privacy in camp was a lost cause.

As we became better acquainted with one another, the latrine section became a congested meeting place for the block residents in the evenings. My sister Masa often departed for an early shower, but several hours later, long after I had put Kay to bed and had reason to go to the latrine building again, I would find her there with friends of her own age. Still in her robe and unshowered, she would be sitting on a bench with them and chattering animatedly. The same conviviality occurred on the men's side, as I could sometimes recognize my brothers' voices and hear bits of conversation through the intervening wall.

Construction of some of the barracks at the far end of the camp was still unfinished, and in some cases building continued even after the barracks were occupied. We heard that some of the residents had been rained upon through open roofs, and rumor had it that someone had been severely burned while napping when hot roofing tar had dripped upon him or her.

Eventually the War Relocation Authority permitted some of the possessions we had stored in government warehouses to be shipped to the center. To our surprise, our large wooden wardrobe that had stood in my sister's bedroom in Berkeley with its one door still slightly ajar was unexpectedly delivered to our barracks. The sight of it, homely and unpretentious, recalled so much. For a few days, I would go to it and just touch its worn door as though my fingertips could relate to me the atmosphere of that other home. Now, instead of using paper cartons for storage, we could hang up some of our clothes in a civilized piece of furniture.

The days accelerated after that initial time of unpacking. In the front and back of the barracks, residents who had brought cuttings and slips of plants from Tanforan tried to cultivate new gardens, but the desert soil was not receptive to the transplanting. Father planted radish seeds behind our barracks. He carried water in a bucket from the latrine and used a dipper to scoop out water for the green sprouts. Kay trotted beside him on Father's trips back and forth for water. He would squat down beside his grandfather and participate in this ritual. The vitality of the radishes interested the child as well as the adult. For Father, even the growth of puny radishes in this unfavorable earth was a good sign. Once as Grandfather stooped over, Kay stepped backward to get out of the way. In doing so, he tripped on the full bucket behind him and promptly sat in the water. He came running around the barracks and rushed into our room to be changed into dry clothes. As I helped him, he insisted over and over that he had not needed to go to the bathroom.

Not all the camp residents were interested in gardening, but the non-gardeners did appreciate the efforts of the others. They would saunter around the block, occasionally to other blocks, to see the gardens and comment encouragingly about the plantings. The evacuees favored making Topaz a more livable habitat.

Nonetheless, in the evenings, as I looked about our room and saw the unfinished walls, the cots lined up in a row, Mother and Father quietly reading, Kay asleep, the mending on my lap, my mind protested: How long are we to be here in this forsaken place? What will I tell my son when he grows up? I could not openly speak of the pain I felt or ask the questions that assailed me, and poetry was my outlet:

Time threads the needle.
I sew blindly, because tears
Obscure my slow hands.

Grief chokes in my throat.
I cannot speak; tomorrow
Stretches far away.

Doubt haunts me: I ask,
Will there be another spring
To justify breath?

Was I more prone to think emotionally than my parents? Were they more settled in than I? Or did they too mull over our strange exile?

INTERNMENT CAMP

The parched earth waits for April miracles
    Though spring was done so long ago
(As if the summer sun could be
    Incentive for the grass to grow!)

The dust is blown by strong, wild winds
    And seeds choke in unwatered sand—
How can the roots endure this drought
    Denied the shelter of the land?
    (September 1943)

12

AS 1942 ENDED

Even as Kay grew, Topaz evolved in stages out of a stark desert compound into an organized settlement. Although we knew that we would be confined for an indeterminate period of time, as long as the war in the Pacific dragged on, we could not be resigned to being passive or purposeless. We would hear an outspoken Issei tell us, in the imperative, "*Gambare!*" which meant "Hold out—hang on—buckle down!" Though we inveighed against our internment, or whatever disgruntled us at the moment, we were aware that beyond the daily routine of living, our functioning as a group of people depended on our own efforts. Indirectly, I learned from my own family and other evacuees to adapt to and accept the limitations of this four-cornered, mile-square world.

Despite the striking contrast with California, the camp began to flourish. From September to December, the residents sought employment; mapped out more than two thousand acres for agricultural projects which included plant crops and livestock; developed community government; and turned tight, crowded rooms into homes. Annoyances continued to edge some days, but I could better understand now *shikata ga nai* (it cannot be helped; it is inevitable).

A week after our family reached Topaz, and two days after Kay's uncelebrated first birthday, a large group of former San Francisco people were moved in from the Santa Anita Assembly Center, and they were housed in Blocks 33, 34, and 40 at the opposite edge of the camp from our block. By mid-October, the last of the Tanforan contingents joined us. Before the month was out, the final Tanforan paychecks had been distributed, the elementary and high school children enrolled in school, the hospital dedicated, and a new post office opened.

We were soon exposed to the unremitting dust storms, more violent and smothering than anything we had experienced in Tanforan—and demoralizing. When the fierce winds blew and stirred up the fine silt, visibility became nil. The nearest barracks, just a few feet away, disappeared from sight. Puffs of dust drove in under the door, around the windows and over the sills, and the rough grit sifted over the scrap-lumber table, stools, beds, and the cast-iron space heater. A layer of gray covered everything. When we went outside during a storm, we would return with whitened hair and eyebrows. Chiffon scarves tied over our faces or wet handkerchiefs over our noses gave little protection against the grains of sand beating on our skin.

In the mess hall, the cups of tea, poured as the diners filed in and stood in line, would be powdered with dust, and the food we ate had an added texture that ground sharply on the tongue and teeth. After a storm subsided, a common flurry of activity occurred in every barracks and block. Beds were stripped; covers, blankets, and pillows were taken outside, shaken and beaten; floors were mopped, sills and furniture wiped off with damp cloths. The cleaning continued into the night, with hair-washing, baths, showers, and laundry.

Much later, the roads between the blocks were graded with uneven rocks (rough on the shoes we had to obtain on rationing), and the pathways between the barracks were graveled. The surfacing of the roads and the ground allayed the dust to some extent, but did not prevent the onslaught of sudden dust storms. There were times when I could look down the road and see a narrow funnel of wind twisting and turning in the distance like a wild dervish, and shouting to the people outside to take cover, I would run for shelter. A strong dust storm could last for three days. I railed against this element with this:

Dust Storm

The dust blows up from desert soil
    And taunts air with its maddening dance,
A swirl of gray along the roads
    To mock the cautious glance.

How can a sudden twist of wind
    Veil all the camp in choking cloud
Until eyes cannot tell the sky
    From earth, wrapped in this shroud!

Original plans for Topaz called for a program for landscaping the blocks. Each residential block was to be provided with a small park with trees, shrubbery, and lawns in the open space beside the recreation hall barracks. But the parks never materialized. The open space in our block remained a dry sandlot where my brothers sometimes played baseball with their friends.

It was not until late in November when Arbor Week was observed that trees were brought in from a distance outside the camp and transplanted. Willow saplings were planted in thirty-five occupied blocks (unoccupied blocks were used for the public schools). Larger trees like the Siberian elm and the Utah juniper, obtained from the Forestry Department of Utah State Agricultural College, were set in the ground around the administration and hospital buildings. The saplings looked spindly, but these slender trees did take root and showed green leaves the following spring. However, not all survived.

The days turned cold, and the briskness in the air penetrated our sweaters and jackets. Soon the rain turned the ground into gummy mud, and the snow and biting winds became another source of grumbling comment. Going outdoors for the half-block walk to the latrine made us wish for a bathroom within our barracks. When we arose in the morning, the first blast of chill air we breathed when we went outdoors was a real eye-opener. On the way to the mess hall for breakfast, Kay would sidle more closely to me and with a mittened hand over his nose say, "*Samui!*" (cold).

The barracks had been constructed rapidly, and initially they had not been insulated. Now Japanese work crews came to the blocks to put up sheetrock and celotex panels over the exposed two-by-four uprights on the walls and to cover the ceiling. Outside, they also placed a wooden skirting around the foundation of the barracks for more insulation. The men warned us that the winters in this region were bitter and long. The only means of heating the interior was by burning coal. The shortage of coal at this time concerned us, and the residents, without thinking of a fire hazard, began to hoard piles of coal in their rooms, right beside the stoves. Father, whose job was to tend the furnace and keep a supply of hot water available for Block 4, had to guard the low supply of coal piled near the laundry-latrine building. We were relieved when the War Relocation Authority did contract for delivery of more coal for the cold months ahead. I thought it was a good thing that the fire station was completed then.

When the strong winds and steady snows blew furiously through the flat land of the camp, our barracks did seem thin and unprotected. The snow, propelled by fierce gusts, heaped against the doors, which made half-circles when pushed open. It edged the window sills and sometimes forced itself inside, just as the dust had. The contrast of the black barracks against the expanse of snow and unobstructed gray skies made a drab view.

The first blizzard we experienced was a startling phenomenon to us from the West Coast. We sank knee-deep into the snow, which came over the top of our boots and melted under our socks. The snow hampered our walking, but we thought the winds were more troublesome. During one blizzard that lasted for several days, the snow scaled off the surface of the ground and mounded at the end of the barracks. As flake impacted on flake, pounded by the force of the wind, the drifts grew as tall as the barracks. The solid drifts became firm and broad enough to bear the weight of several boys. One noon hour my brothers waited for me with a supply of snowballs as I returned to our block for lunch. The first two or three well-aimed snowballs hurled at me made me run for cover to the women's side of the latrine building. Shaking the snow off my head and shoulders, I waited until I saw the boys enter the mess hall. When I joined the line to be served, my brothers, presenting a picture of decorum, grinned at me, while I frowned back at them.

At the year's end, the construction work throughout the camp was practically finished except for the hospital boiler house and its laundry, and the four eighty-foot water towers. Work on the water towers was completed after the new year was under way. After priorities on building materials were cleared, other construction was authorized, not by the United States Engineer Corps but by the War Relocation Authority. The building projects included the high school, elementary school, administration dwellings, community church, slaughter house, meat packing plant, bakery, engineering and agricultural office, garage and repair shops, chicken brooders, and hog pens. In another project, two thousand acres beyond the boundary fence, where the soil was least alkaline, were to be cultivated for crops to supplement our food in the mess halls.

Consumer enterprises were started with the opening of the canteen in Block 19, a dry goods store in Block 12, and shoe repair and electrical repair shops in Block 26. Two movie houses were created in recreation halls although, without seats, we had to take blankets to sit on the floor, and there was a radio repair shop. Other services were added later, but private enterprises developed on a very small scale, mainly in personal services such as barbering, beauty care, tailoring and dressmaking, and watch repair, on cash payments or a barter basis. They did not compete with community enterprises in any way.

Because of wartime shortages, the canteen and the dry goods store never had enough merchandise for the demand, and items we needed were invariably scarce. When pinking shears were announced for sale at the dry goods store, only seven were to be had. I was able to acquire one because my brother Howard delivered supplies to the stores and had advised me to be in line early before the shop opened. On another day, cantaloupes were shipped in to the canteen and word spread through the camp that fresh fruit, a rarity, was available. A long queue waited for hours, but I was able to purchase a small melon. The melon was something new to Kay, so when I served it, he smelled his portion, looked at it closely, nibbled a bit, and then ate it with great relish. If I could not obtain a tube of toothpaste at the canteen, I brushed my teeth with salt from the mess hall.

The block managers under the direction of the camp administration were mainly Issei evacuees appointed to their position, and they supervised the activities in each residential block. The block manager was the person we saw when a fuse was blown, when we needed more coal, or had complaints to make. It was his responsibility to deliver letters and the occasional packages addressed to us, keep records, issue supplies, notify us of administrative policies, and look after the welfare of the residents. He was the liaison officer between the residents and the administration in the management of the camp, and in his role, he was effective in developing block cohesion.

When our block manager was able to have three foot-pedal sewing machines assigned to our area, the women rushed to have their names placed on a waiting list. Many of the women had sewed and mended for their families, and they were now able to refurbish meager clothing. I took my turn in signing up for the use of a sewing machine, which could be borrowed from the block manager's office for a few days at a time. There was little choice in the selection of fabrics at the dry goods store, but I made a brown cotton print dress for Mother, a tan cotton dress for myself, and patched the knees of Kay's worn coveralls.

By now, most of the evacuees had applied for work, ranging from the manual to the professional, and 77 percent of the able-bodied residents found employment. In the wage classifications of the professional, skilled, and unskilled workers, more than five hundred were in the top salary bracket of nineteen dollars a month for professionals such as the doctors and teachers. Those in the skilled category earned sixteen dollars a month. Father, who could have taught mathematics, was hired at sixteen dollars a month because he did not specify his college education on his job application. When I, who earned more than he did, asked him why he did not request a reclassification, he simply smiled and replied, "I work as a furnace man for our block, and the furnace does not need attention every minute. I am near home. So you see, I have time for my oil painting." As far as we knew, there was only one worker classified as unskilled who received twelve dollars a month. Mother refused to work for she was fully occupied in taking care of Kay while I was away during the day.

The snowfalls continued as the autumn days passed, and we huddled in our rooms around the coal stove. *Samui gozai masu* or *Samui desu, ne?* (It's cold, isn't it?) were the greetings we exchanged when we met other block residents. The young and old seemed to reflect the philosophical acquiescence of the Issei in bearing the rigors of the weather. In November, I composed a series of haiku which I mailed to a friend:

A small thing to give,
But I give you the silence
Of moonlight on snow.

The petalled snow falls
Too gently where not a blade
Of grass has grown—see!—

The flowers of snow
Conceal the barrenness—
Oh, that I should know!

But take the silence,
If you will: it holds substance
Of my heart's still song.

On the same day, conscious of the weather we were now exposed to, I also wrote:

In Topaz

Can this hard earth break wide
  The stiff stillness of snow
And yield me promise that
  This is not always so?

Surely, the warmth of sun
  Can pierce the earth, ice-bound,
Until grass comes to life,
  Outwitting barren ground!

A week before Thanksgiving, Caucasian family friends who had visited us in Tanforan sent us a gift box of food, followed by a letter shortly afterwards. In the box, the mother had packed dried corn and dried cherries, products of her garden, and chocolate candy. She had pre-cooked the kernels of corn before drying, so that all I had to do was soak the corn in water or milk and simmer it until softened for eating. She wrote that winter was in the air in Berkeley, but that it was not very cold and that the smell of catsup was gone for the year. With that mention, I could almost smell the spicy tomato odor from the catsup factory that I always associated with the crisp autumn days in Berkeley.

In the same letter, she remarked that people on the outside were as mindful of food as we were in camp. She described the way store shelves were being stripped of grocery items such as butter, particularly after rationing. She sent news clippings from local papers so we could know what was happening in the city we had left behind.

In camp, meat, coffee, and sugar were served sparingly, and dairy products were still limited to little children and the elderly. The government allowed thirty-one cents per person each day for food, so there were no special or extravagant dishes. Mother missed having butter for breakfast, the only meal at which she ate bread, and she would not touch the uncolored margarine that resembled chunks of lard. I took to saving her portions of the margarine in a jar and using it later for cooking in our barracks. Therefore, we had not expected a special dinner on Thanksgiving Day, but as it turned out, the kitchen crew took pride in serving roast turkey, which was pronounced "tahki," with accompanying side dishes and dessert.

Away from California, this first winter in Topaz was especially rugged for us who were unaccustomed to the freezing weather. It was the first time that I saw milk frozen in a bottle left on the window sill, with its paper cap sitting an inch above its top. Many of us ordered yarn by mail, and we knitted sweaters, caps, socks, and mittens. I had learned to knit years before as a volunteer for the Red Cross, and I was certainly thankful that I had acquired the skill. Besides, I enjoyed the relaxation I found in knitting. One afternoon I saw two tall boys, dressed in heavy plaid mackinaws and thick caps pulled down over their ears, walking down the road and chatting companionably. One of them kept tugging at his pocket with a regular motion of his right hand. After a moment I realized that he was knitting on a sock from a ball of yarn tucked into that pocket.

Later, when I heard that surplus navy pea jackets could be had for the asking at the camp warehouse, I decided to go and obtain one for myself. I trudged to the warehouse blocks away. As I stood at the counter to inquire, the clerk could scarcely contain his amusement on seeing me, standing not even five feet tall. Grinning all the while, he informed me the sizes up to thirty-eight had all been issued, and that the only ones left were in men's size forty. He added that it would take two of me to fill that large size, and that size forty was even too large for most Japanese men. Some of the women residents, I eventually learned, had purposely requested the large sizes, which they were able to remake for their children. As it was, I continued to wear my old coat, fast becoming threadbare at the edge of the sleeves and around the collar, with an extra sweater underneath.

Toward the end of the year, the constitution of Topaz was drafted and ratified, and civic government was established. Late in December, a general election of a stable community council was held in the camp's nine electoral districts. The candidates for the thirty-three council positions, both Issei and Nisei, had been nominated at district meetings the week before. With the election of the council, the residents gained a liaison body to approach the administration. The Issei were then declared ineligible for the office, but in April of the following year, the War Relocation Authority rescinded its prohibition against the Issei sitting in the community council.

The snow deepened on the ground, and as our first Christmas drew near, we were homesick for California and reminisced about former Christmases. Here we were so far removed from the holiday atmosphere of a city, the festive lights and the Yuletide decorations of the shops and streets, the throngs of shoppers. My son, now a year old, would not have known what the tinsel and glitter meant, had he been able to see them. But for his sake, I took two pieces of cardboard, pasted green tissue paper over them front and back, cut out the outline of a Christmas tree, slotted and fitted the bottoms so it would stand, and I placed this crude imitation near Kay's bed. On the angular branches, tiny bows of yarn added color. How could I have described a real tree with its fresh-scented needles, its graceful shape, to a child who had never seen one? We had no cards we could buy and send, except brief notes to friends scattered in other states, but they remembered us and encouraged us with their Christmas messages.

On the freezing cold Christmas Eve, we gathered near the coal stove. The air in the room lacked any touch of hilarity. Suddenly we heard caroling outside. It had been a very long time since I had gone caroling. Hurriedly pulling on coats, we went out the door to see. A slowly moving truck with high school students in the back was on the road. Neighbors popped out of their doors also. The singing sounded sweet and clear in the night. "Joy to the world" was their blessing to us. As the truck passed by, their voices dimming in the distance came back, "We wish you a Merry Christmas; we wish you a Merry Christmas, and a Happy New Year!"

On Christmas Day, I dressed Kay in his mail-ordered snow suit and carried him to the mess hall, where we had turkey served again. As we gathered around the mess tables and sat with friends, a pervasive loneliness kept our conversation subdued. While we were eating, some of the kitchen crew and the girls serving tea walked among the tables and asked us to return to the mess hall after the cleanup chores were done. At the unusual announcement, we looked at each other and asked, "Why? What kind of surprise has been planned?" No one seemed to know, and the questioning glances towards the kitchen helpers were met with noncommittal smiles. After the gong rang for the second time that evening, we returned to the mess hall, and then we learned that Christian churches in distant cities had sent boxes of gifts for the children in the camp, and the boxes had been distributed to each block. The little children, their faces scrubbed and straight dark hair recombed, some shy, some eager, waited expectantly as the gift-wrapped presents were placed in their hands. The parents looked on in wonderment. Kay received a warm cap in two soft shades of blue that some kind hands had knitted, a box of crayons and a coloring book.

And so, 1942 drew to an end.

13

BLOCK 4-8-E

The residents of our Block 4 were mainly from the east side of the bay—Alameda, Oakland, and Berkeley—with some from San Francisco, but we were a conglomerate of personalities with dissimilar occupational backgrounds, and we had not known each other before the internment. Now, we were bound together by circumstance into an extended family or clan. For this disjointed period of time, we all practiced *akirame* (resignation, acquiescence). Sharing in the communal living, eating together in the mess halls, or meeting informally at night in the latrine building, wearing bathrobes and carrying towels, we learned of one another.

I observed a slim, dignified woman, past fifty, who seemed aloof although she greeted others with a smile and courteous bow. She would come alone to the mess hall and after receiving her food at the serving counter, she would glance around swiftly and go to an unoccupied table. Occasionally, if she were invited to sit with a group already seated, she would then join her acquaintances. I noticed that she did not become involved in the table talk, although if a question were directed to her, she would reply with a friendly, attentive look.

There was a grace to the movements of her hands and the bow of her head. The people of the block always spoke deferentially to this gentle Issei woman. I was told that her husband, a Buddhist bishop, was an invalid and did not venture out of the barracks, and that they had no children. She could understand the English that the younger ones spoke as they greeted her, and she seemed pleased when they did.

She carried an indefinable air of cultured descent in her appearance, unobtrusive dress, and softly modulated tone of speech; her manner gave her a bearing of imperturbability. When she and Mother greeted each other, they both exhibited something distinctively similar that must have been derived from their past. Whenever she saw my son, as I led him by the hand to the latrine building for his bath, she would chat with him and ask him questions with unpretentious interest. She would listen closely to his childish chatter about his nursery school and his playmates.

One evening, when I went to the laundry room to wash some dishes, I saw the young woman who lived at the end of our barracks rush past me into the latrine side with a blanket in her arms. Sounds of agitated voices came to me then from that area, so I too dashed into the latrine side. Then I saw the cause for the alarm. The gentle woman whom I had seen earlier at supper was now lying motionless on the cement floor. I went towards her and saw, between others' heads and shoulders, how pale and still she was, with her head cushioned on the knees of another Issei woman and her legs covered with the blanket. Several women went out to let the block manager know what had happened.

People did not know whether or not she had simply fainted. Moments elapsed, and she still had not opened her eyes, but we did not dare move her. The faces of the women who knelt beside her expressed their concern. One whispered that she suffered from high blood pressure and that she had not been feeling well lately, but had not complained. I felt helpless, unable to do anything, so I returned to the barracks to put Kay to bed.

Later, after Kay had fallen asleep, Mother and I went back to the washroom. There we learned from another neighbor that the block manager had notified the hospital, and that she had been taken there in the ambulance without regaining consciousness. How vivid in my mind was the sight of that still, almost lifeless figure. The neighbor added that the prognosis was poor. Several others who overheard this remark shook their heads with sad faces, murmuring that she might not be expected to live through the night. They lamented the fact that she had no children to mourn for her, that her husband was ill too, and that her relatives in Japan could not be notified. My sense of helplessness deepened.

The women commented that had we been in our former communities, we would have access to a hospital better equipped and better staffed to cope with emergencies like this. What could you expect in a camp, miles from a city? Salt Lake City was too far away for quick transport to a good hospital. Besides, arrangements would have to be made through the administration, and that would take too much time. Here she was without a family to care for her and no one to be at her bedside. The doctors at the camp hospital were overworked, and the few professional nurses and practical aides were burdened with other patients. Without the special care she had received in San Francisco, her health had been jeopardized by the rough camp life, but she had never complained, not wanting to impose on others. The conversation went on and on, Mother listening quietly. I kept hearing interspersed in the talk the phrase *shikata ga nai,* which meant simply that one must bear what one must. Anger at the futility of the situation welled up in me even though I knew necessity compelled acceptance. The women hoped that she would recover and be among us again.

My thoughts revolved around that patient woman who must have been lonely taking care of her husband in the small barracks room. She had cloaked herself in reserve as she had been taught in Japan, yet reached out with warmth and kindness even to a little child. Living as closely as we did in our bare boxes that allowed no privacy, we each had to create inner corners of the self that were altogether our own even while aware of the others around us in the same existence.

What I sensed in the conversation of these women was that had our internment not been imprisonment, living would have provided choices. It was bad enough to be so isolated, but deprivation of familiar creature comforts was not always tolerable. Nevertheless, we had to endure. The women identified with their stricken acquaintance, but they had no power of their own accord to ease her illness or rescue her from what we feared.

The following noon, the nurse's aide who had previously taken care of Kay told me that the patient was too far gone and that the doctors were not hopeful. She inquired about Kay, whom I had kept home from school since he was having another siege of asthma. The women in the block went to the hospital to see how she was, but she was still unconscious. Within the day we learned that she had died in a coma from a cerebral hemorrhage. All I could tell Kay was that she had gone away and would never return.

On my way back from the mess hall, where I had heard the news of her death, I saw her so clearly in my mind, bowing to me. I bent down to clutch up a handful of the soil, not the dark moist clods of earth I had felt in my hands in Berkeley, but fine grains of sand, long parched by the sun and ground to a soft powder by winds. I let the soil dribble from my hand, and I thought: dust to dust. Gradually with time she was no longer mentioned in company. It was as though the winds had scattered the sand over an immense desert. But Mother and I sometimes spoke of her, and I could not forget her gracious presence.

Though remote from their everyday thoughts and routines, the elderly in the camp must have dreaded the idea of dying in a strange land that would not accept them, although California, at least, had been more a home than this wilderness. In facing the death of another, they themselves would not want to dwell on their own future death but would turn their attention to the present. It occurred to me, as I thought about the woman who had lived among us, that the Japanese usually do not offer gifts or serve portions in amounts of four because the Japanese word for the numeral, *shi,* sounds like the beginning of the word *shinu* (to die). And then I thought, we lived in Block 4.

A few days later, when the winter cold gripped us, and the chill seemed to be woven into our clothes, I was able to write:

Lament

She who was so gentle now is dead;
Cover her softly with the still
White peace of snow; her head
That grew so heavy knew no will

Except to sleep, alone, alone.
She lay so grave and motionless,
And uttered nothing, made no moan,
Bequeathing earth her gentleness.

There was another woman in the block who impressed me in a totally different manner, who was much taller than most of the other women, and who usually wore a bright, splashy head-covering. Her features were like those of an Indian, with high cheek bones and rough-hewn features, a wide mouth that could smile rather cynically, and dark, cautious, snapping eyes. She walked with a loping gait, with her youngest child slung on one hip, followed by several others of her five children. Her stringy black hair was brushed back into a loosely pinned knot.

The other women in the block, on the whole, had been hard-working people, a number having been employed in domestic service as housekeepers or cleaning maids. They were older than Setsu, so their children were in grammar school and high school. They had somehow managed to support and raise their families, though now they often found that their children had absorbed more American ways than they could understand.

Although these women were themselves unlettered and totally immersed in their family concerns, they were shielded by their own value system, by their own judgment of conduct. When they would see Setsu in the laundry room inevitably followed by her brood, their remarks were spoken with a smile, but also with a gibing tone. It was rumored that each of Setsu's children had a different father.

She was not at the laundry tub as often as the other women, and because her oldest daughter, about thirteen or fourteen years of age, would sometimes be washing the children's clothes, Setsu was, in the eyes of the other women, a slattern. She usually wore faded, well-worn clothes that did not really fit her, evidently discards given to her. Her children's attire was much the same shape, shrunken out of the original freshness and in sizes not intended for the particular child who wore the outfit.

One brusque woman who had a mean tongue would patronizingly comment on how closely the baby resembled Setsu, who would then look straightforwardly at her critic and shrug, "Like father, like son." Another would bait bitingly, "Nice to have such leisure time to walk around the block with nothing else to do." To that Setsu would reply, "If you took care of my small children, I would go to work like you." The malice was not too adroitly concealed, but Setsu held her own. She had a way, too, of noticing the unusual about these women and would not hesitate to comment herself, not as stingingly as these women but with greater subtlety. Mother would often say in the confines of our room that Setsu could take care of herself.

Setsu's children were intelligent and well-mannered, poorly dressed as they were. I was sensitive to the use of the honorific term, *san,* attached to a person's name, since this was the form of address we had been taught to use in talking to others. Setsu's children were well-trained in this courtesy, and the eldest girl, a gawky, near-sighted child, with the dark skin of her mother and the same stringy hair, would often chat with me and Kay. Sometimes she would pick Kay up and hold him, always in a gentle and kindly way. While she talked with us, she would keep an eye on her younger brothers and sisters and interrupt her chatter with "Stop hitting him, Ken," or "Now, don't you do that again, Taro," or "Come over here and I'll wipe your nose. See how clean Kay-*chan* is!"

Mother invariably greeted the people she met with quiet courtesy and a bow of her head. And she did not single Setsu out for different treatment, but exchanged pleasantries of the day as she would have with any close neighbor. She also made it a point to speak to Setsu's children. I noted that Setsu's attitude and even the tone of her voice towards Mother was always respectful. At first Setsu was inclined to address Mother as *Okusama*, or *Okusan* (mistress or madam), but after a few times of being addressed in this fashion, Mother demurred. Thereafter, she greeted Mother with the more customary form of Suyemoto-*san*.

Mother, with her quick perception and ability to discover points of interest about people she encountered, found out that Setsu read a great deal, including Japanese newspapers and the popular women's magazines published in Japan. Her reading probably made her isolation from the other women in the block more bearable, and it certainly made her alert to the news of the world. How far she had advanced in schooling, we did not know, but Mother claimed that her newspaper reading would have increased her vocabulary and knowledge. Mother was delighted that Setsu could converse intelligibly about many things, even fashion, whenever they happened to meet.

The other women could not comprehend Setsu's unfailing courtesy towards Mother, and often when the two were together chatting, the others would saunter over out of curiosity to join them. Setsu would look at each of them in turn and calmly tell them that the conversation was private. Then the women would withdraw, with comments under their breath about the upstart and her airs, leaving the two ringed by the children. The children were not boisterous, and sometimes one of the smaller ones would shyly take hold of Mother's hand.

One day Setsu came to our barracks and hesitantly invited Mother to tea, and seeing me at home, she asked me to come also. So we went to her room in another barracks. She had superficially straightened the beds, gathered up the children's clothes and piled them on one bed, and found some beaten copies of a few magazines that she offered to lend to Mother. I had to leave to finish some chores, but when Mother came home, she said that Setsu had talked about herself, without a trace of self-pity, of her impoverished childhood, of her marriage and coming to the United States with her husband only to be abandoned, of the hardships of earning a living and caring for her children. Somehow, she had managed the care on a day-to-day basis. Though Setsu's solutions to her problems, magnified by relations with different men, would not have been hers perhaps, Mother recognized in Setsu a similar temperament that would not be overwhelmed by difficulties.

Sometime later Setsu returned the call, and Mother served tea and cookies bought at the canteen. That afternoon I saw a considerate, genteel Setsu, truly a lady, conversing as though she had been accustomed to this exchange of social visits. She accepted the cup of tea gracefully and ate a cookie daintily. It was on this visit that we discovered that Setsu had a richly pitched, though untrained, resonant singing voice. She had learned her repertoire from listening to singers on Japanese records. She sang popular songs and folk songs, some that were familiar to me. When I glanced at Mother, I saw she was listening intently, and I realized with a start that for that moment the Japanese songs had taken her far away in time.

Setsu's nonchalant behavior continued towards the other women, aggressive when she had to be, quick-witted and disdainful. Mother remained unchangingly herself, accepting Setsu as another human being, brought together by chance to the same place, so Setsu always felt comfortable with Mother. And Setsu, and her young children, never called me other than Toyo-*san,* the polite form of address.

Mother came to know another resident of the block who was somewhat of a mystery to the others. I never learned his name, but he lived in the barracks across from ours. He was a tall, lean man who gave the impression of being unfriendly and taciturn as he seldom spoke, though he would bow to people as he passed by them. The general gossip was that he had worked as a butler for a wealthy Caucasian family in San Francisco, but no one was sure. Now he worked as a cook in a mess hall in another block.

Mother often remarked on his neat appearance. For a bachelor who did his own laundry, as we did ours, his clothes were clean, starched, and pressed. I often wondered where he had come from, what his former occupation had been. A few acquaintances would visit him from other blocks, but he made no overtures to those in ours. When he did his washing in the laundry room, he did so silently. When one or two of the women nearby would throw bantering remarks about his being single and unencumbered by family worries, their remarks seemed to fall off an invisible armor of reserve.

We knew that he read because we would see him returning from an evening walk with books in hand. We assumed that he had gone to the Japanese library or the public library to borrow the books. Mother was able to tell me later that he was well-read. Knowing how little he spoke to the others, I was surprised that she had discovered his interest in reading and had enabled him to talk with her. Having seen me with Mother often enough, he would give me a curt, quick nod when we passed each other.

When I thought of it later, I realized that Mother herself had a reserve about her that was much like that of the quiet man in the next barracks. At some time they must have met in the laundry long enough to talk about more than the weather. Occasionally I would see women staring at Mother when she would be bent over the washboard at a laundry tub. She would greet them pleasantly, but beyond the niceties about the temperature of the day, or reference to their children, she kept to herself and to her task. So how a conversational gambit had been established with the reticent man, I did not know. But it must have been her interest, untouched by idle curiosity, that had evoked a cordial, respectful response.

By this time we had acquired a small radio to catch what news we could and to listen to musical programs, but I still missed the concerts and plays that I had attended in our former freer life. The popular music on the radio broadcasts was the current jitterbug, nothing that could be considered profound or a satisfactory replacement for a classical concert. But one afternoon, when I was returning from the laundry with an armload of dry clothes, I was startled to hear the strains of *La Traviata* coming from somewhere.

I could not bear to go inside immediately, so I stood at the door to listen. How alive and beautiful the singing of the familiar arias sounded as the music soared into the air. In my mind, I could picture the fragile Violetta and her lover on the stage. Even Mother knew the story, and as a child, I had first heard from her about the lovely *Tsubaki-hime* (camellia maiden).

While I stood transfixed, the taciturn neighbor came out of his barracks. Seeing me standing there, motionless and intent, he glanced at me rather quizzically. I bowed to him quickly and blurted out, "Oh, that is simply beautiful!" In an instant, I discovered he spoke fluent English, as he asked, "You mean the music—*La Traviata*?" "Yes, it is beautiful," I repeated. "I have not heard that opera for so long. It just seems amazing that I am hearing that music in a place like this." To that he said, "*Traviata* is one of my favorite operas, but I only have a part of my record collection here with me. I enjoy music very much." I breathed, "Thank you, thank you for playing *Traviata* today."

He smiled at me, nodded in response, and went on his way briskly. From then on when he saw that I was at home late afternoon or early evening, he would occasionally play his records—chamber music, concertos, opera, selections that seemed to assuage the spirit. And I was grateful for the unspoken thoughtfulness of this stranger whom no one in our block ever came to know closely.

Another neighbor in the barracks across the way was a dear old gentleman, probably near eighty years of age. Like Mother he did not work, so his days at home must have been long and drawn out. He was a slightly stooped, compact figure, and bald. In the summertime, at midday, when the desert sun burned our faces, he would tie the corners of a clean, white, man's handkerchief into knots to make a rounded beret and would perch it on his head when he had to go outdoors.

The old man would reach out to his neighbors and offer help where he could. One day, he tried to join in a rescue effort for Kay. By now Kay was quick in his movements, energetic, and fast on his feet. When I had to take Kay for his bath in the evenings, Mother would accompany us so she could hold on to one hand while I clutched his other. One day, after supper, on just such a walk, Mother and I became engrossed in our conversation, and we let go of his hands.

In that instant, he suddenly darted away from us, with a gleeful look over his shoulder. He ran for the open space beyond the recreation hall. I handed the towels and bath items to Mother and started after him. Mother called after him, but the spurt of freedom winged his feet. My younger brothers were in the recreation hall, so, running past the open door, I yelled to them, "Joe, Lee, Howard—help me catch Kay!" They came out to join the chase. Like a little fox, he changed his course and zigzagged to break away from his pursuers.

Our elderly neighbor had been standing on his porch to watch us go by. When he saw Kay escape and the rest of us running after him, he called out, "I shall help you!" He began to jog after Kay with the slow measured pace of the aged, but his unsteady legs were no match for those of a determined three-year-old. My brothers, converging on the culprit from different directions, caught up with the runaway, and one of them carried back a wiggling armful and set him down in front of Mother and me. Mother took his hand firmly this time and admonished him in Japanese all the way to the latrine building. When I looked back, I saw our old neighbor, winded by the chase, returning to his barracks.

The neighbors, young and old, in our block were one small segment of the entire camp. After we had settled in Topaz, we tried to bring some order into our disrupted lives. Some of us brought a few cherished books or tools for handcrafts, or phonographs or radios, to add some normality to our shared existence. Yet a number of the people simply waited out the days as though we were rooted permanently in the dry soil of exile.

14

SCHOOLING IN TOPAZ

In Topaz, schools opened for the young people just a little over a month after the advance group arrived in the camp. The War Relocation Authority provided for the education of elementary and high school children in all the centers, and in Topaz registration for the schools took place on October 20, 1942. John C. Carlisle served as superintendent of the system for the first four months, until he left to resume teaching at the Utah State Agricultural College. He was succeeded by LeGrande Noble. Education was highly regarded by the Japanese, and the Issei parents were relieved when schools opened and a regular schedule was established for their children. It was crucial to them that their children receive the education they so honored and which they themselves had had to forego in many cases. Their own lives had been difficult ones of self-sacrifice to support their families and to keep their children in school. I knew this was true of my parents.

Although he was not able to find work in the field, Father had a university education in mining engineering, and Mother had completed normal school in Japan. She taught for a short time before coming to this country, which was probably one reason why she never condoned lax study habits on our part. I suppose it was because of their own education that they wanted us to make the most of our schooling. As the older of us entered college, we were constantly cautioned not to indulge in a "hash curriculum," but to take substantial "meat and potatoes" courses. Other parents must have advised their children in a similar fashion.

In my childhood, "playing school" on our front porch seemed as natural as hide-go-seek or tag. When we advanced in grammar school, vacation days were not all fun and games. If we did not go to the church summer school, Mother saw to it that the mornings were spent in reviewing arithmetic and spelling, or in reading and expanding our vocabulary. Only the afternoons of vacation days were free and unencumbered. The truth was, however, that prior to the war, the Nisei often found themselves without prospect of employment after college, even as my Father had in his day.

Hakujin (Caucasian) teachers who had credentials and experience were employed at prevailing salaries, but the schools still had to be partly staffed by Nisei who were educated, but untrained. The Nisei worked for the camp professional wage scale of nineteen dollars a month although they carried full teaching loads and responsibilities. The teachers, both Caucasian and Japanese, came from as far west as the Pacific coast and as far east as the Atlantic. The two racially differentiated groups were known as the appointed and the resident faculty. Other school employees—the assistant teachers, school library staff, secretaries, and clerks—were all evacuees. Inevitably, there was a constant turnover among the resident teachers as the evacuees began to relocate outside for better opportunities.

At the beginning of September, I received a mimeographed form and personal letter from Drayton B. Nutthall, principal of the high school. The former stated:

> We are impressed with the important part that education must take to stabilize the life of our Topaz youngsters. It is thus that we solicit your assistance in securing an adequate resident faculty for our high school which opens next week. Our first plea is, would you be interested in taking over a teaching post? We have vacancies in practically every field. This is unquestionably a responsibility to be assumed by our educated residents.

The second, addressed directly to me, read:

> We are appealing to certain qualified residents within the center to join our faculty for this coming school term effective next week. According to the records, we feel that you might be able to handle a class in English.

So it was that I taught English grammar and composition and Latin in the high school, as well as Americanization and basic English classes in the adult program. As it turned out, I was teaching high school students at the same time as I had some of their parents in the evening program.

The school curriculum conformed to the standards of the state of Utah, and the credits the students earned in the camp schools were recognized in regular public schools after relocation, and accepted for college and university entrance throughout the country. High school students had an opportunity to receive vocational training along with the regular courses of study.

A six-six division of grades for the elementary and high schools was adopted, a modification of the California and Utah educational systems. The courses offered included social living, language and home arts, mathematics, social and general sciences, drama, public speaking, music, art, modern languages and Latin, agriculture, business, physical education, and library and supervised reading. Special emphasis was directed toward organizing a complete college preparatory program. Nonetheless, instruction in the Japanese language was forbidden. I taught first-year Latin and Caesar's Gallic wars. The beginning Latin class in the second year dwindled to a handful.

New to students and faculty was the core curriculum, recommended to the WRA by Stanford University's summer class on curricula. It focused on the concept of the community school in which the facilities and resources of the community were considered part of the school's educational tools. In theory, the core included a broad field, combining social studies and language arts (oral and written English). It might have been the lack of qualified teachers, but in practice it became necessary to divide the teaching of English and social studies.

The elementary schools employed seven *hakujin* and twenty-eight resident teachers for almost 700 students. The high school had the largest staff with four counselors and directors, a school librarian, and twenty *hakujin* teachers augmented by twenty-five resident teachers. The high school, grades 7–12, had a student body numbering 1, 037 young people. Enrollment in the adult education courses varied seasonally, but more than 3,000 adults attended, primarily the Issei and the *Kibei* (born in the United States but educated in Japan), perhaps for the first time in all their work-filled years; and they enrolled in 165 different classes. In all, there were about 2,000 children and several thousand adults involved in school despite the shortage of instructional supplies and equipment.

At first, the high school was not a single building as in the world outside, but an entire block of barracks, Block 32. The barracks rooms were the classrooms, as bare as the ones we lived in, and the paths between the tar-papered buildings were the open-air corridors for the students when they changed classes during the day. Not only the high school, but two elementary schools (appropriately named Mountain View in Block 8 and Desert View in Block

41), nurseries for pre-school children, and adult education classes all began functioning by the end of that first October.

The nursery schools in Blocks 9, 13, 27, and 37, staffed by resident teachers, enrolled 182 toddlers. Placing the children in nursery school during the day enabled their parents to work in the project program. I would see the little children trudging along the rough roads with their parents, glad to be in school like their older brothers and sisters. I thought back to the time when I too had a handkerchief pinned to the front of my dress, and I was bemused that mothers still did the same. Now the little ones carried washcloths to school for lack of paper towels. The second year in camp, I enrolled Kay in the nursery school across the road from the public library. His school supervisor lived in our block, and her uncle was our block manager. On mornings when the snow reached a depth well over the top of my knee-high boots, I would carry him piggyback to his school before I went on to work.

The Adult Education Department, located in Block 8-7-E, served students who had graduated from high schools or who desired vocational training. By January, 62 percent of the camp population over eighteen years of age were enrolled in adult education with an average class attendance of 50 percent. Taught by resident teachers, both daytime and evening classes were offered for adults in art, flower arrangement, bookkeeping, cabinet making, first aid, music, sewing and knitting, mathematics, penmanship, basic English, and creative writing.

Construction of a new school building was delayed because of wartime priorities on building materials, and classes continued in the barracks of Block 32. When the building was finally completed on the open ground in the middle of camp that we referred to as "the high school plaza," a Caucasian teacher in charge of the dedication ceremony asked me to write a brief speech and participate in the event. Several decades later, after I had become an academic librarian at the Ohio State University, a professor of speech and drama in the OSU College of Education, Dr. George Lewis, visited me in my library office one day, after he had read in the campus newspaper of my internment in Utah. I had known and seen Dr. Lewis for years, and I was glad to have him stop by. Now he stood before me with a quizzical look in his eyes and asked me whether I remembered him from Topaz. Puzzled, I exclaimed, "You weren't there!" Then he smiled, and as soon as he said, "I planned the dedication program for the new high school there," my mind flashed back to that time in Topaz, and I remembered.

Regaining a sense of normality from the schools, the young people had a good attendance record, did their homework—though not without an occasional protest against assignments—and were active in student government, clubs, sports, and social events. The high school yearbook was called *Ramblings,* and the weekly student newspaper, with its logo taken from the horned mountain sheep, was named the *Ram-bler.* The student staffs on the two publications worked under wartime restrictions, but expended lively enthusiasm on them. To raise funds for the publication of their yearbooks, the high school students became involved in community projects and directed their energy towards presenting a musical fun-tasia, a winter carnival, and benefit motion-picture showings. They enlisted the help of individual residents as well as organizations within the camp for their programs. A notable feature of the 1945 *Ramblings* was the double-spread endpapers displaying two photographic views of Topaz, one from the side of the camp showing the blocks in rows and the other at the north end looking towards the camp hospital, an elongated building with wings jutting forward with room for 128 beds, modeled after an army field hospital.

When school first started, some older students were discontented with the limitations of their barracks classroom. They were thinking of the more spacious, better equipped schools they had attended in California. There were a few for whom school had no significance who became truants. They would mutter, "Waste time!" when urged to improve. I had not heard such disgruntled expressions of futility before. Formerly, parents had been able to discipline behavioral problems, but for many, now, family unity was lost. "So what?" was as common as the current "Waste time." The serious students sometimes referred to the rebels as *yogore* (dirt or blot) or as *buta* (pig) head.

The high school students I taught were like their *hakujin* peers on the outside, sometimes uneven in performance, often questioning their future, yet frank and open, resilient in coping with the rough conditions of their present school. They made my teaching enjoyable, although occasionally I would overhear an Issei parent comment, "*Rambo-na kodomo*!" (unruly or rowdy children). A class of 196 graduated from the high school in June 1943, and there were more to follow.

Mother helped me with Kay's care, but as I adjusted my time to a tight schedule of teaching English and Latin at the high school during the day and conducting adult classes in basic English in the evenings, I sometimes took refuge in re-reading the "Prayer for Teachers" that was printed in an April 2,

1943, issue of the weekly adult education bulletin. Parts of that prayer I needed to reassure myself:

> O Lord of Learning and Learners, we are at best
> blunderers in this godlike business of teaching.
> We have thought more about our subject
> than about our object.
> We have schooled our students to be clever competitors
> in the world as it is, when we should have been helping
> them to become creative cooperators in the
> making of the world as it is to be.
> May we realize that it is important to know the
> past only that we live wisely in the present.
> Help us to realize that, in the deepest sense, we
> cannot teach anybody anything; that the best we can do
> is to help them learn for themselves.
> Give us, O Lord of Learners, a sense of the
> divinity of our undertaking.

15

TOPAZ PUBLIC LIBRARY

The Topaz Public Library provided a rich benefit both for the camp residents and for me personally as my experience working there, from December 1943 until my release from internment, led directly to my career after the war as an academic librarian. The library originated in October 1942, a time when the camp as a whole was not yet completed, and the library grew along with the camp. The library's official opening was delayed until December, after the transfer of approximately five thousand books, cartons of periodicals, and boxes of supplies from the Tanforan Assembly Center. The books, crated in boxes made from the dismantled shelves of the Tanforan Library for shipping to Topaz, were donated by California schools, colleges, and public libraries as well as by individuals. The library was organized by two professional librarians, Misses Ida Shimanouchi and Alice Watanabe, with the assistance of a bookbinder, Mr. Yoshiharu Tsuno.

The public library was a unit in Community Activities within the Community Services Division. In addition to support from Community Activities, the public library depended on small fees and donations to purchase needed supplies and new books. Other libraries were organized under the Community Services Division at the grammar school and high school, although the school libraries were administered by the Education Section.

Later, we felt a need to provide books for the Issei who could not read English, so we added a Japanese branch to the library. All the books in this collection were on personal loan, to be returned to their rightful owners when the camp closed. To accommodate the Japanese branch at one end of the library, the office work room was shifted, and book shelves rearranged. At first, the circulation was limited only to those who had donated books, although any Issei or Kibei patron could read in the library. But when the collection grew in size, the books were made available to non-lenders as well for home reading. Eventually, the Japanese branch was moved to Recreation

Hall 40, and finally settled in Recreation Hall 31, a central location for the residents.

When the unpacking of the public library collection began on October 2, 1942, the library was housed in Recreation Hall 32 at a time when the roof still had to be tarred, coal stoves installed, the walls and the ceiling sheetrocked, and the electricity connected. Occasionally, one of the staff would bring her own electric heater to work, but on some days the staff members had to close the library because it was impossible to work without heat. Throughout October and November, camp residents contributed more books and periodicals until the collection was increased by two thousand books to a holding of almost seven thousand books and several thousand issues of periodicals.

Before long the public library was moved to Recreation Hall 16. The building was not partitioned like the regular residential barracks though outwardly it was tar-papered and looked like any other. The interior was left as one open hall for a reading room. Entry was by a double door in the center front of the barracks, or by a single door at the left end of the building.

Half the space in the library was used for adult fiction and nonfiction, and the other half for children's books and magazines. Bookshelves, left unpainted, stood along the walls, under the windows, and up the walls between windows. There were two small end rooms; the one near the adult books was used as a workshop for Mr. Tsuno, our genial bookbinder, and the other by the juvenile collection provided an office for the staff members.

The staff used the Dewey classification and the Cutter table. They decided to catalog only the nonfiction books because of limited funds for purchasing catalog cards. In order to familiarize themselves with library procedures, staff members made frequent visits to the Delta Public Library, where they were welcomed and given helpful suggestions.

Instead of typical library furniture, mess hall tables with attached benches, inadequate as they were for comfortable reading and study, were placed down the center of the long room. When the number of tables was found to be insufficient, a few more were acquired, slightly crowding the adult section. Almost two years after the library had been established, plans were made to accommodate the increasing number of library-goers with regular tables and chairs with backs, but even though engineers came in to measure the walls, the plans failed to materialize. Some bookcases were constructed out of the dismantled crates from Tanforan, others from requisitioned lumber. The charging desk, work tables, desk stools, display stands, and bookends were made by Mr. Tsuno. For the juvenile section, he made unusual sets of bookends out of scrap lumber and tin in the shape of little boys dressed in blue jeans and T-shirts. The jaunty little figures looked as though they were pushing against a load. The children who came to browse and borrow would often run their hands up and down, or pat, these bookends.

Mr. Tsuno also made a wooden card catalog cabinet which was well used in the reading room. Later the library acquired a metal card catalog, so we moved the wooden case into the office workroom. After the library had begun to function and serve the needs of the camp population, we were permitted to requisition library supplies.

The current issues of our magazines were heavily used, so when they were first received in the library, Mr. Tsuno would make them more durable by carefully removing and backing the covers with heavyweight wrapping paper and sewing them back on the journals. To add color to the interior, we decorated the walls with book covers. Sheetrock plaques had been put between the two by four uprights to serve as bulletin boards, and we thumbtacked the covers in patterns or color combinations. Sometimes the combination of titles on the book covers would evoke a giggle or a chuckle, as when I placed *A Tree Grows in Brooklyn* over *Behind the Rising Sun.*

The library officially opened to the public on Tuesday, December 1, 1942. The rental collection had its inception then, and thirty-five cents in rental fees were collected on that first day. Staff members worked rotating shifts of morning, afternoon, and evening hours so that the library could be kept open on weekends and evenings as well as on weekdays. Only later, near the closing of the camp, was it necessary to curtail hours. Then the library was placed on a quota of workers employable, and as workers became unavailable because of relocation, the Sunday and evening hours were discontinued.

The day after the library officially opened, the staff held a concert of recordings as a feeler to see what the patron response would be. The interest of the audience that evening was so great that concerts were continued every Wednesday night. That first concert presented Bach's *Toccata and Fugue,* Tschaikowsky's *Nutcracker Suite,* Moussorgsky's *A Night on Bare Mountain,* and Schubert's *Ave Maria.* On December 9, when we started the regular series of one-hour library concerts, we had selections from Verdi's *La Forza del Destino,* Delibes's *Lakmé,* Puccini's *Madame Butterfly* and *La Bohème,* and Wagner's *Die Götterdämmerung.* Program notes were designed in an attractive layout by one of the staff members and mimeographed for those attending the concerts. The program notes contained explanations of the selections, brief biographies of the performing artists, and an announcement of the recordings for the following week.

Plans were made to have lectures and demonstrations in art, drama, and literature once or twice a month. At times, rock and fossil exhibits were placed in the library. The Japanese Library had a Hawaiian Exhibit in May for several days, and the donations received at that time were divided, after expenses for the exhibit, among the Community Activities, the public library, and the student Scholarship Fund.

In various ways the library reached out to the camp population. Elementary school teachers brought classes to acquaint the children with our collection. Library notes and book reviews were printed in the *Topaz Times* to draw readers. Nursery school teachers were given the use of one shelf for their own books so they would have a place for studying. Since the collection at the school library was not adequate for high school assignments and barracks rooms were not conducive to study, girls in bobby socks and hand-knit sweaters and boys in jeans and mackinaws—the jitterbugging set—crowded into the library to do their homework, prepare research themes, and read. Usually their studying kept them quiet so that all one could hear from the circulation desk was the sibilant turning of pages, subdued whispers, and occasional laughter. But the weekends brought more students into the library, and then the place sounded like a locker room of many voices. Once in a while I had to walk over to a table and ask the young people to tone down their exuberant conversation.

Beginning on January 18, 1943, we were able to borrow books from the Salt Lake County Library at Midvale. The books, shelved in a special section and circulated on regular loan, were popular and filled a need for new reading material. Mrs. W. M. Tyler, librarian of the Salt Lake County Library, and Mr. L. H. Kirkpatrick of the University of Utah Library visited the library to see how it was being managed.

On January 21, an interlibrary loan service was put into effect with the cooperation of college libraries in Utah and the University of California Library in Berkeley. Patrons who wished to read books on special subjects not available in a small library like ours were able then to request what interested them. This service extended the scope of our library, and often a borrower returning a book would express his appreciation. Correspondence between our public library and the college libraries, the payment of postal and insurance charges, and the receiving and return of the requested books were tasks undertaken by the library staff. This interlibrary loan service was maintained until the library closed.

A pamphlet file supplied current materials for students as the library's reference books were too frequently outdated. The files grew from one box to two, and more, before the camp schools were ended. The library sent for government publications and pamphlets from other sources that were useful for term papers. Beginning on July 13, 1943, we also provided service to the hospital, with two staff members walking the considerable distance to the hospital to take books to the patients. The first visit saw one book from the public library and sixteen from the Japanese Library loaned out to the patients.

To keep the residents posted on world news, the Project Reports Division sent weekly news maps to the library to be posted on the bulletin board by the door. Any timely information regarding relocation and camp concerns also appeared on the bulletin board. The library subscribed to several newspapers including the *New York Times,* the *Chicago Tribune, P M Daily,* the *Salt Lake Tribune,* the *Oakland Tribune,* and the *San Francisco Chronicle,* the last two because most Topaz residents were from the San Francisco Bay area.

The library paid for the first magazine subscriptions, fourteen in all, but later the War Relocation Authority arranged to pay for subscriptions, and the number increased to fifty-two periodicals, ranging from fashion magazines and news weeklies to literary journals and technical journals.

A rental collection was established, and it expanded at a steady pace. This popular collection started with a few books purchased with funds from overdue fines, charged at a rate of two cents a day. For a rental book, people paid a fee of five cents a week. Suggestions for new titles came from enthusiastic readers, although we also depended on book reviews in the newspapers and magazines for reliable selection. As rental fees accumulated, we were able to purchase more new books. A waiting list of saves on the books was kept at the desk, but as soon as a book outgrew its demand on the rental shelves, it was removed for regular circulation without fees. So there was a constant turnover in the collection, and at the closing of the library there had been about seven hundred books bought out of the rental fees. In the end, since the rental books had come out of money from the residents, I placed these books on sale at very reduced prices during the last week of May in 1945. The sum accumulated from the book sale I then turned over to the Topaz Scholarship Fund.

There were certain titles that did not circulate, like closed reserve books in an academic library, because they would have been stolen. Among them were such titles as *Studs Lonigan* by James Farrell, *Forever Amber* by Kathleen Winsor (whom I used to see as a student at the University of California Library), a tetralogy of novels by Vardis Fisher, and other particularly popular works. A few restricted books had already disappeared, and I would hear that a certain novel was passed from hand to hand without ever being returned to the library.

Nonfiction on current world affairs was much in demand. William Shirer's *Berlin Diary* was always checked out. Newspapers that the library did not subscribe to were donated by camp residents, a little late but still welcomed by our patrons. The *Vogue Book of Etiquette* and *Emily Post* were in demand as weddings, receptions, and church affairs occurred. And occasionally we would be asked for a cookbook.

The little children who came to the library were better behaved and quieter than their older brothers and sisters. The parents who accompanied them would sit patiently while the children looked over the selection of picture books, the Bobbsey Twins series, the Lucy Fitch Perkins books on children in different lands, folk stories, and fairy tales.

Late in February 1943, gravel was laid down from the road to the library doors so that patrons no longer slipped in the mud which turned to glue when it rained. Attendance rose to almost five hundred people a day. Three of us worked at night, and circulation increased. When Mr. Tsuno relocated, Yukio Hayashi and his wife, Sue, library neighbors in Block 16, joined our staff. Yukio replaced Mr. Tsuno as our bookbinder, and many a morning, Sue brought us doughnuts or rolls and coffee and enlivened our break period. There were other turnovers on our small staff as young people moved out of camp. My sister Masa worked for a while as an assistant before she relocated. One day she shared a box of prunes that our mess hall had given out freely because cooked prunes had not proved to be a popular breakfast item; the following day she and two other girls had to make frequent trips to the latrine.

Many outside visitors came in to see the public library and made favorable comments on its place in the community. On May 29, 1943, three representatives of the Dies House Un-American Activities Committee, then investigating the relocation centers, also visited our library and complimented us by commenting that ours was the best library of all the centers they had seen. They were investigating the quality and kind of books, and they had the authority to remove anything considered un-American from the shelves. Strangely enough, the only title they insisted on removing was *Christians Only!*

At the end of the month, June 1943, the Topaz Public Library and the Japanese Library closed so that the entire Community Education staff could go to the project farm to hoe weeds out of the onion field.

One Christmas, the library had fantastically lovely, unique decorations designed by a graduate engineering student, Alfred Sawahata. He made wheels out of flat wooden boards graduated in diameter, the largest approximating in girth the circumference of a medium-sized conifer. He bored evenly spaced holes into the sides of these wheels, inserted dry willow branches which he covered with green crepe paper. Using patterns he created, the library staff members made geometric ornaments out of colorful bits of paper, envelope linings from fine stationery, and snips of fabric gathered from friends who sewed. The ornaments were fastened to the branches, and then our designer suspended the circles of wood from the ceiling, the narrowest at the top to the widest on the bottom, to make a mobile Christmas tree. Whenever the doors opened, the tree swayed and turned gently, delighting everyone who came to the library.

He found in our collection a photographic book of snowflakes. Under his direction, we cut out hundreds of six-pointed snowflakes of silver paper, then threaded and hung them at various lengths from the ceiling between billowy clouds of pale pink and blue crepe paper. The wonder in children's eyes, and even on the faces of adults, as they looked up to the clouds and at the Christmas tree warmed our spirits.

February 22, 1944, was declared a No Fine Day, and long overdue books quietly returned to the shelves. The month of March brought in several days of a blizzard when the windblown snow packed into sloping hillocks as tall as the barracks. No one ventured out unless it was necessary, and the attendance fell, so we spent the time shelf reading, mending worn books, and cataloging.

In June 1945, when the relocation program gained speed and the schools had finally closed, the public library merged with the elementary and high school libraries and moved a great number of juvenile and adult books to the science building, located in the annex to the community auditorium. Thus, the Topaz Public Library closed officially on June 23 and lost its identity to this newly formed Community Library.

It is clear, however, that while it was a separate entity, the Topaz Public Library occupied an important place in the life of the camp. The physical facilities were never adequate, but the library succeeded in providing not only a place to gather, a place conducive to study and exploration, but a varied program of cultural interest for a people cut off physically from the outside world. Because it played a vital part in this war-made community, it will be remembered for a long time by those who created the library.

16

SENSEI

The Issei in our block understood my English better than I first imagined from their speaking skills. When I asked them questions in English, since I myself lacked a command of Japanese, they would usually answer me in Japanese, with a goodly mixture of English words. When I began to teach Issei and Kibei students in the adult classes, I found the same pattern.

The Adult Education Department, directed by Dr. Laverne Bane, started its Basic English Division when the public schools opened. A small group of Nisei, interested in teaching adults, first met together in Dr. Bane's living room in the administration quarters in October 1942 to discuss plans. A friendly woman, Dr. Bane listened to our discussion about teaching methods. After listening to us for a while, she teased us about being "foreigners from another state" because of the way we pronounced Utah, and she told us how the state had derived its name from an Indian tribe.

We held a series of meetings at which we continued discussions of whether we should conduct classes entirely in English or use some Japanese to explain idioms. A few of the teachers read and spoke Japanese well, so they offered to teach the beginning students. We agreed that Japanese translation might also be necessary for the elementary groups. We decided to group classes into four levels: Elementary, Low Intermediate, Intermediate, and Advanced. Each class session was scheduled for two hours in length with classes meeting on alternate days. We scheduled classes on Monday, Wednesday, and Friday morning, afternoon, and evening, and on Tuesday, Thursday, and Saturday afternoon. We reserved Tuesday, Thursday, and Saturday mornings for teachers' meetings at which we could help one another with problems or suggestions.

The autumn registration for classes brought out 250 adults who wanted to study Basic English, and the program began under the supervision of Nori Ikeda on October 22, 1942. After three sessions, we found that we were hampered by the weather and other physical conditions despite the willingness of our students to brave the distance to our classes. We postponed classes until the barracks where we taught could be insulated, and cast-iron heating stoves, tables, and benches installed. It was not until November 16 that classes were resumed. During the forced recess, the teaching staff met in one another's barracks rooms for further discussion of teaching methods, lesson materials, class records, testing, and promotion. The first quarter we saw the beginning and development of twenty Basic English classes taught by eight (later ten) Nisei teachers.

We had trouble obtaining appropriate textbooks for our adult students. The children's books we first considered were too immature for our purpose. Consequently, we selected or wrote materials on our own, such as the history of Topaz, the origin of American holidays, or familiar stories like Charles Dickens's *A Christmas Carol,* scaled down to the level of our students' vocabulary. For the Intermediate and Advanced students, I gave differently worded versions of the history of Utah and of Topaz from which they gained details about their settlement in the desert and the state in which they were now interned. When the holidays came, the Advanced students read about the origin of Thanksgiving Day, and, casting knowing glances at each other, they commented, "Oh, so that is why we have roast turkey for dinner on that day in America." The Intermediate students enjoyed the simplified account of *A Christmas Carol* and, because Japanese literature abounds in tales of the supernatural, they thoroughly savored the descriptions of the three ghosts. As we planned materials, we kept in mind that attendance by the adult students was not compulsory, so lessons and mimeographs had to be interesting and pertinent.

During the first week of classes, we gave vocabulary tests to our students, both Issei and Kibei, ranging in age from fifteen to seventy-nine, and discovered that students knew the meaning of many words but could not always use them. We decided to concentrate on sentence construction and conversation practice rather than on rote learning of single words. Within the class levels, we divided students into units for fast and slow learners. For the Elementary level, we prepared a vocabulary list of words commonly used and focused on improving students' reading comprehension. For the Low Intermediate groups, we emphasized conversation, and they practiced greetings and familiar social exchanges. They eventually were able to read short stories and write letters.

The program for the Intermediate level in general stressed reading. Along with the text materials written by the teaching staff, we introduced them to current periodicals and books. The chief aims of instruction for this level were to stimulate the understanding and application of facts, the ability to visualize the ideas that words convey, speed in skimming, and skill in writing.

The students in the Advanced classes had freedom in the choice of lesson texts, as personal interest motivated their reading. Teachers presented grammar and English idioms only as needed, or requested. Because they could read with ease, they expanded their fascination with history, art, philosophy, and the government. They often spent time outside of class reading books and magazines from the public library.

When I prepared lesson plans for the Elementary and the Intermediate levels, Father would sit down with me almost every day to read through them. For difficult sentence structure and vocabulary, he would give me Japanese equivalents. When I was teaching from *A Primer of Democracy: Why Is America?* by Ann Mersereau, I underlined idioms with a blue pencil and words that needed to be translated into Japanese with red on my mimeographed copy of the text. If Father had not translated for me, I could not have explained the meanings of democracy (*minshu shugi*), government (*seifu*), continent (*tairiku*), majority rule (*daitasu no sansei shita kisoku*), governors (*shu chiji*), self-government (*jichi seifu*), or cooperation (*kyoryoku*). He teasingly remarked that this was one means of my acquiring some knowledge of the Japanese language.

I became supervisor of the Basic English Division in March of 1943 when Nori Ikeda resigned from her position to relocate. Shortly after that, Dr. Bane requested prepared statements from each of the Adult Education supervisors describing the objectives and outline of our programs. The objectives of my division were (1) to enable students to learn usable English through the practice of reading, vocabulary, spelling, writing, and conversation; and (2) to facilitate the readjustment of our students to community life after the war by timely selections in reading materials and by class discussions of possible problems.

Father, who spoke English fluently (though he wrote with a Germanic sentence structure), thought the program was much needed. He said that when he came to this country he could read and understand English, which he had learned in Japan, but his pronunciation was not always correct. He was of the opinion that the Issei had failed to be assimilated into their former communities because they did not have English-language skills. In Sacramento, he had often accompanied his Issei acquaintances as their interpreter when they had business transactions or had to consult a lawyer or doctor. The Japanese, both the Issei and the Nisei, had remained a minority group, unassimilated into the total community on the West Coast. The society of the white majority failed to recognize or accept Japanese cultural mores and ideals. The majority resented the presence of a group who could not speak or write English, could not become naturalized citizens, a people apart because of race. The Nisei felt the same social and economic pressures their parents had endured, and it was these strictures that contributed to our internment.

We teachers were agreed that a knowledge of the English language would help the Issei students to understand the country they had lived in for so long and the ways of their American-born children. This in turn would help them to cope with the outside world once the war ended.

Adult English classes had actually started at Tanforan and had been very popular, especially with the Issei women because the camp situation gave them time to study, meet, and learn from one another. When we asked our Topaz students about their reasons for studying English, their range of answers included a desire to learn, to be able to read and answer letters from sons in the army and children relocated to colleges and outside employment, to comprehend newspapers and magazines and radio broadcasts, to prepare for their relocation, and to enjoy life.

English clubs were formed in each block as well for the study of English. A paid supervisor was available to help any group with special problems, but for the most part, the groups operated under their own power as semi-social, semi-educational self-improvement groups. In addition, the Topaz English directors placed English-speaking helpers in the Flower Arrangement, Flower Making, and Issei Sewing classes to encourage those students to use English.

My adult students were delightful, and I was often overwhelmed by the profound respect shown to me as their *Sensei* (teacher). As I stood before them and saw their faces with time-drawn laughter and worry lines, their dark eyes attentive, their firm hands gripping pencils a little awkwardly, I felt humble. I wanted to ask: Who are you? Where do you come from? What have you endured? Will I be able to reach out to you and communicate? I thought, too: I am so young, compared to you, and untried in many ways. Perhaps, you can teach me of your strength and quiet endurance.

When I met with this group and greeted the students with "Good evening," they would bow to me and murmur, "*Konban wa, Sensei*" (Good evening, Teacher). A few of them ventured, "Good-o ebuning!" Although we were to use as much English as possible in class, for this level, I discovered that some Japanese words were necessary to convey the meaning of the English idioms. Somehow their Japanese salutation always sounded gracious. As instruction commenced, I found that their ears were not attuned to differentiate certain similar sounds, and that they were not used to tongue and lip movements in distinguishing *v* from *b, r* from *l, s* from *th,* nor adept at cutting off consonants at the end of a word.

One evening, as I looked down the list of some troublesome words, I asked for the pronunciation of "very" and "berry"; the students responded with a prolonged "be-e-e-ry." When I asked for the difference in "celery" and "salary," they wrinkled their brows and sputtered a rolled "sa-ra-ri." One man exclaimed, "No, no, no, not right!" And the Issei women, eyes twinkling, could not suppress their amusement and put up their hands in front of their mouths to giggle. Then one woman, more determined than the others, tried again, but with no better effect. She paused, shook her head, and remarked in Japanese, "Teacher, I cannot do it." They all did try hard, and they wanted to learn.

Though unable to converse easily in English, these adult students had minds of their own, and they expressed themselves in witticisms and spontaneous puns. Their humor lightened our lessons. During one session when the internment camp of Minidoka was mentioned, a man solemnly and slowly uttered, "Mini doka?" The question in colloquial Japanese had become, "Minnie, how are you?" This time it was I who had to put up a hand before my face to laugh.

My Advanced class was composed mainly of young Kibei and a few Issei whose comprehension of English was on the junior high school level. The Kibei girls in the class had the same gentle manners as the Issei. Although they were fairly fluent in conversation, they needed practice in idiomatic English. The ease that the Kibei had in speaking English sometimes made me forget that I still had to key my vocabulary to theirs. One night, when a student had recited exceptionally well, I commended her, "You are certainly right on the ball!" Puzzled, she looked back at me and hesitantly asked, "Sensei, what do you mean?" I tried to explain the slang expression, but I was not sure that she understood.

In the fall of 1943, I also taught a class of a totally different nature, an extension course sponsored by the University of Utah that required thirty-six semester hours and was listed on our schedule as College Composition. Students each paid one dollar for tuition. We met two evenings a week in Block 32. This class consisted of a small group of high school graduates, some of whom had attended college. Several young men from Hawaii wrote vivid nostalgic essays about the islands. One student who enlivened this class was older than the others, an English woman named Hester Shironitta, who had been married to a Japanese seaman and who came into camp to be with her teen-age son. She was from Yorkshire, England, and in one composition, imaginatively projecting herself to her seventieth birthday, she wrote:

> Although the plane trip from the United States was quite a stormy one, I now feel rested. It was so wonderful to visit York Minister en route and to hear the choir boys sing at vespers. The singing and the sacred atmosphere in this old cathedral touched me beyond expression, and I thanked God most fervently that World War II was but a bad dream.
>
> This afternoon I visited the old Haworth Church of the Brönte family, the old Manse, and the Druids' altar. This is such a lovely part of Yorkshire, and so dear to me with all the carefree school day memories.
>
> I was thrilled to find a little tea shop, where once again I could partake of English strawberries and cream, tea, and the famous Yorkshire tea cakes. Next door, I purchased a box of ginger snaps, so famous on Guy Fawkes' Day. Oh, what memories!

So Hester and her classmates, the Japanese Americans, wrote of their memories, which I found most moving in the time and the place where we were.

Name Edward B Marks Jr.

From Washington, D.C.

Date July 23, 1943

Comment

Name Prof. Ray Aite

From Wyoming River

Date Sept. 25, 1943

Comment "Silence is Golden"

Name Raymond Prior Sanford

From Topaz

Date Nov. 6, 1943 (THE DAY AFTER ARRIVAL — INTRO-
DUCED TO LIBRARY BY 'BILL FUJITA)

Comment NO — IT WILL NOT "ALL BE THE SAME 100 YRS F
NOW' — WHAT YOU DO COUNTS!

Name Toyo S. Kawakami

From Berkeley, via Tanforan, California

Date December, 1943

Comment "A word to the wise is sufficient" concerning the good books here!

Page from the Topaz Public Library guest book containing the signature of Toyo S. Kawakami, circa 1943.

Thomas Toyota
Oakland — Tanforan — Topaz — ?
February 4, 1944
Gee, they got books here.

Bill Shinoda
The country is my home. (U.S.)

July 10, 1945
Many Thanks Tozo for the hours spent at "your" library, but the books are ours. They were the best times while at Topaz.

George & Evelyn Wilson

California

June 21, 1961

There is much pleasure in spending hours of enjoyable conversation with one who cares.

G. I.

17

INTO ANOTHER YEAR

New Year's Day 1943 came quietly after a fresh snowfall during the night. The morning chill of the barracks was laced with anticipation for the start of a new year. Long icicles, glistening like glass pendants, fringed the eaves of the barracks. The sun touched the transparent spears with a wand of light and created a sparkling beauty. Breakfast that morning was not the usual cereal and toast and coffee, but traditional *mochi,* small round cakes made from steamed glutinous rice that had been pounded into thick dough. The pleasure of having *mochi* served to start the new year was so evident that the cooks and the young waitresses kept smiling back at us. Elation sounded in their voices, as the residents bowed ceremoniously and greeted each other with *Shinnen omedeto gozai masu!* (Happy New Year!)

As a child growing up in Sacramento, I had witnessed *mochi*-making when several families gathered in one household and combined efforts to prepare this treat. I had seen the neighborhood women cooking the special rice in wooden steamers and rushing out to the backyard to put a batch of the rice in the huge stone mortar. Five or six men with large wooden mallets would slowly begin to circle the mortar and beat down in steady rhythm. During the pounding, the rice had to be moistened slightly and turned over. One of the women stood by with a bowl of water, and she would sing a folk song with a deliberately accented flow as the pace of the pounding quickened. Regularly, throughout the pounding, in the split second when all the mallets were raised, she would deftly turn over the mass of rice with wet hands; her singing timed that swift movement. When the rice had acquired the consistency of smooth, kneaded yeast dough, then the young girls like myself would shape the bun-sized cakes with hands coated with rice flour. As I enjoyed my bowl of *mochi* on this morning, I knew that the men and women on our kitchen crew had performed the same ritual a few days before.

Back in our room after breakfast, as I tidied the beds, I watched Mother carrying Kay in her arms as she talked and sang to him in Japanese. He looked at her face intently as he listened. He especially liked the melody about baby chicks, and he chortled as the song ended with "Peep, peep, peep." It occurred to me then that the three of us here represented not only the generations, but time itself, time past from an ancient culture, time present of mine in a country of blended origins, and the time future of my young son who would benefit from both. The image I retained of the two I described in a sonnet:

New Year's Day, 1943

I wish you well, my mother and my son,
Joy held securely, in strong arms entwined,
As this new day glitters, the old year done,
Over drab, smoky barracks, now outlined
In sharp whiteness aggressive to the eyes.
What do you meditate, proud-gentle face—
The being here, restricted to room-size,
Or childish laughter innocent of space?

I cannot say the greetings I should speak
This morning—happy signifies too much—
Yet on this moment is transposed before,
The once and long ago, less cold and bleak,
And so I fasten with imagined touch
The *sho-chiku-bai* to this snowbound door.

In that instant of inarticulate awareness, I remembered out of my childhood how Mother had welcomed family friends on this day, not only with spoken greetings, but with well-wishes implied in the decoration tied to the posts of the porch and made of *sho* (pine for longevity), *chiku* (bamboo for rectitude), and *bai* (plum for fragrance and grace).

On this New Year's Day, the mimeographed camp newspaper with its English and Japanese sections featured sketches drawn by Chiura Obata, who had been professor of art at the University of California in Berkeley. One of his drawings was of a flock of sheep to celebrate 1943, which by the Chinese calendar was the year of the Sheep, symbol of peace, sacrifice, and docility. The singular appropriateness of his design did not escape me. Several other sketches by him recalled scenes out of the previous eight months: the departure train, a severe dust storm, and barracks in a block, with the mountain ridge in the distance.

Except for its format of legal-size pages, the *Topaz Times* was like any other small town paper, transmitting news of community events and activities. This holiday issue also carried greetings from the Inter-Faith Ministerial Association that "we adhere to the meaning of the spirit that lies behind the greetings of the new leaf on the calendar" and the suggestion: "Though we are in relocation centers where the meaning of material life has diminished, let us be thankful that ours is a life not limited to material wealth alone. . . . With faith in the religion of our hearts, we can sustain that hope. . . . [W]e can see that day when once again we shall be a part of a normal community."

That hope was not so buoyant when we wondered how long we would be detained and what would become of us once the war ended. Although we could talk about happier times in our former homes, some of us had the premonition we would never return to California. The fantasy of the world outside, far from our present situation, still engaged our imagination.

Miné Okubo was another recognized artist whose sketches and illustrations enlivened the covers and pages of the camp literary journal. She, with other Nisei writers from the Bay area, was instrumental in starting the magazine *Trek,* the first issue of which came out in December as a special holiday publication of the Reports Division.

Miné, whom I had known when we were both students at the university, stopped by our barracks one afternoon to ask whether I could contribute a poem to the journal. I countered with, "How soon do you need the poem?"

"Oh," she said, "I'll be working late tonight, so I'll come around 3:00 a.m. to pick it up."

I just looked at her, and when she saw my expression, she laughed, "I won't wake you up. Just tack the copy to the door, and I'll come by with my brother and get it!"

During the night, when all was still in our room, I awakened to the sound of footsteps crunching on the gravel outside, the voice of Miné murmuring to her brother, a soft chuckle from him, the front entrance to the barracks opening and closing as she lifted off the copy of the poem I had thumbtacked to our door. The first poem I submitted to *Trek* at her request was this:

Gain

I sought to seed the barren earth
  And make wild beauty take
Firm root, but how could I have known
  The waiting long would shake

Me inwardly, until I dared
  Not say what would be gain
From such untimely planting, or
  What flower worth the pain?

Her prompting enabled me to keep writing poetry. The journal provided a needed medium for the creative writers in our camp. Some of them were familiar names by-lined in the Japanese American newspapers published on the West Coast before the war, and I had long been familiar with the literary talent of these writers from the Bay region. Although the publication was monitored by the Reports Division, there was no suppression of what could be printed in *Trek.* With the final issue in spring 1944, the publication changed its title to *All Aboard.*

Those who were not writers found diversion in other forms. Artists besides Obata and Okubo continued to draw and paint, in oils or with *sumi,* or to practice calligraphy. Men with skills in woodworking made shelves, cabinets, and other pieces of furniture for their families, so their barracks rooms gained a home-like appearance. Their artistic vision and patience made odd shapes of polished driftwood a delight to the eye. Even peach pits were saved and smoothed into buttons for hand-knit sweaters. Picturesque plaques carved from scrap wood decorated interiors and doors.

The Issei women turned to hobbies of their own. Some of them knit sweaters of intricate designs with yarn ordered by mail. Others who had had the foresight to pack the materials at the time of evacuation worked on needlepoint and exquisite embroidery. On the way to and from the laundry, I would sometimes visit with an Issei acquaintance and admire her needlepoint, which she had learned to do when she had been employed as a housekeeper before the war. She had seen me exasperatedly trying to thread a yarn needle with slow success, so she demonstrated an easy method. Thereafter I had no trouble with the threading.

Ingenuity, when craft supplies were unobtainable, found surprising materials. Some of my students found they could soften the plastic handles of discarded toothbrushes by boiling them and make rings out of them, sometimes in layers of colors. Rocks of unusual shapes and mineral stones were polished with care to a high gloss and displayed on shelves. Shells dug out of the ground were bleached and tinted with nail polish to fashion into jewelry.

Father continued to paint in oils, and occasionally he used the reverse side of a piece of scrap Masonite board for canvas. He and Mother often read when books began to circulate from the Japanese Library, the collection of books on loan from the residents of the camp.

Among some Issei men the games of *go* (checkers) and *shogi* (chess) were popular, as well as some forms of card games. The younger ones found sports more to their liking than handiwork or sedentary games. The residents provided their own equipment and, when the weather permitted, used the open ground by the recreation hall for impromptu baseball or touch football. A baseball game sometimes had Issei fathers watching as spectators.

Entertainment in the form of musical programs revealed talents of long training and study, and these drew appreciative audiences. Those who had performed as dancers, actors, and musicians in classical Japanese theater sent for their instruments and rich costumes. When in the middle of a stage stood a slim, young girl, radiant as a butterfly in her *kimono* (gown) and *obi* (sash), a fan in an upheld hand, a transformation of time took place. Her face immobile, she would slowly turn with the beginning of the music and move gracefully forward into her dance. How quietly the audience breathed; for the length of her performance, all else was forgotten—the hard benches we sat upon, the unpainted rafters, the bare walls. The light focused on that dancer; her grace and gestures transfigured the commonplace into something remarkable.

Not all were such stately performances. In contrast, the jitterbugging set preferred gatherings of their own and liked what the Issei called the "modahn" (modern) approach to music and dancing. At some of the dances on occasions like New Year's Eve, a small combo played the popular tunes for the blue-jeaned boys and their partners wearing swirling skirts and bobby socks. An Issei peering in the mess hall where the dances were held could only mutter, "Such energy!"

Other leisure time programs included variety shows and motion pictures like "Going My Way," the first movie Kay and I saw. Once it was opened in

December of 1942, the public library sponsored weekly evening record concerts. Organized youth groups like the Boy Scouts also had recreational activities.

The earth was not as barren as my poem stated. The people were able to add vivacity and movement and color to their otherwise lackluster existence. Even the lifeless ground yielded hidden treasures to the seekers: an occasional arrowhead, stones, and small shells buried in the silt of the dried up lake bed. Later, when I was teaching Basic English to adults, one of my students, an Issei man, shyly gave me a brooch made from such shells in the form of a tiny basket holding a bouquet of flowers. The little basket was woven of narrow strips of dark blue crepe paper twisted tightly into a cord, and the flowers, even to the miniature sprays of lilies of the valley, were painstakingly wrought from shells that had been cleaned and tinted in pastel colors. The whole brooch was no larger than a silver dollar.

With another year under way, we tried to keep pace with the news of the world outside and the course of the war. The Issei relied on the Japanese-language newspapers from Denver and Salt Lake City; the Nisei read the American dailies and the weekly news magazines which we could buy at the canteen—if we were fortunate or early enough—or borrow from the public library. Those of us who had portable radios listened to broadcasts and knew that American forces were fighting the Japanese enemy in far-flung parts of the world that we had never heard of till now. The Issei spoke anxiously about their kinfolk in Japan, and the Nisei about the outcome of the war, but none qualified as prophets. It was impossible to predict anything beyond the next meal.

Then, at a press conference on January 28, 1943, the Secretary of War, Henry L. Stimson, announced that the War Department had approved the formation of a volunteer all-Nisei combat team and that recruitment for the unit would soon begin. By late afternoon of that day, the camp administrative office received a message teletyped from Washington, D.C.:

> The War Department announced today that plans have been completed for the admission of a substantial number of American citizens of Japanese ancestry to the Army of the United States.

And on February 1, almost a year after mandating our exclusion order, President Roosevelt stated:

No loyal citizen of the United States should be denied the democratic right to exercise the responsibilities of his citizenship, regardless of his ancestry. The principle on which this country was founded, and by which it has always been governed, is that Americanism is a matter of the mind and heart; Americanism is not, and never was, a matter of race or ancestry.

And so began the year of 1943.

GUILT BY HEREDITY

"Guilt by heredity" presumes enough
For accusation and the summary.
The verdict but sustains unreasoned proof
Against our suspect race, as history
Repeats itself, and this unfriendly land
Now acts to wash the yellow stain from sight
And, conscienceless, wills not to understand
That being born here constitutes a right.

No self-defense assures, when slant of eyes,
The tinge of skin, and black hair mark, as well
As any badge, the racial difference.
How many others, lost beneath cold skies
And exiled from their homes, like us, can tell
Of judgment that exacted such sentence?
(N.d.)

18

REGISTRATION FOR LOYALTY

From the previous autumn of 1942, the atmosphere of our camp had gradually stabilized as in a remote Japanese town and had acquired an even tenor from our daily routines. Thus the news, as reported in the *Topaz Times,* of the possible military induction of Nisei volunteers from the ten relocation centers, the no-evacuation zones, and the Hawaiian Islands had the impact of a huge boulder hurled into placid waters. The ripple effect rocked the sensibility of every block.

Until now in our fence-bound world, momentous happenings on the outside were like the mountains we could see in the distance, too far for us to know firsthand. But the words of Secretary of War Stimson had shifted the mountains, and through the opening the outside world arrived at the gates of the camp.

As rumors mingled speculation, approval, and resentment, we were made suddenly aware that a reversal of opinion regarding Japanese American servicemen had occurred. Earlier, in mid-1942, about five thousand Japanese Americans were allowed to remain in the service, including my brother Roy, who was still serving in the medical corps of the army. But many Nisei soldiers had been reclassified to 4-C, aliens not acceptable to the armed forces, and others, already in service, had been given honorable discharges. The news stirred us all; we could talk of little else.

Within twenty-four hours after we read the announcement in the camp paper, some young men sought out the camp administration to ask for more details. Through the Topaz Community Council, the administration sponsored a mass citizens' meeting at which questions could be asked about the War Department's plan for recruitment. A crowd of more than six hundred men and women attended the assembly. They raised questions from the floor about the organization of a separate combat team, the draft, the different branches of the armed forces, equal privileges, acceptance into the Officers Training School, working in defense industries, the treatment of the Issei parents as friendly aliens, and the security of dependents. After the meeting was concluded, a committee of fifteen residents was selected by the chairman of the Community Council to compile the questions raised from the floor to present to the army recruiting team expected to arrive the next day.

Block meetings to discuss the issue resulted not only in citizens' committees, but also—unusual for Issei women—in a mothers' organization. Another consequence was the Issei's appeal to the Spanish consul, the neutral intermediary between the warring countries of the United States and Japan, that the Nisei be given equal rights in selective service. By contrast, the Nisei, on the whole, agreed that they did not need the intervention of the Spanish consul.

The War Department, in need of manpower, had become convinced that most of the Japanese were faithful to this country and that they should have the opportunity to prove their loyalty. Consequently, and despite the suspicions and opposition from General DeWitt and legislative representatives, the War Department had devised a plan to register all the Nisei of draft age and to call for recruits. The plan worked out by the War Department and the War Relocation Authority was to have the Nisei men fill out a questionnaire to ascertain their loyalty before they could volunteer.

The project director explained that the registration was also a means to expedite the relocation program. Months before, the WRA had decided that camp existence was numbing the aspirations of the once independent people and had begun to press residents to relocate out of camp. Since the American public was still suspicious, an educational campaign had been started through newspapers and periodicals to encourage communities to accept the evacuees.

But relocation out of camp was slow. Part of the reason for the residents' reluctance was the experience of people taking part in the seasonal leave program. The leave program, instituted with the cooperation of the WRA and permission from the army, had begun even while we were at Tanforan. When available farm labor had been reduced by our internment, urgent calls came from California state officials for workers to help save the crops. Then in September 1942, in Utah, sugar beet companies hired the Nisei for the beet harvest, among them my brothers Howard and Joe. The work furlough was temporary, and after the harvest season the young men returned to look for other jobs in camp. However, while out on leave, they had encountered rank discrimination. They had been refused haircuts in barber shops because they were considered enemy, or denied service in restaurants, and they had begun to think that this would be the treatment accorded them if they relocated outside.

Now, however, in its commitment to the relocation program, the War Relocation Authority decided to register all adults seventeen years of age and older regardless of gender and to administer a version of the army questionnaire with the title, "Application for Leave Clearance." Although constantly heckled by outside organizations, newspapers, and legislators demanding tighter control over the evacuees, the WRA expected that this registration could distinguish the loyal from the disloyal. Critics would be satisfied, the loyal would be considered eligible for resettlement in cities outside, and the relocation program could be accelerated.

On February 5, 1943, the army recruiting team, headed by Lieutenant William Lee Tracy (better known for his motion-picture roles than as an officer) and including Technician Fourth Grade William T. Ishida (a Japanese American), Sergeant Raymond Condon, and Sergeant Luke P. Rogers, arrived in Topaz and met with the administrative personnel concerning their mission. Several days later at a special invitational meeting on February 8 in Dining Hall 1, 350 representative residents heard Lieutenant Tracy read the War Department proclamation to clarify the new enlistment program. The proclamation issued to all the relocation centers explained the government's desire to permit loyal evacuees to reinstate themselves in the normal life of the nation through service in the armed forces and in war production.

The War Department stated that the formation of a Japanese American combat team was not motivated by any thought of racial segregation. Its proclamation, in one section, referred to this particular point:

> The reason is that if your strength were diffused through the Army of the United States—as had already been done with many Americans of your blood—relatively little account would be taken of your action. You would be important only as manpower—nothing more. But united and working together, you would become a symbol of something greater than your individual selves, and the effect would be felt both in the United States and abroad. . . . To the nations abroad, and especially to the peoples of the East, you would provide a measure of solidarity of people who get together in the name of democracy.

After the general meeting, Project Director Charles F. Ernst declared that the indisputable evidence of loyalty could be manifested only by the voluntary action of the Japanese themselves.

Two nights later, the proclamation was read again before a larger audience of almost a thousand young citizens. At this meeting, the specific questions compiled by the committee from the earlier assembly were answered by the army team, although the questions about the opportunity to enter the Military College Training School, the security of dependents, and compensation for damages and loss incurred during evacuation were deferred to the War Department. Those answers came within a few days.

There were strong mixed feelings in Topaz among both the Issei and the Nisei about a segregated combat team. Many Nisei believed that such a distinct group would help regain the confidence of the public in Japanese Americans, but for some people, the idea of a segregated combat team seemed another instance of discrimination. The Issei insisted that the camp unite in a refusal to serve in a separate combat team. They argued that the evacuation had been forced upon them because the Nisei had not stood firm on their constitutional rights of equality. The Kibei, whose opinions were partial to Japan, openly protested against the volunteering. At first, the Nisei attended the block meetings, where dissension grew stormy, but refrained from outright comments. Argumentative speakers at these meetings were the Issei and the Kibei, and after about a week, the majority of the Nisei stopped going to them as they saw the volunteer program as of no concern to the alien Japanese.

In my own family, talk revolved around the purpose and the validity of a segregated fighting unit. We were mindful that we had been interned even though Roy was in the army at the time and aware of what had happened to him when he had tried to visit us at Tanforan. When selective service was still in effect for the Nisei, Bill had been deferred because of college, and Howard had been classified as physically unacceptable. The two youngest, Joe and Lee, were still under age for enlistment. In the end, Mother and Father advised my brothers to wait until selective service was reinstituted and not volunteer for the combat team. (Not until we had relocated to Cincinnati after the war ended did Bill, Joe, and Lee take their turns in the army, although not in the special combat team.)

In a special, February 9, number of the *Topaz Times,* a summary of the project director's explanation of the purpose of the registration appeared side by side with the text of the War Department's proclamation. The prefatory paragraph of the proclamation tied in with the intent of the War Relocation Authority to expedite relocation:

> Our mission is not an experiment but marks the radical extension and broadening of a policy which has always intended that ways should be found to return you to a normal way of life.

On another page in the same issue appeared the procedures for the center-wide registration slated to start on February 11 with a staff of interviewers trained to interpret the questionnaire and to ensure that the form would be answered correctly. The block managers asked for a delay to determine whether willingness to volunteer by the male citizens meant a commitment to enter military service. Lieutenant Tracy responded that an affirmative answer was simply a profession of loyalty and did not constitute an enlistment.

Registration was rescheduled to begin on Saturday, February 13, according to the procedure outlined in the *Topaz Times,* with recruitment into the armed forces taking place simultaneously. The people in Block 8 were the first to register, followed by Block 11. Each block was notified in advance of the schedule so that people seventeen years of age and older could arrange to remain away from work in order to register. The process of registration proceeded block by block and was completed by February 28, with the total number of registrants reaching 6,100.

The questionnaire, as I read it at registration, resembled ordinary application forms except for the final questions that were the most troublesome for most of us. The first part of the questionnaire called for personal information as to age, occupation, relatives, membership in associations, and other interests. It was the last two questions, numbers 27 and 28, that proved controversial and that aroused strong reactions of apprehension and anger:

> No. 27: Are you willing to serve in the armed forces of the United States on combat duty, wherever ordered?

> No. 28: Will you swear unqualified allegiance to the United States of America and faithfully defend the United States from any and all attack by foreign or domestic forces, and forswear any form of allegiance or obedience to the Japanese Emperor, or any other foreign government, power or organization?

A variation of question no. 27 was asked of the young women:

> No. 27: If the opportunity presents itself and you are found qualified, would you be willing to volunteer for the Armed Nurse Corps or the WAAC?

Question no. 28 was particularly problematic for the Issei, who were ineligible for citizenship although they had lived in this country for many years. If they answered affirmatively, they would become a people without a country. Eventually the question was revised for them:

> No. 28: Will you swear to abide by the laws of the United States and to take no action which would in any way interfere with the war effort of the United States?

After the change in wording, most Issei replied to this question strongly in the affirmative.

A staff of trained interviewers helped people interpret the questions in a uniform way and explained how to fill out the registration form correctly. Block managers were reassured that "Yes" to question no. 27 was simply a proof of loyalty and did not constitute an enlistment.

Nevertheless, the registration and the implications of the two questions unsettled the entire camp, disrupting families and dividing blocks into groups at cross-purposes. The questionnaire evoked serious debates of citizenship rights, suspicions of government motives, and misunderstandings. Hearing vehement statements, pro and con, from fellow evacuees, and knowing that homemade stink bombs had been thrown under cover of night into some barracks (one of them into the barracks fronting ours, where a bachelor lived with his aged father) and that several innocent Nisei had been assaulted, I asked of myself, Who is right? Was our loyalty to be measured by those who had prejudged us by our racial origin? Did the quality of devotion have no more weight than the paper on which the questions were printed? Why were our law-abiding parents, who had to register yearly as aliens, subjected to the questionnaire?

In my own reply to question no. 28, I qualified my positive answer of allegiance by adding the words: if I were granted former liberty and could resume normal living immediately. Even though I had not replied in the negative, I was summoned to a hearing afterwards. Because of the addition, my sincerity was doubted. Since segregation of those who had written "No-no" to the last two questions had been rumored, I asked the members of the hearing board what would happen to me and Kay if my answer were construed as negative. I was casually told that my son was my own problem, not that of the board, and that if I did not rescind the qualification I might be transferred out of the camp. After a moment, I asked those bland faces watching, interested, yet impersonal, to delete my qualifying remark and let my answer be simply "Yes." I said that I would remain in Topaz with my son.

A committee of thirty-three, drawn from the original committee of sixty-six Nisei and Issei block representatives, found WRA national director Dillon Myer to be responsive to their protest, and they reacted positively to an official message from the War Department which emphasized: "It is only by mutual confidence and cooperation that the loyal Japanese Americans can be restored to their civil rights." The residents' committee then agreed: "We accept this registration as an indication of the government's good faith."

With the call for volunteers during February and March of 1943, more than a thousand Nisei entered the army from the ten relocation centers. These men joined the volunteers from Hawaii and others who had enlisted on the mainland outside of the camps. This combined group became the core of the hard-fighting 442nd Regiment, whose wartime record in Italy and France gained favorable public opinion toward Japanese Americans.

The loyalty check in our camp showed that most of the Nisei and Issei had retained their allegiance to this country. The young men in Topaz who chose to be inducted as volunteers rather than as draftees formed a committee of the whole. They published a booklet entitled *Volunteers for Victory,* a compilation of articles that stressed the significance of volunteering. The title of the booklet was adopted as the official name for the Topaz volunteers. Their credo read:

> We believe in democracy and dedicate ourselves to the furtherance of its principles. To uphold these principles, we must destroy every form of tyranny, oppression, and violation of human rights. We place our faith in America, and bear our hope in the future of that faith. Therefore, we believe that our volunteering in the armed forces of this country is a step towards the realization of these ends, and a positive manifestation of our loyalty to the United States of America.

The ages of these volunteers ranged from seventeen to sixty.

Thirty-two percent of the Nisei men answered "No" to question no. 28. Some of them had replied "No-no" to both questions in sheer protest against unfair treatment even though they had complied with evacuation orders; others answered "No" because of family or peer pressures, or because of unrealized careers or dissatisfaction with camp life. A few even thought that expatriation would restore to them a sense of worth as human beings.

With the February issue, *Trek* began to contain articles emphasizing relocation and the return to more normal ways of life. Fashion notes in the journal suggested buying clothing suitable for the outside instead of rugged jeans and flannel shirts. A columnist also advised good etiquette, including proper table manners instead of "the slurp, guzzle and clutch" rudeness that she had noted.

But in the period after the loyalty registration, there was no rush by camp residents to resettle outside.

19

WEIGHED IN THE BALANCE

Throughout the turmoil of the registration, ordinary activities continued, even as the temperatures dropped below thirty degrees. Church groups sponsored meetings for their youth groups. The camp hospital appealed to all the residents to return any prescription bottles they might be keeping, since new ones could not be ordered. High school seniors contemplating college after graduation met periodically in each other's barracks to talk of their future; they kept in touch with friends who had preceded them to colleges outside. The schools remained in session, and I kept busy with teaching. A memo went out from Superintendent of Schools LeGrande Noble to parents that the yearly promotion system in the high school was being changed to the semester schedule as of the coming summer.

As spring came to Topaz, the confusion and turmoil over the loyalty registration subsided and animosities faded. The sunlight became a degree warmer, the air softer, and the sky a more intense blue after the long gray winter. But there was nothing green and alive in the earth. One evening, while I was trying to put a wide-awake, still exuberant Kay to bed after his bath, I overheard Father remark on what might now be sprouting and visible in the Berkeley yard. As I glanced over my shoulder, holding on to my squirming child, who was distracted by what he could see in this room that had no partitions, I saw Mother nod in reply, "*So ne* (that is so), the perennials along the fence should be coming up (the Japanese term she used meant 'returning to life'), and the *boke no hana* (the flowering quince) must be scarlet again." That garden was miles away; here there was, in abundance, the stifling dust.

Long before this season, an American friend, a former schoolmate in Sacramento, had sent me a package of woolen fabrics. Between the layers she had tucked a brown, lumpy bulb. Father planted the bulb behind the barracks close to the wall to protect it from the rough winds. Now, each day on his way back from tending the furnace, he would stop to inspect the spot and water the mysterious plant from the bucket of water intended for our drinking. He speculated on what it might be but was not sure. He carefully watched for signs of growth, and when the first blade of leaf showed its tip above the ground, his joy was unmistakable. Mother even took to returning from the mess hall around the back of the barracks. As the stalk grew taller, she and Father wondered what kind of flower it would bear. The plant flourished and opened into a Madonna lily, incredibly pure and stately, and utterly incongruous in the desert setting, a miracle in itself. The block residents shared our delight, and by word of mouth, the news of the lily spread. While its glory lasted, people from the other blocks came to admire also.

The walk to the mess hall or the latrine building was no longer such a hardship. With little entertaining to do in our own rooms, we made the most of our encounters with block friends in those places. I looked forward to having our meals with an attractive young woman, Hatsuyo, whom I called *Nesan* (elder sister) as her own younger sisters did, along with her mother from Hiroshima. No matter when I saw her, Nesan looked neat and fresh, her long hair brushed smoothly back from her classic features. She generally spoke to me in Japanese although she understood English well. She called my son Kay-*chan* and always used the diminutive form of *san* in talking with him. My family called him Kay-*bo,* probably the abbreviated form of *botchan* (a boy or son). Kay liked to sit at their table, and when Nesan saw him in line with me, she would beckon him to join her. Mother enjoyed their company, and our table would be enlivened with our conversation as well as with Kay's chatter.

This was our first spring in Topaz, and because there were no trees, we had yet to see birds flying close around the camp. Then one morning on her way to the laundry room Mother called to me as soon as she had stepped outside. Her voice was urgent: "*Hayaku, hayaku*!" (quickly, quickly). She was looking, with a hand shading her eyes, up at the sky. I rushed out to join her. There in the sky a flock of seagulls, the state birds of Utah, swirled and slanted in undulant motion, in graceful flight over the open area that stretched between the hospital and the front row of blocks. Almost unmindful of me standing beside her, she kept looking and looking until they vanished. Long afterwards, I tried to recapture that incident in a poem:

Seagulls

The seagulls came out of nowhere
That morning to the camp, and air
Seemed brighter for their clean white wings,
As music wakes from quiet strings.

Their shrill cries called her to the door,
Where she stood still, as on a shore,
To watch them circle, dip and rise
Against the wide, unclouded skies.

Did they not know the desert land
Was alien, unwatered sand?
Oh, had they come to cleanse her sight
Of dust with their cool, liquid flight?

Shielding her eyes against the sun,
She felt she must escape and run
Beyond the heavy barbed-wire fence,
Could wings be hers, strong and intense.

And then, as strings cease to vibrate
And silence palls, the noon seemed late.
The gulls vanished. She turned to go
Indoors, eyes blind, feet leaden-slow.

Although the temperatures had turned milder, Kay had another siege of illness. Instead of lobar pneumonia as at Tanforan, this time he contracted bronchial pneumonia, and he was admitted to the hospital. Members of the family could visit, but he wailed so forlornly when I had to leave that on one occasion the nurse asked me to simply peek around the door to see him and stay out of his sight.

A nurse's aide from our block, Fumi, assisted with the little patients on the pediatric ward. When Kay was beginning to recover, she told me with a sigh, as we sat at dinner, that she had to change his bed three times that day. Because he was dehydrated from fever, the doctor had ordered a Murphy drip to be inserted in his bottom, but Kay, annoyed by this strange treatment, pulled out the catheter and proceeded to spray not only his bed, but others nearby as well. After the third removal, and change of bed linens, the doctor canceled his order.

By and large, the loyalty registration had progressed smoothly in all the internment camps except in Tule Lake, where a dissident faction resisted the process. Fortunately, in Topaz the project director was in touch with the residents, and he kept the council informed of administrative and community concerns. The chairman of the Community Council, in a letter to the project director on March 13, 1943, made recommendations that later favorably influenced the policy on transportation costs to job destinations, on the hearings granted to those who had answered negatively to the crucial questions no. 27 and no. 28, and on the changes in camp employment to relieve the manpower shortage caused by people leaving to resettle in outside cities.

On March 20, the project directors were authorized to issue leave permits to those wishing to relocate permanently, provided that clearance had been granted by the Washington office. Taking advantage of this option, Bill and Hisa then made plans to leave camp, the first out of our family. Bill relocated to continue graduate work at the University of Maryland in the winter quarter, but shortly afterwards transferred to the University of Cincinnati. Hisa left for Chicago in the summer to work as a medical technologist at the Walther Memorial Hospital and remained there until the rest of the family was out of camp.

After the registration questionnaires were evaluated in our camp, those who had answered "No-no" were interviewed. The reasons they gave differed from person to person. They ranged from unfair treatment by the government; fear of conscription because of responsibilities for elderly parents, wife, and children; too little opportunity to enter the professions because of discrimination; to the loss of status as citizens. Thirty-six people applied for repatriation and were sent to Rohwer, Arkansas, until they could find passage to Japan. From these interviews, it became apparent to the administration that, in the main, the desire to keep families together had been the deciding factor for many negative answers.

The reinstitution of selective service was first received as good news in Topaz, but contrary reaction set in when the residents learned that the drafted Japanese Americans were to be replacements for the 100th and 442nd Battalions in action. People had believed that selective service was to be reinstituted on an equal basis. Because they felt that this feature of the draft was discriminatory, they formed a citizens' committee to discuss the issue. Even the Issei mothers, in an uncharacteristic move, banded together in an organization of their own.

To meet together on their own initiative was an important event for these mothers. They had admired the way American women participated in community and national affairs, but had not been able to emulate them until now. The Issei mothers did not object to the draft itself, but they did object to what appeared to be an arbitrary separation of their sons into an all-Japanese combat team. When they first met, with two representatives from each block, they appointed a committee of five to draw up recommendations to the government concerning the draft for their sons. The committee worked closely to write the resolutions, which opened with the paragraph:

> We mothers of American citizens of Japanese descent have fully cooperated for years with the American educational system so that our children would be worthy American citizens. We have taught our children to affirm their loyalty, especially in a time of national emergency. This idea is in keeping with the traditional spirit of Japanese mothers. As you may know, before the evacuation we did not oppose the drafting of our sons, but willingly sent them with our encouragement.

The resolutions continued:

> We mothers deplore the discriminatory measures directed against them. We desire for our sons the privilege of entering the branch of the armed services which they select and of receiving full benefits accorded American citizens.

The resolutions were respectfully worded.

One week later, when copies of the statement were distributed to each block for signatures of interested mothers, the women in three blocks refused to sign. Their opinion was that the resolutions were too mildly stated to make any impression. At an emergency meeting called the next night to discuss a compromise, the dissenting blocks sent two Issei men to present their views. The men disrupted the meeting so completely that no agreement was reached. Although the majority of the blocks had accepted the original statement, the dissenters composed their own version. The revision resembled the original in gist, but was written in a more florid and sentimental style. Very few mothers of the men who had already volunteered would sign the second version for fear their sons would not approve.

When the results of the registration became public, members of Congress probed into the camps for examples of disloyalty and interpreted their findings as though the interned were related to the enemy overseas. The scapegoating of the evacuees turned into a Roman circus, and the thumbs-down cry of anti-Japanese organizations, politicians, and news media echoed everywhere.

Discomfited by the extremely biased misinterpretations of the registration that we heard and read, we became apprehensive about being dislodged from Topaz. The situation must have been true in other camps as well. Work performance in the project operations began to deteriorate. Employment in camp had already been reduced by administrative order and made more stringent, so there was dread of layoffs. What troubled me was the effect the harsh judgment of the public at large had on my high school students, whose helplessness and vulnerability showed in their doubting attitudes. They lost interest and neglected their studies. Even those who until now had spoken enthusiastically of relocating with their parents seemed to hang back. After the registration was completed, the rumor spread that the War Relocation Authority intended to force us out of camp. The anxiety felt by the residents rose to an unbearable pitch.

In keeping with General DeWitt's statement made in April, right after the army had recruited Nisei men from the camps, that "A Jap's a Jap. They are a dangerous element whether loyal or not," and Damon Runyon's opinion the following month in his syndicated column that "only the future can disclose the wisdom of putting any Japanese in uniform or war production," the West Coast legislators opposed letting the Japanese enlist. One of them sponsored a resolution to keep the Japanese under permanent surveillance, or keep them from ever returning to the Pacific coast. The steady supply of hate propaganda from the politicians printed in the West Coast newspapers made us all uneasy.

When the Un-American Activities Committee, headed by Representative Martin Dies, was investigating the War Relocation Authority, the WRA national director was denied attendance at the committee's hearings. With agency officials and evacuees themselves unable to defend against allegations, the newspapers ran distorted, sensational stories as they reported on food shortages attributed to oversupply in the camps, on the danger of uninterned Japanese roaming the country, and on the charge that the agency was subservient to the people in its charge. The majority of the public believed what appeared in print. Eventually, the investigations of the Dies committee petered out for lack of evidence. But the harm had been done; the very fact of our evacuation and internment was taken as an indication of disloyalty.

The Town Meeting Broadcast on the radio for July 15, 1943, which I heard in our barracks, focused on the question, "Should all Japanese continue to be excluded from the West Coast for the duration?" The speakers on the program were Congressman John M. Costello, from California, and Carey McWilliams, the author; the interrogators were Robert R. Gros, lecturer and former member of the Stanford University faculty, and Max Radin, professor at the University of California Law School; serving as the moderator was George Denny. When Denny asked why feeling ran so high against American citizens of Japanese descent whose loyalty had been established beyond doubt, Costello responded, "The only persons on the Pacific coast urging the return of the Japanese at this time are those who feel that their individual servant problem might be solved, or that the price of vegetables might be reduced." McWilliams countered, "We cannot ignore the fact that this current agitation is being largely predicated, now as in the past, upon dangerously irrelevant so-called racial considerations, unsupported by a shred of scientific evidence."

A thin margin of hope was offered to us by steadfast *hakujin* friends on the outside who still kept in touch with us, and by some educators and church groups. Berkeley friends wrote that they had heard "all kinds of talk about the food the camps are getting in comparison to what the Army gets, but we think we know enough of the actual conditions from what you have told us, to realize that these tales are influenced, of course, by vicious prejudice. It will be such a relief when this whole thing is over."

Another Berkeley friend, to whom I had sent the June issue of *Trek,* commented on my poems appearing in that issue: "Your poems are an experience in themselves. . . . [A]ll three poems seem a far cry from the way you wrote even two years ago, a kind of ferocity new to your mind. In a way I miss the skeletonized oriental quality in these while applauding the newer strength."

One of the poems that prompted her remarks appeared on the same page with an article by one of the administrative personnel:

Transplanting

No anchorage in shallow dust,
No searching hold has found
More than shadows to grasp
Where hope withers in the ground.

Oh, guard the exposed roots against
Untimely sun and wind;
Some other soil may prove
More flower-wise and kind.

So let a richer earth restore
What once had died in need;
Strong roots will then respond
And bear tomorrow's seed.

Another poem in *Trek* appeared on the page where the editors announced that it was the final issue of their "record of growth in a concentrated atmosphere, an expression of the moods and modes of a transplanted people":

Retrospect

No other shall have heard
  When these suns set
The gentle guarded word
  You may forget.

No other shall have known
  How spring decays
Where hostile winds have blown,
  And that doubt stays.

But I remember yet
  Once heart was stirred
To song—until I let
  The sounds grow blurred.

And time—still fleet—delays
  While pulse and bone
Take count before the days
  Lock me in stone.

Yet another Californian friend who had read the issue thought that the emphasis on relocation was pathetically optimistic. His letter, almost harsh in tone, read:

> It makes me, in the comfortable safety of economic and racial security, unhappy and somewhat unworthy to read how you folks still believe that this devilish world will willingly accept you soon. Don't you have any papers or radios? Don't you know the stinking things that have been said and resolved and done about minorities in these past few weeks. Here we are, oh so sanctimoniously fighting for the "four freedoms" which we cavalierly deny our own people.

The unrest in camp climaxed on April 11, 1943, when an elderly resident, James H. Wakasa, said to have been deaf, was shot and killed in broad daylight by a sentry on duty in one of the watch towers as the Issei man approached too close to the boundary fence. Conflicting stories were told, but none was satisfactory to the people in camp. The old man, in the habit of strolling along the fence for exercise, had no intention of escaping. The incident alarmed all the blocks. Protests erupted and were made known to the administration.

Before the funeral, the women in each block gathered in their mess halls to make hundreds of paper flowers. They brought crepe paper, scissors, artificial leaves, wires and buckets and worked at the mess hall tables. I joined the volunteers in our block, and an Issei woman patiently guided my clumsy hands to curl cut-out petals and shape them into a rose. I observed my skilled Issei acquaintances making other flowers, besides roses, and adding the green wire stems and leaves. They filled the buckets with a profusion of artificial flowers, a mass of colors. At the camp-wide outdoor Wakasa funeral service, attended by more than two thousand people, huge and beautiful floral wreaths decorated the platform.

After the incident was reported to Washington, the *Topaz Times* put out an extra issue on Friday, April 16, with a report bearing the banner headline: "WRA Gives Assurance":

> Full assurances have been made that everything possible is being done by the Project Administration and the national WRA to eliminate all possibilities of future occurrences similar to the recent killing of a Topaz resident by a Military Police sentry. As some of the first steps now being taken to protect the residents, Caucasian Internal Security representatives will be stationed at all gates through which work trucks pass and will accompany resident crews leaving the city limits to work in the Project area. These WRA employees will report in detail any action taken by the Military Police here.

Concurrent with the announcement of these assurances came the official notice from Lieutenant H. H. Miller, the commanding officer of the Military Police, who may have feared an uprising, that emergency armament such as riot weapons and tear gas bombs had been withdrawn and that the sentries on duty at the main gates of entrance and departure were now carrying only side-arms. The most telling part of his communication was that no more soldiers who had seen service on the Pacific battlefront would be sent to Topaz, and the soldiers present who had seen such service would be withdrawn within a few days.

The *Topaz Times* article continued:

> Lt. Miller also emphasized that the Military Police personnel are under orders not to molest or injure the residents or to exercise any unusual surveillance upon the evacuees. Moreover, orders have been issued that M.P.'s are not to enter the city except on official business approved in advance by the commanding military office and the Project Administration.

A large committee composed of sixty-eight block representatives was convened after the incident. On April 15, the committee released a statement discouraging any proposed work stoppages and assuring residents that another camp committee (the Committee of Fifteen) was negotiating on the Wakasa case through the War Relocation Authority and in conjunction with the Spanish Embassy and the State Department.

The following week, another *Topaz Times* extra edition announced the order from Washington that all sentries except one were to be withdrawn from the gates and the observation towers during the daytime hours. The one sentry on duty was stationed at the main gate by the administration area, and his function was limited to routine checking of incoming baggage and people. Guards were retained at the checking stations at the boundaries of the camp along the main roads to Delta, and soldiers continued to patrol the outer boundaries of the project area. The residents were cautioned to carry authorized passes at all times when they left or reentered the project area.

On the outside, the clamor to separate the disloyal from the loyal persisted, and on July 6, the U.S. Senate passed a resolution to "take such steps as may be necessary for the purpose of segregating persons of Japanese ancestry in relocation centers whose loyalty to the United States was questionable or who were known to be disloyal."

As a result, in mid-July the War Relocation Authority issued a directive that Tule Lake had been chosen to serve as a segregation camp, and that people weighed in the balance and judged disloyal would be separated out and confined there.

20

WE BE BRETHREN

Spring slanted quickly into summer. The weather turned intensely hot, the temperature rising during the day to 105 degrees, sometimes even higher. The morning was pleasant, but as the sun ascended, the black tar-papered barracks without trees around them for shade absorbed the heat. By noon the mess hall was a veritable oven, and I wondered how the kitchen crew managed to cook at the old-fashioned stoves.

During the afternoon, as I looked down the road, I could see heat waves blurring the distant blocks. When it became unbearably warm and I had to be out in the sun, I found it helped to tie wet handkerchiefs around each wrist. Once the sun went down, the air outside cooled, although the interior of the barracks retained the heat, and then we sat outside to chat with our neighbors.

The warm weather brought insects, especially mosquitoes, into our rooms. Eventually screens were issued to us, and when they were placed over the windows, staying indoors became more endurable. We could then open the sliding windows to let in the air if a dust storm was not brewing. Kay, relieved to be out of heavy clothing, scampered about in a sunsuit or shorts and top, and he tanned easily. Some women carried fans and parasols along with their handbags. Straw hats sold out at the canteen.

Life, not abundant, had a practicality about it that kept me occupied: saving the monthly clothing allowance so Kay could have new shoes, which he seemed to outgrow every few months, preparing lesson plans for the high school and adult students I was teaching, meeting with other teachers, both Caucasian and Nisei, and visiting with people in our block.

I began to see an occasional runty dog in some of the blocks. Workers returning from seasonal leaves outside must have brought back pets. My brothers, too, had somehow captured a prairie dog. Father turned a crate into a home for the little animal, and we shredded newspapers into the box.

The prairie dog shredded the paper even finer and made itself a nest in the corner of the box. He would peer out at the curious human beings looking at him. At first, he remained hidden under the mound of paper, but hunger enticed him to nibble on the scraps of fresh vegetable we brought back from the mess hall. Before long, he became accustomed to his imprisonment in a confined space, as we had, and accepted water and food from us.

Kay would hunch down in front of the box to watch the rodent eat and scurry around the cage. Once in a while the animal would emit an odd barking sound which Kay interpreted as the animal's talking to him. Other boys in the block kept on the lookout for more of these animals to keep as pets. Mother urged us to set our pet free. She said that this creature of the open fields should not be kept caged, but we were fascinated by its activity. Then, as a few more residents captured prairie dogs, a warning was issued throughout camp that we were not to keep them because of the likelihood of their transmitting ticks to human beings. Reluctantly, the boys released the animal beyond the block, and the wooden cage was broken down for kindling.

Workdays were work days, but on Sundays I would see friends dressed in their best, often wearing hats and gloves, on their way to church. Religious faith, whether Christian or Buddhist, had bonded groups of Japanese together in our former home communities on the West Coast. In the camps, people could attend any religious services of a nonpolitical nature, and the churches were the first camp-wide organizations to be established. From the beginning of our internment, the weekly church services were the largest social gatherings for the people. In Topaz, except for Father Stoecke, the Catholic priest, church leaders were the Issei and Nisei who willingly volunteered their time and enthusiasm, even as they worked in other camp jobs.

The War Relocation Authority could not build separate churches because of wartime priorities, so some of the recreation buildings were turned into churches. The Buddhist church held services in Recreation Halls 8 and 28; the Catholic church shared Recreation Hall 14 with the Seventh Day Adventists; and the Protestant denominations met in five other recreation halls. In camp, as outside, the Buddhist congregation outnumbered the Protestant groups combined. To coordinate the churches, the Inter-Faith Ministerial Association was formed, and members of this group met regularly at Recreation Hall 33, where the association had its own library for the use of camp worshippers.

The Christian churches held young people's worship and social hours in the evenings. I could not attend them because of the adult classes I supervised and taught, but I learned of the effect they had from my students. The churches gave them an inner support that the government could not. One brisk Christmas Eve, we were surprised to hear fresh young voices caroling outside our barracks. Kay and I rushed to the door, and out there in the cold air stood a group of high school students with small song books and flashlights, singing to us. I looked down at Kay, who was completely absorbed by the carols. I looked ahead at the next barracks and noticed that our neighbors were also at their windows and doors. As the young people moved on, the words of "We wish you a merry Christmas, we wish you a merry Christmas" drifted back to us. On their first Easter Sunday in camp, the Protestants observed the day with a sunrise service in Block 32, but an unpredicted, violent dust storm routed the congregation. I saw people from our block who had started out early in new Easter attire returning to their barracks with heads bowed against the wind and handkerchiefs held over their faces.

As elsewhere in the world, the churches were an essential part of the weddings, christenings, baptisms, and funerals as they occurred in our restricted existence. There was a flurry of excitement in our block when a friend in a neighboring barracks announced her engagement. She and her mother came to the public library to consult the etiquette books, *Emily Post* and *The Vogue Book of Etiquette,* and leaf through the fashion magazines. Later I was invited to her wedding in the recreation hall church where there were no pews, but only benches. To everyone present, and to me especially, she looked so lovely, smiling shyly and walking slowly down the aisle in the white gown that her mother had helped make. At the simple reception afterwards, the young bride and groom greeted me warmly. The joy in her face as she took my hand, and the smile on her husband's face, erased my momentary regret that her married life was beginning in such a dreary place. They were happy, and that was all that mattered.

When we were children, Mother had sent us to the Japanese Baptist church nearby because we received excellent discipline and teaching there. Because of her efforts, we were known to have the best attendance record year after year of any family in town at the Baptist church.

In Sacramento, our two-story house was just across from the Buddhist temple, impressive in size when compared to the Baptist church I attended. Adjoining it was a huge, open playground, enclosed by a tall wooden fence. At the far end of the playground stood a square building where Japanese-language classes were taught. After the regular public school hours, the playground usually buzzed with children, many of them our schoolmates who attended the language school. The Buddhist church always drew a larger congregation than the other three Japanese churches, the Baptist, Methodist Episcopalian, and Presbyterian. Belonging to a certain church was most often decided for the children by their Issei parents, but the Nisei sometimes transferred from one to another as they grew older.

In mid-August, the Buddhists celebrated the *Bon,* the Festival of the Dead. Although a serious, religious commemoration, the event was also festive and joyous, with candles lit to welcome back the souls of the departed. I remember from my childhood in Sacramento how the temple ground was transformed by a large platform in front of the schoolhouse where young and old, wearing the traditional kimonos and obi, danced in the communal *Bon odori.* For the length of a block, our street would be closed to traffic for several days. Vibrant paper lanterns were strung through the branches of the elm trees along the sidewalk, and in the evenings, the temple ground was alive with spectacular performances of folk dances from the different provinces of Japan. Since we did not belong to the Buddhist church, I could not go to the playground to see the *odori,* but I would sit entranced at the window of our second-floor bedroom and absorb the pageantry and rhythm of the folk melodies that floated across the street. In Topaz, also, more than two hundred residents observed the *Bon* Festival on August 15, and, graceful in unison, they danced to recorded Japanese *odori* music in the camp square.

Some of the non-churchgoers observed religious rites within their own rooms at little homemade shrines. One individual form of worship I witnessed almost every day early in the morning was that of a rugged old man in our block. He would walk out to the road, face towards the east, and clap his hands three times as he bowed reverently. He did this in all kinds of weather. The image of that burly bowed figure, praying alone, solemnly, in the open air, with the ritual clapping of his hands, I was able to capture later in a poem:

Approach the Day

Approach the day with reverence:
    Bow low, clap once
To greet the dawning of
    The sun of suns.

Clap twice to bless expanding noon,
That ampler glow
May open budding hours
To lucent know.

Clap thrice amen for dusk at last
That in the night
The mind may magnify
Fragmented light.

In October 1943, Kay was on his way to becoming two years old. He loved to explore the outdoors, so we had to keep constant watch to see he did not wander too far off. He talked a mixture of strangely garbled Japanese and English. Somehow aware that Grandmother spoke more Japanese than English, he would tell her after breakfast, while nodding his head positively, that he had eaten all his portion of egg and translate the word "egg" into *tamago* and "bread" into *pan.* Hearing his chatter, the Issei women in our block sometimes suggested that I teach him better English.

A slim, lanky boy named Tommy, the son of the Block 4 chief cook, occasionally visited our barracks. Although rumored to be tough and rowdy in his manners, he was gentle with the little one. When Kay would sight Tommy coming, he would run, kicking up the dust, as fast as he could into the outstretched arms of his tall friend. Tommy would bend down and swing him upwards in one movement. One afternoon, ensconced in Tommy's arms, he patted his friend's cheek and tilted his head back to look squarely at the grinning face. Then, as he patted Tommy's cheek again, he enunciated, "Tommy—*tamago.*" As Tommy was grimy with dust and perspiration, Kay added, "Tommy—*batchi tamago* (dirty egg)!" Tommy understood the remark was made affectionately, and I was glad he thought the pun amusing. I met Tommy's mother in the shower room that night, and she laughingly said Tommy was telling other people about Kay's new name for him.

The residents in our block were like an extended family, but *hakujin* friends kept me in touch with the world outside through their letters. I felt nostalgic when a brief note from a friend in Berkeley ended, "Oh, it makes my heart ache to think of you so far from home and longing for the eucalyptus smell of Berkeley." Or when I read the description of a full moon in a clear sky over the Berkeley hills in a letter from another friend, Joe: "The

Campanile was lit for the first time, I believe in years—or so it seems. The dim-out had been removed, and while there is not enough illumination to compete with former times, it is quite a contrast with what we have been accustomed to recently. Let us hope that we shall be able to watch the moon together before too long." An encouraging letter came from my high school Latin teacher, who wrote to say that she had attended the Institute of International Relations at Mills College and recalled that Hisa and I had been her guests at the previous convention. She noted that she was glad that Hisa and Bill were out in the real world again and asked for Hisa's address in Chicago in case she traveled there (although at this time railroads were urging people to stay home). She also mentioned seeing an exhibit of Japanese art from several camps at the conference, and she wrote, reassuringly, that the evacuees had many well-wishers among those attending the institute.

Earlier that year I had finally saved enough from my camp salary to begin paying my obstetrician, Dr. Josephine Borson, who had never sent me a bill. I wrote that I would continue to send small payments until the prenatal care that she had given me was completely paid for. She wrote back soon afterwards: "I am more than repaid by your confidence and wish to give to your son that which he should have, so please consider your bill paid." In her letter she returned every cent I had sent to her in the form of a war savings bond in Kay's name. Her gift to Kay was as comforting as the kindness and concern she had shown even before he was born, and I was deeply touched by her generosity.

The friends in camp and on the outside made me realize, when I became disgruntled, that brotherhood did not simply mean kinship by blood or ancestry as the scaremongers wanted to imply, but understanding and kindness. Between the old residents and the newcomers from Tule Lake, who were being well assimilated into camp, were formed family relationships, renewed friendships, and the acceptance of one another. The always anticipated letters from the outside created an invisible fellowship as strong as the friendship I had come to know among the people in our camp. I was reminded of Genesis 13:8:

> Let there be no strife, I pray thee, between me and thee,
> for we be brethren.

The kinship I was learning in exile extended beyond the immediate family.

GROWTH

Have I so changed with time
That songs I once wrote pall
By judgment grown mature
And thus more critical?

The one who sang was then
So young, not yet aware
That doubts and questions were
To be her daily fare.

And now in wonderment
I ask: how did that child
Develop so her songs
And life were reconciled?
(September 12, 1945)

21

IN THE LENGTH OF DAYS

In the length of days in camp, we arrived at the camp's first anniversary on September 11, 1943. A week after that milestone, the day came for the separation of families and the removal of people to Tule Lake. Originally scheduled for July 13, the process of segregation was postponed until September 19. Twenty-two repatriates left camp for the long overseas journey back to their homeland, and the number of transferees to Tule Lake increased to 1,466. At the beginning of September, provisions were made for the residents to send telegrams to Japan if they wished to contact their relatives.

The mood of the residents was reactionary. The emotionally tense situation caused uneasiness which spilled over into disputes and rebelling on the job. Some workers argued with their supervisors, and the wrangling resulted in temporary walkouts. A few evenings before the departure by troop trains for Tule Lake, some men took to drinking to revive what little confidence remained to them. The Hawaiians in Block 1, mostly bachelors and still resentful of their treatment on the islands and the mainland, held a noisy party. The others who were leaving had no cause for celebration. The strain was noticeable throughout the blocks as we assembled for our meals or met one another at the work place.

The administration categorized the transferees into several groups: those who had applied for repatriation or expatriation; those who had replied "No-no" to the loyalty questions, or refused to answer, or qualified their answers; those who could not obtain clearance for relocation after their hearings; and those, mainly young people, who wished to stay with their parents. One reason why Tule Lake was chosen as the segregation center was that so many of the original population there had wanted to repatriate. "Transfer to Tule Lake" was the euphemism for the segregation.

The transferees themselves had their own reasons for opting for segregation. For some, the evacuation and the internment seemed to show there was no future in this country for people of Japanese ancestry, especially when California pressure groups were ranting against their return to the state. For others, parent authority still prevailed. We Nisei had grown up deferring to the decisions of our fathers and mothers, and many of the Nisei transferring had no intention of expatriation, but had agreed to move with their parents. The Issei had seen a lifetime of work wiped out, and those few who had a little money and property in Japan did not want to lose all they ever had. So economic considerations rather than the question of loyalty to either country motivated them. The group who had been unable to secure passage to Japan before Pearl Harbor were the ones who expressed loyalty to Japan.

On the dull, cloudy morning of the departure day, the weather reflected the gloom of the people. Those leaving gathered quietly at the mess halls to wait for buses going to Delta. They were returning to California, but not to their former homes.

Some of my students were leaving, and I wished to say good-bye to them. I went from block to block to the barracks where they lived. Families clustered in quiet groups with their luggage and packages. For some, this was a moment of separation among themselves. A few of my high school students, minors, were going in order to stay with their families. But a few, I well knew, were remaining in Topaz against the wishes of their parents. The farewells were agonizing but said with emotions under control. As I looked into the eyes of the Issei, stoic and courteous, and of the young children, solemn on this occasion, I could not speak, but could only bow to them. I sensed a reluctance to say the final good-bye. *Sayonara, sayonara* (if it must be so, if it must be so). The division of families and friends depressed me. The students whom I would never see again held onto my hand and whispered their thanks. They left in silence, except the Hawaiians, who wore leis around their necks and shouted defiant *Banzais* (may you live ten thousand years) as their buses drove away.

To accommodate the people being transferred, many loyal Tule Lake residents had to be moved out and scattered among the other centers, though some elected to remain there rather than endure another uprooting. About two thousand came from the California camp to Topaz. The camp administrators wondered how the Bay area residents of Topaz would accept the new people coming from Tule Lake in their blocks.

On the cool October evening when the new arrivals were expected, many of us went to the intake gate and waited until nightfall, when we had to use flashlights and torches. A pathway was roped off at the entry gate, and we crowded close to it. As the buses arrived and people came out of them, they filed past us. The newcomers looked forlorn and very travel-weary, and I thought we must have looked as tired when we first arrived. Among them were farmers our family had known in Sacramento when I was a child.

The drum and bugle corps of the Boy Scouts provided a fanfare. As the camp residents recognized incoming acquaintances, they called out their names. Heads lifted and smiles lit drawn faces, and voices called back and forth in Japanese, "*Ashita* (tomorrow) we shall meet once more!" The Tuleans were led to the induction hall where "Welcome to Topaz" signs had been tacked on the walls. After the intake and inspection of their baggage by the military police, the Boy Scouts and bystanders helped carry their baggage and escorted them to their assigned barracks.

The Tuleans wondered about jobs in Topaz now that the War Relocation Authority had begun an employment retrenchment program in June. When they were settled in, they petitioned the Community Council to intercede with the administration so they could be part of the camp labor force. As it turned out, the Tuleans merged harmoniously with other Topaz residents and adjusted well to living in the same camp.

In the same autumn season, word came from the West Coast that workers were needed to help harvest the half million dollar vegetable crops grown at Tule Lake. The produce was intended for other centers as well as Tule Lake itself. Camp administrators approached the Community Council to determine how the Topaz residents would respond to the call for volunteers. The council disapproved of the recruitment and announced that Topazans would prefer to have less food in the coming winter months than be accused of unfriendliness or strike breaking given the fact that more than a thousand of the people now in Tule Lake had formerly been in Topaz. About thirty residents were willing to help, but many hesitated for fear that harm might come to their families if they volunteered.

The project director contacted Tule Lake administrators and ascertained that there were no longer any strike or labor problems then at Tule Lake. The Tule Lake residents had earlier balked at harvesting crops going to the other centers. The last week of October, the *Topaz Times* reported that there was no strike at Tule Lake, and thereafter thirty-five workers left to help salvage the vegetable crops.

At the end of October a visitor of note came to Topaz: E. Stanley Jones, the liberal Methodist clergyman. His message to the residents was that Japanese Americans were not a problem; they were possibilities. He stated that he did not know of another race that would have been so disciplined under the same circumstances.

So much had happened since the beginning of the year. I mulled over the sequence of the drastic events as we tried to maintain normality as best we could. If I had not rescinded the qualifying clauses added to my reply on the loyalty question, I too might have been among those transferred to Tule Lake. I said to myself, under my breath, "There but for the grace of God . . ." What good would protests have done? I found nothing consoling in the thought. Rethinking the events of previous months, in August I wrote the following tanka:

My thoughts twist and twist
Till the beginning and end
Are snarled together.—
Can your sensitive fingers
Disentangle them for me?

If I could but see
Flame-points of scarlet against
The spring's frosty air!—
There was a time, remember,
When quince-blossoms warmed our hearts?

Haunted still by the same mood in September, I wrote more tanka:

Tell me, you who know,
What hope can outlast the long
Winter of the mind?—
Can the hidden roots survive
The ravaging ice of time?

The heart must believe,
Though exiled and forsaken
That spring will return—
When, after winter, fair days
And live roots keep their promise.

In the evening, as I would lead Kay back from his bath in the latrine building, he and I would see the stars dotting the firmament. He would point at the sky and say, "Many stars." So I was moved to write a haiku:

Though the sun now sets,
The dark night has countless stars
To befriend us here.

In the days that followed the upheaval of the segregation, I wryly appreciated what my high school students muttered under their breath, "Waste time," whenever I assigned them homework. The term was aptly descriptive of the months of internment and of living in this wasteland, isolated as we were. The passage of time I could gauge by Kay's development as he outgrew his shoes as fast as his infancy. The present environment—all he knew—sheltered us, but he would have much to learn of the outside world later.

Even though the War Relocation Authority stressed orientation toward the future, the thought of it was not as immediate to me as urging a stubborn child to eat his lunch. Holding a spoonful of peas towards him, after he refused to touch what was on his plate, I would say, "Now open your mouth. This is good." He would shake his head, or turn his face aside, or simply hold the food in his mouth without swallowing until I gave him milk to wash it down. The repetitious daily fare of the same menu bored him.

Relocation now took our attention. It was long before the segregation that the War Relocation Authority had decided that the sooner residents were relocated, the better their adjustment would be to the outside. Now, immediately after segregation, the Relocation Division became active in camp and began to coordinate the relocation procedures. The residents saw signs of the greater emphasis on resettlement in the tightening of camp employment.

As early as May, I had received, as did all residents, a pamphlet about the relocation program. In it were listed the field offices of several cities in the East and Midwest, established to assist camp residents in locating jobs and housing. The first field offices were located in Salt Lake and Chicago. Before long, other offices were opened in Cleveland, Minneapolis, Des Moines, Little Rock, New York, Denver, Kansas City, and Boston. Hostels were established by churches in Chicago, Cleveland, Cincinnati, and Des Moines so that people going to those cities could have temporary accommodation at reasonable prices until they found an apartment or a house for rent. The hostels served as halfway houses for short-term living quarters and meals while the people became oriented to a new community.

In the pamphlet's preface addressed to all camps, the national director of the War Relocation Authority explained that the loyalty registration had been carried out to expedite indefinite leaves. The pamphlet urged all able-bodied residents in the camps, especially those who intended to remain in the United States, to seize the opportunity to leave as soon as proper clearance was granted. The pamphlet made it evident that the agency had already been opening the way for resettlement in the previous spring.

However, there was reluctance among the residents to relocate. The tales of workers returning from seasonal leaves, the accounts that the Issei read in their Japanese-language newspapers, and the information that the Nisei gleaned from outside sources continued to indicate various kinds of discrimination outside camp.

A further problem in considering where to resettle was that the expectations of the parent generation did not always coincide with those of their children. An unease persisted even among my family members. Although we often talked about the prospects for relocation, lack of money plagued us all. In our discussions, our parents could only advise, no longer direct as when we were younger. So it must have been with other families where the decision making gradually shifted from the first generation to the second.

Mother, I knew, wanted to keep the family together wherever we went and was especially reluctant to have the family scattered over distances. Father did not insist that we return to Berkeley, and with Hisa and Bill resettled in the Midwest, Mae and Howard now favored going to Cincinnati. So it was that we decided against returning to California.

For the Issei, relocation was a huge problem. They wavered in their thinking about what to do. About one-third of the Topaz Issei had no inclination to resettle anywhere as long as the War Relocation Authority housed and fed them. Many of the elderly had no families, no property, and no money, and the Issei who could not speak English fluently were dependent upon their Americanized children. However, a number of them still hoped to return to California.

An old Issei man without relatives said wistfully to me, with a faraway look in his dimming eyes, "How I wish I could go back to *Kashu* (California). I feel so *Kokoro-bosoi* (helpless, disheartened). I just cannot go to a strange city.

There nobody would speak to me. If I went back to *Kashu,* maybe I could live in my old neighborhood again and see friends I had there." He could not realize, even had I told him, that time had no doubt changed the composition of his old neighborhood, that new people from other states had moved in after the Japanese were evacuated. A few Issei clung to the unrealistic hopes that the government would reimburse them for their losses and finance a new start for them on resettlement.

A small fraction of the Topaz residents, about one-half of 1 percent, was against relocation for political reasons. This group was convinced that the agency was forcibly pushing the people out for purposes of its own. They were vocal in their opinions and tried to influence others against relocation. Others less vehement said that the internment was not of their choosing and that they were being rushed into resettlement without adequate means. Some Nisei hesitated to leave because they felt that wartime conditions would prevent them from finding suitable jobs. Aware of the antagonism of these residents, the administrative staff tried to avoid the constant use of the word "relocation," which to us meant dislocation again.

The antagonism stemmed, in part, from the disparity between the governing and the governed, from the obvious differences in status and salaries. Our barracks were primitive; the housing of the administrative personnel was better constructed and furnished with equipped kitchens and indoor bathrooms. Even the distance between their quarters and ours seemed to set an unstated barrier. Moreover, they had the privacy we could not have. The residents felt that the administration would not listen to grievances and that major issues would be decided without their input. On the other hand, the appointed *hakujin* personnel believed that the residents had developed an organized resistance to the entire relocation program.

Most of the people who had already relocated or who were considering moving out were young, from teenagers to those in their mid-thirties. The population of Topaz was predominantly urban, people with specialized commercial skills, college education, and technical training. The former urbanites who had social contacts before the evacuation found it easier to go to new cities than the farmers. The farmers, mainly Issei, in their years of coping on the West Coast had confined themselves to relationships within their own families or to a small number of acquaintances in their rural area.

The camp workers were asked to fill out a personnel record form for the Community Services Division. The form I filled out asked for information about qualification by county, state, or federal civil service examination. (At this time I had not taken any examinations, although in the following year I took a federal civil service examination in Provo, Utah, for a subprofessional library position.) The personnel record also asked about my educational background and majors, my professional memberships, and my work experience and requested a list of five persons as references. I could also indicate the kind of employment I preferred and any special qualifications I possessed.

In June, following close on the publication of the relocation pamphlet, I had received a memo from the chief of the Community Services Division, and to it was attached a carbon copy of my personnel record. The memo read:

> As you perceive [*sic*] to make your own definite plans for relocation, the information you have developed on this form will prove to be important and valuable. Therefore, I suggest that when you go to the Relocation Office and have your interview regarding work opportunities you take this form with you. The information as to training, experience, etc., contained in this individual form will expedite your own relocation.

In addition to the personnel records, the Community Services Division had card indexes that listed the skills of each family member, and the indexes were used in family relocation.

To acquaint the residents with conditions outside, relocation forums organized as panel discussions were conducted for potential relocaters. The panelists, made up of administrative staff and resident leaders, explained rationing, warned of housing problems, gave information about transportation and the allowable weight of freight and baggage for each train ticket. They emphasized the need to be conscious of personal appearance, conduct, and job ethics since animosity still prevailed in some communities.

Jobs on the outside were well publicized. As announcements arrived from outside, the notices were sent to the block managers, section heads, and others in administrative or supervisory positions. Usually the notices of new openings were posted on the mess hall bulletin boards or relayed by word of mouth.

Despite the flutter caused by talk and plans for relocation, the daily business of camp work continued uninterrupted and took precedence over future concerns. In mid-July, as a teacher of Basic English in the Adult Education Division, I met with the other teachers in my section to discuss what changes could be anticipated with the loss of students and faculty through segregation, and how much would have to be absorbed by the remaining staff. As it turned out, the reduction of our staff was affected not so much by segregation as by the relocation program. I found that I did not have to be overly concerned because enrollment in the Basic English classes continued to be steady, with about one-third new students and two-thirds continuing. Some drop-in attendance did occur for other reasons such as changes in camp jobs or summer schedules, the uncertainty of available classrooms, the turnover among teachers, and even the scheduling of classes at night.

In September, the principal of the Topaz High School appealed to qualified residents to join the teaching staff, and I was again asked to teach secondary English as I had done before. With the approach of the fall semester, I had enough to keep me fully occupied.

When autumn was finally in the air, and the chill grew sharper, we could hear the wild geese honking in the sky, and Mother and I would stand outdoors to watch the birds flying overhead in their wedge formation. Once we saw a wedge break formation and stretch out into a long, sinuous line against the color-drenched sky. As she watched, Mother murmured, "*Watari-dori*" (birds of passage), a Japanese term applicable also to migrant people, poetic in imagery, but somehow sad as she spoke.

Afterwards, I wrote a series of haiku about the flight I had witnessed with her:

The geese flew over
At dusk—I shivered, not with
Cold, but sense of loss.

Where do the geese go?
Can they escape from autumn
And return to spring?

Let me follow them:
The geese know better than I
Which way leads to spring.

For a certainty
Autumn is now in the air:
The heart took warning.

The second week of December, a letter addressed directly to me by the project director was delivered to our barracks. The letter pointed towards a definite relocation program:

> We are about to initiate on the project a most important program, the purpose of which is to learn from families at first hand their personal plans for relocation, to assist them in the making of long-term plans, and to provide WRA with valuable data.
>
> It is proposed that this interviewing be conducted by teams composed jointly of appointive staff members and resident personnel. Some will be asked to carry on this function on a full time basis, while others will be asked to carry on a limited number of interviews on a part time basis.
>
> You have been chosen as one capable of assisting in the interviewing. If this program is to succeed, and we are confident that it will, it must have the full support of everyone asked to assist, and it must have high priority.

So it was that I was teamed with LeGrande Noble, the superintendent of education. In the interviews I mustered what Japanese I could to translate and explain while Mr. Noble proved to be a kindly, sympathetic interviewer able to put the Issei at ease.

Our project director believed that the Japanese people were not destined to remain confined in camp interminably, but he was also firm that there would be no "pushing out" in Topaz. His intent was that these relocation interviews would help allay the misgivings of those who were thinking of resettlement. Because family cohesion was so powerful a factor in making plans, the emphasis was to be on families relocating together.

Like grains of sand, the days sifted through our consciousness and flowed into each other. By this time of the year, as we once again used our heating stoves, I noticed that the walls and ceiling of our barracks room had become dingy from burning coal through the previous winter. One day, in fun, Joe printed a wall with the sides of fisted hands and finger tips, starting up from the floor and stopping midway across the ceiling near the light fixture, so that it seemed as if an invisible goblin had walked up that sooty wall and vanished into thin air at that point. At night after he was put to bed, Kay would stare up at the ceiling and point to the false footprints and ask, "No more?"

By Christmas of 1943, Hisa had saved enough meat ration points to send us an unexpected, unsurpassed gift of a whole ham, wrapped in sturdy brown paper and labeled with our camp address, 4-8-E. We learned afterwards, much to our amusement and wonder, that after she had purchased the ham and packaged it for mailing, she did not have the time to go downtown in Chicago to a post office. She knew the weight of it, so she affixed more than the sufficient number of stamps to the package to cover the mailing cost and left it sitting on top of a street mailbox. It arrived untampered, intact, and on time.

ROOTS

The roots of being will endure,
    No matter what,
To probe the earth for whys
    That time forgot

To answer when the blossom died
    And green leaves curled,
As long as roots can grasp
    This wherefore world.
    (March 1962)

22

THE DUST BEFORE THE WIND

As we tried to foresee the future, our imagined relocation was as clear as the attempt to sight our barracks in a dense dust storm or a blinding blizzard. No amount of wishful thinking could clarify the unknown. In my family, we talked about the possibilities of homes and jobs outside, but could only guess what they might be. The New Year of 1944 began with crisp, cold days and snow, and an acceleration of concern about the approaching upheaval. Mae was finishing her requirements for a degree in dietetics through correspondence courses with the University of California. Masa was just out of high school, and Joe and Lee were still attending high school, with Joe considering college. In spite of the calendar and the news of the war, time somehow seemed to be suspended between "before the segregation" and "after the segregation."

A dust storm was no doubt a more apt metaphor than a blizzard for the obscurity and apprehension surrounding the coming relocation. Some months before, I had had a firsthand experience of a storm. I was terrified. That morning I had gone to Block 1 to meet with the Basic English teaching staff, early enough, I thought, for me to go to Block 32 to teach my high school class. A strong wind was blowing and threatened to push me over as I started out from our barracks. With a bandanna tied over my head, I had to lean forward to shield myself against the blast. I made my way to Block 1, and after the meeting with my staff members, who had all come from other corners of the camp, I started out for the high school, located in the center of the project area.

There was an awesome eeriness about pushing through that gray, dust-laden atmosphere, all sounds deadened except for the whining rush of the wind; the barracks huddled out of sight until I was right up against one of them. Instead of going diagonally through the camp as I usually did on a clear day, I thought that with such poor visibility I should go in a straight line for several blocks and then turn at a right angle toward the center of the camp to end up where I needed to be. I knew that I had just enough time to reach the school before the beginning of my class that morning.

I walked and walked in the storm, and blocks and barracks disappeared, emerged barely visible, disappeared again, all looking the same. I then lost count of the blocks I had passed since I could no longer distinguish where one ended and another began. Although the scarf partially screened my face, I had to keep my head down. Sharp particles of dust bit into exposed skin. I was uneasily aware that time was passing and that I was nowhere near my destination.

I felt a slight slowing in the velocity of the wind, and I looked up. To my consternation, I saw that I was directly under the tall water tower at the opposite end of the camp from Block 1. I had groped the entire length from one side to the other. Baffled and lost as I was, with little else recognizable in that murky air, wisdom suggested that I try to find my way home. Following the camp boundary from the water tower to Block 4, I was able to get back to our barracks. My class had a holiday that day.

With relocation looming, the Issei in my evening classes were not interested in talking about the thirty-below-zero cold, the snowdrifts on the roads that made walking to work or school laborious, or the breaking down of water pipes and sewage system. Instead, they speculated on cities they had never seen or visited. They asked questions I could not often answer since I had never traveled in the Midwest or the East. Nodding seriously, they would remark that camp existence was *yoku-nai* (not right) or *warui* (bad or wrong) for their children. As I looked into their earnest faces, I realized that even with the losses they had incurred, they were willing to chance another relocation so their children could attain what had been denied them.

After a year of teaching both day and night classes, my schedule became so exhausting that I was released from the Education Division and transferred to the Topaz Public Library. The transfer eased my workload; no more massive amounts of lesson plans to prepare and papers to correct. However, a handful of my second-year Latin students wished to continue and complete their two years of study. So for the remainder of the semester, they met with me in the evenings in the small side room in the library, a combination workplace and office, and we finished reading Caesar's Gallic wars. A library assistant—sometimes my sister Masa—manned the circulation desk while I taught. The review of Latin grammar and translation had occasional lapses from strict scholarship. One night, for example, we were discussing the conjugation of the verb *to be.* A student started reciting the perfect tense of the verb, and she uttered, "*Fui,* I have been, I was." A classmate interrupted, "Phooey! Latin certainly can be phooey!" Moments later as another student read, "*Locus castris idoneus erat*" (the place was suitable for a camp), the other students chimed in, "Absolutely!"

When I was first thrust into camp among so many Japanese, I felt hampered in trying to converse with the Issei. Unlike many of my Nisei schoolmates, I had not been sent to a Japanese-language school when I was growing up. My brother Bill was the only one who had taken courses in Japanese while he was a student at the University of California. His one complaint at that time was that because he was Japanese he was not admitted to the elementary course, and even with Mother's tutoring, he had to struggle in a more advanced course. Both Hisa and Masa had acquired some knowledge of reading and writing Japanese from Mother when they took turns accompanying her as a babysitter while she taught in a country school. However, now in camp, with the help of Father and Mother, the language I had acquired by ear revived, and I was able to speak Japanese more freely.

In the length of days we had been in camp, an understanding of my people came with our closer communication. Language, spoken or written, Japanese or English, drew us together, in exchange of greetings and bows or in individual conversation and group discussion, even through the camp publications, the newspaper *Topaz Times* and the literary quarterly *Trek.* I discovered another dimension of that communication through teaching Basic English to the Issei and both English and Latin to the high school students. My appreciation of the connecting power of language was further strengthened when I began work in the public library.

As winter eased into spring, the morale of the people—in direct contrast to the rising temperature—dropped. The newly constructed auditorium in the middle of the camp had been used by the high school students and young adults for sports events, dances, motion-picture showings, and other entertainment. But by now, many able recreation leaders had left camp to relocate or join the armed services, and their absence created a vacuum in activities. Some people pursued individual hobbies, but in general there was little organized recreation, especially for the elderly.

However, in April, the elementary school group proposed a spring program which the administration approved. First, there was a campaign by the administration, resident officials, and block managers to give the camp a spring cleaning. The War Relocation Authority agreed to furnish the trucks, and the blocks would furnish the labor to resurface the gravel walks between the barracks and to tidy the area surrounding the coal pile in each block. The War Relocation Authority was also willing to furnish calcimine and paint, if the residents would provide volunteer labor.

After the spring cleaning, a camp-wide, week-long celebration of spring commenced on May 5, the day for the traditional Boys' Festival, a meaningful occasion for families with sons. There were hobby shows that featured lapidary skill, delicate shell creations, wood carving, art, and needlework. The women were attracted to the flower arrangement exhibits and the fashion show. To appeal to all tastes, there were *go* and *shogi* (like checkers and chess) tournaments, competitive baseball, marble and kite-flying contests, marathon dances, and talent shows. The residents flocked to the exhibits and the performances. The heat and the dust were overlooked for the time being, and thoughts about relocating receded. The two nights of a high school minstrel show were attended by capacity crowds and enjoyed by the students and parents alike.

About two weeks later, a visit from Sergeant Ben Kuroki, born and raised in Nebraska and a member of a bomber crew active over Europe and Africa, gave residents a view of the outside world. They gave him a hero's welcome, and a reception was held in the auditorium, followed by luncheons and dinners. He addressed the high school student body, and people crowded around him to get his autograph. A modest and gentle soldier, he was able to tell of actual combat and of his opposition to prejudice and discrimination. He was an exemplary figure for the young men expecting to join the armed services, and his visit was a stirring interval before the quiet summer when heat, rising to 108 degrees or higher, laid its spell upon the camp.

Relocation to date had not accelerated, but recruiters for labor in canneries and on the railroad came to offer seasonal jobs. More aged Issei men began applying for temporary jobs, and even the urban Issei inquired about farm work. Their savings had been exhausted, and they knew that the future outside the camps would be difficult without financial resources. In addition, they were growing restless after two years of camp existence. On the other hand, they were very cognizant of the hostile attitudes on the outside.

Enough manpower had been drained off, however, by the relocation, draft, and seasonal work that there was concern that there would not be sufficient labor to run the mess halls, the hospital, the agricultural project, and other necessary services. Other worker shortages included teachers, social welfare workers, office staff, laboratory technicians, farm hands, and plumbers. Even the students grumbled about the teacher turnover. Teachers, on their part, contended that their pupils had become rowdy and irresponsible towards school property. Block managers insisted that parents were to blame for student misdemeanors. With the closing of two mess halls for lack of kitchen crew, some of the residents applied for work in the hospital diet kitchen. A combination of weariness, boredom, need for money, and minor irritations from confined living worked against total harmony, and a nagging anxiety overlaid any considerations.

In the following months, servicemen in training were permitted to visit camp on furloughs. Among them was Roy, who was in the service unit of the medical detachment of the Vaughan General Hospital in Hines, Illinois. In his uniform, he was the center of Kay's attention. When he sat in our room to chat, regaling us with tales of his training period and current work in a veteran's hospital, Kay would lean against his knee and look up at him with a rapt stare. In the mess hall, Kay had to sit right next to Roy. Mother and Father agreed that Roy looked well, and though he was the shortest of my brothers, he was still taller than I, so he could tease me about being the smallest of the family: "You are a little bit of a runt, aren't you, Sis?" When I reached out to protest, he lifted me off the floor and swung me around and around, as Kay, astounded, clapped his hands. After Roy returned to Illinois, he wrote that he worried about the welfare of the family and inquired about Kay, who had just recovered from an asthma attack at the time of his visit.

I had inquired about treatment for Kay's allergies and asthma at the hospital, but there were no specialists, particularly in pediatrics, on the medical staff. That summer, the hospital had troubles of its own. The dental staff had been reduced from seven to three, and the pharmacists from four to one. When the new chief medical officer arrived, with a new head nurse, a dietitian, and auxiliary personnel, it was hoped that the hospital would fare better. However, the chief and the resident medical staff were not able to see eye to eye, especially when, because of the shortage of registered nurses and nurses aides, the chief ordered the cancellation of clinic appointments for one week and made other changes without consulting the Japanese doctors. A strike was imminent when Kay was hospitalized with pneumonia again, but a Japanese doctor who knew the severity of Kay's previous illness assured me that he would be responsible for his care. I was relieved that after a series of meetings and consultations the hospital problem was resolved, and the residents came to know the chief medical officer better.

By August, the touchiness in camp was evident as rehearsals for the annual *Bon Odori* (festival of the dead) began. Several families had received news of casualties on the Italian front, and they felt that the gaiety that normally characterized the festival was out of keeping. The Buddhist Church issued a letter to the camp populace to explain the meaning of the event, a ceremonial service for the dead expressed through dancing.

Even as these incidents occurred, people uneasy about the relocation began to use the family counseling program that had begun in the spring. A staff of case workers interviewed families, analyzed specific problems, and tried to assist them in a relocation plan. Discussion teams, including the one in which I partnered with LeGrande Noble, spoke with the Issei about relocation.

In February of 1944, President Roosevelt signed Executive Order 9423 to transfer the War Relocation Authority to the Department of the Interior under Secretary Ickes, and government officials expected that soon the War Department would revoke its exclusion order for the Japanese on the West Coast. Finally, in an announcement on December 17, 1944, the exclusion order was lifted by the War Department, effective on January 2, 1945.

The day after the revocation announcement, the War Relocation Authority announced that all centers would be closed in the period between six months and a year after January 2, 1945. On the same day came news of the termination of seasonal leaves, the shutting down of farming operations for the camp, and the closing of the center schools at the end of the spring term in June 1945. This policy applied to all the relocation centers except for the Tule Lake Segregation Center. Disbelief and anger were the immediate reaction, and the program of liquidation was denounced as brutal and inhuman.

INVESTMENT

Answers life sold as gilt-edged bonds
  Are safely under locks,
Away from prying eyes
  In time's own secret box.

If later, when you need to see
  The record of each year,
Note I invested self
  When living was most dear.
  (September 1945)

MEASURE

What I once was, and am,
  To state the change one sees,
Is better gauged by time
  Than bibliographies.

However erudite,
  No data can explain
That when a grief is done
  The heart may live again.

Fair measure is attained
  When love grants wisdom late,
This last degree conferred
  As being ultimate.
  (December 1945)

23

THE DISPERSAL

On the first day of 1945, we taught Kay, now a lively, talkative three-year-old, to say "Happy New Year," and he practiced repeatedly without comprehending its significance. That morning, as he bounced into the mess hall and met the other residents of Block 4, he greeted them with his childishly jubilant "Happy New Year." The day had been granted us as a holiday although we had to take this Monday as vacation leave. The mess hall served only two meals, which eased the work of the kitchen crew. I was groggy with a cold, but I welcomed the clear day, and in that first night of the year, the darkness blazed with sharp starlight.

This New Year's Day we were not served the traditional *mochi* for breakfast. The commissary had reported that the shipment of the glutinous rice had gone astray. Despite the loss, somehow the lightheartedness of welcoming a new year lessened the anxiety about relocation planning and the closing of the centers. We sat at the mess hall tables to eat the American-style breakfast and chatted about the entertainment that was to be held in the auditorium and the special program in our own block.

The following evening, Kay and I were invited to the quarters of a Caucasian teacher, Eleanor Sekerak, with whom I had been discussing relocation possibilities on her visits to the library. It was a long walk to the administrative sector, but Kay walked sedately beside me. Grandmother had impressed upon him that he must behave and not run about as he did in our room. That evening, Eleanor had invited other teachers I knew from the high school, and we listened to her records and enjoyed the talk of the worlds we each had come from. When Kay discovered that whenever Eleanor opened her refrigerator a light went on automatically, he was puzzled and fascinated by the phenomenon. Every time anyone approached the refrigerator, he would dash over to peer under elbows. On his return to our barracks, his wonder about the light in the refrigerator made Grandmother smile, and I knew that she was thinking, as I was, that there would be many new experiences waiting for him on the outside.

That same week, Mae, who worked in the hospital diet kitchen, took a final examination in English for the University of California, and Eleanor proctored the test in her own quarters where it would be quiet and Mae could work undisturbed. Mae lacked one in-residence course to qualify for registry in the national dietitians' association, and her adviser in Berkeley urged her to complete the requirement. Unfortunately, we were totally unable to provide the necessary funds for her to return to the university. She knew the financial situation of the family and recognized the impossibility of school too well, but could not help voicing her regret.

An expert in cooking, Mae was the one who could coax the portable tin oven on top of the space heater to produce delectable baked treats, once Father had the embers of the coal fire under control. One afternoon, with Masa's help, she made cookies. Watching the cookie dough being stirred and shaped, Kay refused to take a nap, especially when the warm smell of baking in the same room was so enticing.

Block-shopping had been instituted in the camp, and one could apply a week in advance for a permit to go to Delta for shopping. A bus provided the transportation, and the sentry at the gate checked our passes before we left and when we returned. The stipulation for such a trip to Delta was that shopping be done for everyone else in the block, so when permission was granted and names posted, the shopper would receive lists and money for desired items that ranged from groceries to a toy for a baby or a spool of thread. The first time I went block-shopping, I was exhilarated by the bus ride because I had not been outside since we settled in Topaz. Instead of chatting with fellow passengers, I kept looking out at the small homesteads, the farm animals, and the open stretch of countryside free of the barracks. I relished this brief spell of liberty. It was on that trip that a woman in our block asked me to purchase two dozen eggs for her, and the grocer put the eggs into two separate paper sacks. On the way back to camp, each time the bus wheels passed over a rock or caught in the rut of the road and lurched, I quickly had to lift the paper sacks off my lap. It was on a similar block-shopping trip that we were able to get the proper ingredients for the cookies that Mae made.

Joe graduated from the high school in January 1945, and his thoughts turned to leaving camp and enrolling in some college. As early as March

1942, when the evacuation had just started rolling, college educators on the West Coast had become concerned about student relocation. That same spring the director of the newly organized War Relocation Authority had appealed to the American Friends Service Committee in Philadelphia for assistance with student relocation. From the combined efforts of many groups was established the National Japanese American Student Relocation Council. The council had the support of college presidents and deans, associations of higher education, religious bodies, and the student YMCA and YWCA. Some military regulations ruled against Nisei enrolling in colleges and universities engaged in work related to the war effort, but schools not under the ban of security opened their doors to Nisei applicants. Antioch College rejected Joe's application, but he was accepted at the University of Cincinnati, and the council made two hundred dollars available to him when he left us before the summer.

I had also considered returning to school to finish the graduate work I had started at the University of California before marriage. I had filled out a questionnaire and drawn up an estimated budget for the council, but funds were not available then for graduate students. How tenaciously my mind clung to the reflections of those happy student days. I thought of the possibilities as I knitted on a sweater for Howard, who was impatient for its completion. Knit one, purl one, I automatically counted, twining the long ago into the garment as the needles moved and the finger flicked the yarn over for each stitch. Nisei friends who had relocated to Chicago to commence graduate studies or to work had recently visited their families in camp, and they had stopped in the library to urge me to leave. I seriously wished I could.

After the lifting of the exclusion order, the War Relocation Authority conferred with the Western Defense Command and established field offices on the West Coast—in Los Angeles, San Francisco, and Seattle. We knew that people had gone back to their former homes on the West Coast, but shortly afterward disturbing news of shootings, arson, assaults, and threats against the returning Japanese swept through the camp and aroused mixed emotions of fear, helpless anger, and uncertainty. In May, Secretary of the Interior Ickes, in response to these vigilante tactics, issued a press release against "the shameful spectacle of these incidents of terrorism." Of the interned Japanese, he said: "In a real sense, these people, too, were drafted by their country. They were uprooted from their homes and substantially deprived of an opportunity to lead a normal life. They are casualties of war."

Mother worried constantly as she talked with Father about the relocation of us all, especially those who had left the family fold. She had been ill lately, confined to bed for a week or more, and had recovered slowly. Even strong willed as she was, she could not fight off illness. She would tell us, "One cannot afford to be sick if we relocate." Then in February, we learned that Hisa was ill with pleurisy and that Bill was to be drafted. To keep in touch with them, she dictated letters to Mae or Masa or me, and we then translated what she said into English. To make sure that what we wrote carried the exact gist of what she meant, we had to retranslate the English version until she was certain and could approve the final writing. When he had time, Father wrote his own letters in English. When Kay was napping, and the room was still, I would sometimes see Mother's eyes leave the book she was reading and gaze off into a remote distance. Even though she explored the broad reaches of the mind, her private domain was the family. Troubled as she was, she sat so quietly, not relaxed, but controlled. However, I had known her to face deeper griefs, and she was stronger than the rest of us.

A snowfall at the beginning of March softened the appearance of the barracks, and the large, feathery flakes caught in the empty branches of straggly willow bushes made them look less wispy. Kay liked to tromp through the snow, and our walk for his bath took a little longer as he would stop frequently to look back at his tracks. This month he was subject to spells of wheezing and difficult breathing. When he broke out in a rash on his hands and mouth, I took him to the hospital, where we had to wait for three hours in the clinic. We were dismissed rather curtly after we received a prescription for the skin irritation. The service was poor, but I had to admit that a little attention, even if it was so galling, was better than none at all.

In anticipation of Easter, Masa and other block girls planned an egg hunt for the small children. They boiled eggs and dyed them in bright colors, and Easter Eve they hid them around the center of the block, under large rocks, in the willows, near the entrance of the laundry room, and under benches. On Easter Sunday, the entire camp was blanketed by snow, but the children braved the raw wind and waited until the mess hall gong signaled the start of the egg hunt. They scurried here and there, mittens fell off, but the weather did not seem to bother them in the excitement and hilarity. Kay found four eggs, ice-cold, and he might not have found the last one beside a rock, dyed stone-gray, if one of the girls had not kept calling, "Kay-*chan,* look down by your feet." She laughed when he held it up for her to see.

At the beginning of the year I had applied for federal employment, and during the first week of April I received a notice from Civil Service that I was to take a library test in Provo, miles away. Not having had library science courses previously, I did not know what to review. One day I remained home to study the materials I had borrowed for the examination, and I had just paused to chat with Mother and Mae, when Lee dashed in from the next room to tell us that the radio announcer, that very minute, had spoken of President Roosevelt's death at Warm Springs, Georgia. We sprang up from our seats and went to lean over the radio for the next bulletin which repeated what Lee had heard. The news spread, and we saw the flag we had always honored flying at half-mast. That evening memorial services were held in the churches.

At the end of that week, with permission granted through the administrative office, I left to take the Civil Service examination. First I took the bus to Delta, where I boarded the train to Salt Lake City. There I was met by one of the relocation advisers from Topaz, and I stayed with her in a hotel across the street from the Mormon Temple. The feel of the pavement under my feet, the traffic, the shops, the city buildings, and the passers-by who glanced at me impersonally seemed all so new. The next morning I went by bus to Provo, where the examination was given at the post office, and I proved to be the only one taking a test. The postal official was friendly and cautioned me to read the questions carefully. After completing the exam, I was able to be back in Salt Lake City by noon.

To make the most of my outing, the relocation adviser, a Catholic convert, and I visited the cathedral towards evening. I had never before viewed such an awe-inspiring, restful place, and I was deeply moved to feel the peace of that beautiful interior. The young priest who met us at the door talked with me while the adviser was at prayer. As we were talking, another priest came to see him, and he apologized that the two of them had another engagement. My acquaintance and I caught a bus to see a motion picture, and while we were in line for the theater tickets, we saw the two priests arrive for the same show. We were amused to meet again so soon. The next day I returned alone to Topaz.

By May I heard from the Civil Service that my the rating on the examination made me eligible for appointment. In the letter I was asked whether I was immediately available in the event I was certified and appointed. I was undecided, primarily because of Kay. Mother and I had discussed the possibilities of going to Chicago, but in the end we thought it best to plan on going to Cincinnati, where Joe had just relocated to start the summer session at the university.

There was an undercurrent of feeling among the residents that the War Relocation Authority was bluffing about the closing of the centers to stimulate out-migration. When the national director (who was greeted on his arrival with a sign reading "Welcome, Dillon S. Myer, the Great White Father") came to visit Topaz, he stated that the camps would definitely close that year. To break through the procrastination of those holding back or intending to remain until the last minute, the War Relocation Authority announced in July the schedule of camp closings, and Topaz was on the calendar for the first of November.

With the pressure exerted to plan for relocation, the residents exhibited an odd ambivalent attitude towards the program. On the one hand, they seemed indifferent, yet they acted as though the closing had to be met on schedule with a gradual shutting down of cooperative enterprises and activities. The interest in vocational training courses increased to the point where there were not enough teachers or equipment. There was an even greater demand for seasonal leaves so heads of families could earn more towards their relocation.

As the majority became convinced that the relocation program was inevitable, the War Relocation Authority faced difficulties in resettling their charges. There was a housing shortage in cities, caused by the shifting of population during the wartime boom. The evacuees were in financial straits because of losses incurred at the evacuation, and the public was still hostile towards them. Then transportation became a problem because the trains were needed to move troops. The program had to be spaced out, so a policy statement known as Administrative Notice No. 289 was issued to cover the scheduled relocation process. It enabled each project director, starting six weeks before the stated closing of his center, to establish weekly quotas for people to be shipped out. The quotas were first filled by those who were leaving of their own volition, but then, if the quotas could not be met, the director had the power to assign departure dates to enough other individuals to fill them. The notice also made explicit that if a resident refused to pack his belongings and leave, they would be packed for him, and he would be escorted by the internal police to the gate of the camp. In what we later viewed as coincidental timing, this eviction notice was announced just two weeks before V-J Day and the collapse of Japan.

Even as I was beginning to prepare for the shutting down of the library, new books were being added and people continued to borrow them. I was informed that the collection was to be merged with the school libraries in another location. The Caucasian librarian who would take charge of the central library came to ask me what I intended to do with the public library collection. I said that the books purchased out of the rental fees and overdue fines belonged to the people. She strongly disagreed with me and said that since we were allowed to live in camp, those books belonged to the government. I remained unconvinced although I told her that she could have the books bought with the agency-allocated funds. I was bothered, so Mother suggested that I consult the head of the Community Activities Section, to which the libraries reported. Eleanor Sekerak held this position now, so I was at ease in talking with her. She listened to my reasoning and recommended that I see the superintendent of education, Mr. Noble, and she accompanied me to his office. Once again I explained the status of the books in the rental collection, and he agreed that these particular books rightly belonged to the people. So before the public library was emptied, I held a book sale, at reduced prices, of the rental collection. The money derived from the sale was donated to the student relocation fund.

In May, the camp relocation office asked me to give detailed verbal sketches of each one in our family as to experience, education, and capabilities so that, as I was told, our relocation might be effected smoothly. The following day I was asked further questions about the property we had left behind. I remembered tagging some of our things for the army to hold in storage with tags left over from labeling our baggage. Eventually, these tagged items were sent to the camps, although I did not find that out until now. Fortunately, Father had a copy of the list he had made for the Wartime Civilian Control Administration when we prepared to leave Berkeley. But the list he had and the one on record in our camp did not coincide, so we had to conclude that much had been lost or, possibly, stolen.

Mother and I had to go to the camp warehouse to see what was actually in storage in the depths of that barn-like structure. We were led to the boxes we had last seen that April morning three years before. Mother stared at the boxes, then ran a hand over the nearest one and, turning to me, said, "They remind me of the heartbreak of that morning." We could not tell what had been packed into them, but asked that several of the small boxes be delivered to our barracks for sorting. In one of them was our portable phonograph and old records, all of which brought us pleasure. On another day, Mother unearthed, out of another box, my worn scrapbook of clippings with my writings that had appeared in print in the West Coast Japanese American newspapers from 1936 to 1939. As I reread the poetry, essays, and weekly columns that I had written in those years, I could visualize the Berkeley hills, the campus, and friends.

After correspondence had passed between the field office and the camp relocation office, Mae and Howard left for Cincinnati in July. Mae found work in a hospital laboratory, and Howard became a stock clerk for a hosiery manufacturer. Their moving to Cincinnati was a comfort to Joe, who had been lonely without the family, and was reassuring to Mother as well. Then Masa left to join them in August, so only Mother and Father, our youngest brother, Lee, my son, and I remained in Topaz. Our family was diminishing, and so was our block since a number of the residents had returned to California.

Into the midst of our preparations for moving out in mid-August was dropped the startling news of the atomic bomb that had exploded and destroyed Hiroshima. The horror of it surpassed imagination. Only later did we see the pictorial news magazines. There were many Issei from Hiroshima who had relatives in the devastated city. The distraught residents stormed the Red Cross office in camp to see whether they could send messages, but it was practically impossible. Their despair and sorrow were tangible, and I sat, without appetite, at meals with a friend and her mother from Hiroshima as they tried to keep from weeping.

Mother and Father were from another province, but they too seemed overwhelmed by the bombing. When they spoke with other residents, they murmured condolences. They had to accept Japan's defeat. Did *shikata ga nai* apply at this time too? Japan's capitulation became a reality when our neighbor told us that she had listened to the Emperor's message in French come over the air.

The *Topaz Times* brought out a special edition with the headlines "Japan Surrenders" and "Center Closing Set." The feature stories were on the ending of the World War and the Potsdam ultimatum, but greater space was devoted to news of forced relocation. The project director was quoted, "It should be obvious now that there will be no residue populations left in the centers after the closing dates and that the WRA will not keep one or more centers open as some evacuees have predicted." A two-day holiday celebrating the war's end was declared for the residents and administrative personnel, except for essential workers, and there was no delivery of mail or packages.

A few days later, I heard from a Caucasian schoolmate in California who wrote: "When the news of the war's end came, I sat down and cried like a baby. Not from happiness, but from great thanksgiving that one aspect of 'man's inhumanity to man' is over. Wherever you go now I fear for that mass hysteria, intolerance, and the closed mind. . . . We were supposed to be fighting for a way of life. I think that one would be very fortunate if he could surround himself with his own loneliness, a few friends, who are sympathetic to his chosen mode of existence, and the wherewithal to live in dignity of mind and spirit."

At this time, Kay's nursery school closed. Many of the young teachers were now gone, although the supervisor was still in our block with her severely diabetic mother. I was profoundly grateful for the patience and care these teachers had devoted to the preschool children. Playing under caring supervision and learning to share with one another were but a part of their development. The love that calmed a temper tantrum, soothed a hurt, and smiled on repeated stories was a quality that drew the children to their teachers. On the last day of school, the children were told that they could choose favorite playthings to keep. Kay selected a stuffed toy dog, a few books that he had enjoyed hearing his teacher read, and a cut-out puzzle. That night, and after, the toy dog went to bed with him.

The first week of September 1945, the Western Defense Command issued Public Proclamation No. 24, revoking all individual exclusion orders and all further military restrictions against persons of Japanese descent. So came the end to a peculiar, catastrophic experience, our American experience. What we now had before us was to decide how we would leave camp and resume a normal life.

STALKED

I had long shaken dust
    From feet that once had walked
The unpaved roads of camp,
    But quietly dust stalked

And would not let me be,
    Sifting upon the wind
Of memory into
    The crevices of mind.
    (November 1951)

GIANT STEP

A giant step advances me
    Past solid wall of years,
Out of incarcerated self,
    Where sunlight newly clears

The air; I must not hesitate
    Or stop: a sudden halt
Or backward glance might alter me
    To monolith of salt.
    (March 1962)

24

TREE OF THE PEOPLE
(TOPAZ COMMUNITY)

A year after we had been in camp, incoming evacuees received copies of a mimeographed booklet entitled *Welcome to Topaz.* A guidebook prepared by the Historical Section of the Reports Division, it was designed to provide residents with general information about the organization of the camp: services, schools, recreation, hospital, the vicinity just outside the fence. It also included lists of "do's" and "don'ts." On its cover was a drawing of what looked like a heraldic shield, the outline enclosing a sketch of barracks in a block and resembling the shape of a pine tree. In January 1943, the design was accepted and used as the official Topaz Shield.

The last page of the booklet provided an explanation of the cover design. The drawing gave a graphic representation of the camp population of about eighty-five hundred people by age groups. We called it the tree of the people.

At the very top, a conic spire, were the Issei eighty-six to ninety years old; the next area, with a slight sloping outwards, included those who were fifty-one to seventy. A little indentation represented those residents who were thirty-one to fifty. The broadest part of the graph, with the widest branches, indicated people in the age range of sixteen to thirty; another indentation represented those who were thirteen to fifteen; another widening out—not as large as the middle of the graph—included those who were eleven to twelve. At the base of the design, the graph slimmed down, like a short tree trunk, to include the young people, from the infants to the six-year-olds.

When Topaz was planted in the wasteland, there were no natural trees to be seen. Into the arid barrenness, hardy trees and growing saplings were brought in from outside the fence and planted in the blocks. With buckets of water and constant care from the interned people, who longed to see green growth, many took root although buffeted by the sweeping dust storms, the snows and ice of winter. Like the trees, the people uprooted from the West Coast grew into a community and survived.

Although the shield's stylized depiction of a whole tree represented the mass of our camp population, within its segments—its branches and leaves—we grew at different rates and in different ways from one another. We adjusted individually to the climate, the harsh earth, and the circumscribed existence. Once the residents were relocated out of camp, the tree would no longer remain standing but would be cut down and removed, its roots, branches, and the smallest twigs scattered throughout the country. What would the place we called Topaz be like then? One could hazard a guess yet be almost certain that the wilderness would reclaim its silence, the prairie dogs would poke their heads out of their burrows and no longer sniff the odor of people, the wild geese would fly over a houseless desert.

During the three years we lived there, changes had occurred in the family structure. The second generation had turned away from the repressed, obedient behavior they had been taught and had become a more vocal and self-sufficient group. Even the girls were able to speak up during the relocation planning to say that they did not want to return to the West Coast after their friends had relocated to the Midwest or to eastern cities. Although the Nisei were still bound by filial ties to their parents, they wished to make decisions for themselves, particularly eldest sons in the armed service or in jobs outside, or college-age students facing the choice of a school.

After V-J Day, resistance to relocation out of the camps began to decrease, and the War Relocation Authority was able to proceed with its program as scheduled. For a while, because of the scarcity of workers, many of us were drafted into service to bring in the last of the farm crops planted in the outer project area. The gnats and the mosquitoes swarmed out there, and we tried to protect ourselves as well as we could. I would go out with a crew in a truck along with the hoes and other tools, work in the field for a day, and return with stinging, red welts on my arms and legs. Somewhat later, when the kitchen staff became depleted, I helped in the mess hall with the food preparation. It was a little different to be peeling onions and potatoes, stirring pots, and serving at meal times than to be on the receiving side of the counter.

As the people moved out, mess halls began to close, and ours shut down after the volunteers dwindled to a few. The blocks were then grouped into areas, and we had to go to a mess hall blocks away where we felt like intruders, or mendicants. Finally Mother refused to walk that distance for her meals, so Father made a wooden tray with a rim around it for me to bring food back for her. I soon discovered that walking back on a cold evening over a rock-strewn road with a filled tray was sometimes calamitous. By the time I had set the tray in front of Mother, the orange that was the dessert had rolled around and jiggled the bowl of soup so that the contents were sloshing around. The rice was cold, the bread slices had soaked up the soup, and the other cooked dishes were also cold. But Mother made the best of it.

As more and more people left from our block, the sight of the empty barracks rooms haunted me. No more friendly voices called out from windows or doors. At night the atmosphere was eerie. Devoid of lights, the barracks appeared to be waiting, blind and soundless. Even in our own barracks, the end rooms were empty. Kay missed the playmates of the block, even the ones he had fought with. He would ask about them, but explaining "the outside" as distance was futile since he had no concept of time and space except what was directly observable through his physical senses.

Farewells were upsetting as we saw friends off at the gate, and there were regular departures now. Even when the harshness of the desert was absorbed into the mind and resented, the remembered faces of those who had lived near us would return, and we would speak of their kindness, a good time shared, the funny and maddening events we had experienced together. I knew that I would never see many of them again. A few I would correspond with over the years because they had been kindred spirits, but the rest would be dispersed far and wide. Of the comradeship and thoughts exchanged during the internment, I wrote:

Deep Roots

So much is said in vain,
   For words are brittle stems
That break off easily
   And bear few fruits.

Some catch the falling rain
   and flaunt a row of gems,
But certain words I know
   That had deep roots.

One weekend when I was working alone in the library, since by then we had abolished evening and weekend hours, I was sorting books to be boxed and sent to the central library. My attention was caught by the title *Humiliation with Honor,* by Vera Brittain, a slim book published by Fellowship Publications of New York. I had read her earlier book, *Testament of Youth,* which told of her experience as a nurse during World War I. The title seemed so appropriate for our situation that I took the book to a table on which the sunlight streamed through a dusty window, and I read, uninterrupted, as minutes passed.

The book was made up of a series of letters Vera Brittain had written to her fifteen-year-old son, whom she had sent to the United States during this war. In them, she explained the meaning of her pacifism. The honesty of her thinking, which I knew stemmed from the First World War, and her compassionate understanding of the opposite views were remarkable. I was not sure that I could be as lenient towards the opposition.

My eyes were riveted to the paragraph:

> Today, across the five continents and the seven seas, you find large sections of that bulk population being subjected to forms of persecution, oppression, victimization, and constraint which were used in the period between the World Wars by the Russian and German totalitarian governments, but which the unleashing of war-time passions has multiplied and extended a hundredfold. These forms of persecution range from the state control of individual travel, to the compulsory emigration of entire populations; from the exercise of autocratic powers to detain "suspects" without trial in prisons and concentration camps, to the imposition of military and industrial conscription; from the seizure or regulation of private funds, to arbitrary restrictions on speech and writing. The one extreme passes easily into a policy of murder which views with indifference the death of the body; the other involves a total disregard of the frustration and atrophy of the mind. (Brittain 1943, 18)

It was in the fourth letter, which bore the title of the book itself, that I came upon a sentence which struck me with the force of shattering waters, and I recalled with a part of my mind Mother telling me that conversion comes in two ways: either when the force of fierce mountain torrents break a rock asunder, or when the water in a steady drip bores a hole through that rock. So Brittain's words were a revelation and balm at the same time: "Only humiliation with honor—the honor of self-discipline and of new wisdom wrought out of bitter experience—can save men and women degraded by war from becoming sources of hatred and vengeance, and enable them to contribute in their unique fashion to those abiding things 'which belong to our peace'" (Brittain 1943, 45).

In another letter she noted the number of people interned in England in 1942, and at the bottom of that page, in fine print, the editorial note states: "No official figures are available on the number of internees in the United States. However, more than 100,000 people are in Relocation Centers, closely resembling internment camps, simply because they are of Japanese ancestry. The majority of these are American-born citizens" (Brittain 1943, 58). For years, I was to remember "humiliation with honor."

The strength of Brittain's words reverberated close to home when I thought about Father's story of his first coming to California and trying to find part-time work for board and room while he put himself through high school. He worked then for a pittance, less than half of what he was now earning in camp, yet he never asked for anyone's assistance, and he bore his disappointments alone. While his children might have seen him as a tough, stubborn man, unable to understand others, this image of him was not accurate. Stubborn he could be, tough when he had to discipline us in our childhood, but he did understand our aspirations. He mellowed with time, and when I would see him napping in our room some afternoons—before he turned to his oil painting—I thought how much he must have endured when he first came to this country. Then I would look over at Mother, ironing as meticulously as she always did, as durable as Father. She still retained her sense of humor; of late she had started to call Kay, whose face had become rounder, "Pancake Face."

In September, we began sorting and packing, as it was a matter of weeks before we were to depart. Even Kay was picking up his toys and putting them in a box near his bed, and he would aver, "I gotta go Cincinnati—that's why!" Our moving out was all he would talk about now. He little knew what precipitated our coming to Topaz, but when he grew older he would learn that humiliation meant loss of face, the discrediting of dignity, an inward shame that eluded words to express it. I hoped he would also learn that honor revived would render humiliation unsullied and would make the years of internment significant.

Almost prophetically I wrote:

LEARNING

Prescience is not conferred
 On unsuspecting heart
To guess the absolute
 Time only can impart.

No gift of prophecy
 Is given me to speak,
Although the wish survive
 Where common words are weak.

Wisdom is not a pledge
 The fickle years bestow,
But certainty endows
 The learning that is slow.

I looked for a tiny box that I could line with cotton wool for protection of Father's miniature painted on the knothole from the stable door. I was holding a part of Tanforan in my hand. In another small box I placed part of Topaz, the shell brooch from my adult student, and the sight of the shells made me muse on the lacustrine creatures that once lived shielded in these brittle casings. The lake between the mountains had evaporated centuries ago and become this desolate place of sage and wind and dust. It was little enough I was taking away from either place, other than what would continue to live in the mind.

The day we were to leave, we had our train tickets, the allowances of twenty-five dollars per person, and additional money for meals on the way. I took Kay's toilet seat out to the open area by the latrine building and threw it on the dump heap, along with discarded magazines. Father banked the fire in the furnace, and we returned the army blankets to the office of the block manager. Mother made sure that the rooms were swept out and the sills dusted even when I protested that no one would be moving in. She cleaned for the invisible household gods. Before starting out for the departure gate, with Kay running in and out in his impatience to be off, Mother and I stood a moment to look around the room, as bare as when we had first walked in except for the stripped cots along the wall. She looked into my eyes briefly, and then, with a formal bow to those invisible beings, she walked out the door, and I followed, closing the door behind me.

Good-natured chattering went on among the passengers as the bus headed toward Delta. When we finally boarded the long train at Delta, we discovered it was filled with soldiers and a few sailors returning from the Pacific battle zones. There was no seat to be had, so, loaded with our luggage, we walked through car after car until we were in the one directly behind the baggage car. The servicemen looked at us curiously but made no comments, though occasionally I would hear a soft "Japs?"

More than a dozen women and children decided they would stay in the small restroom, where the mothers used their suitcases for seats and held small children on their laps. The men and boys, including Father and Lee, spread newspapers on the floor of the aisle outside the restroom to sit down, leaning against the wall. Some had packed lunches, so they had something to eat. As night fell, the travelers dozed off, but the crowded restroom and the motion of the train made some of the children sick, and they gagged and vomited. I had Kay on my lap, but he would not go to sleep, so long after midnight I went out into the aisle with him in my arms. I stood by the window, but there was nothing to see in the darkness. How long I was there I do not know. Just then a tall, burly soldier came to the fountain for a drink of water. He looked at us for a moment, then down at the men and boys sleeping on the floor, and stepping carefully over their legs, he went back to his car. Ten minutes later he returned, stood for a moment looking at Kay and me, and then he asked brusquely, "What are you doing with the kid up at this hour?"

I hurriedly explained how crowded it was, and smelly for lack of fresh air in the restroom. The soldier said, "Wait a minute. I'll be back," and turned on his heel. By this time I had misgivings. He soon came back and said, as he reached out for Kay, "Here, hand me the kid, and come with me." Kay went to him, and I followed him into the next car. He had the first seat with another soldier, who was standing in the aisle. He said, "You sit down now, and I'll put the kid on your lap. My buddy and I are going back to another car to play poker, so we probably won't be back till dawn." Before handing tired Kay to me, the soldier pulled down his duffle bag from the overhead rack and placed it under my feet. With a casual "So long," they disappeared. As soon as Kay became comfortable, he dropped off into sound sleep. A major across the aisle had watched us in that dimmed light while we were being seated, and he kept looking over at sleeping Kay. After a few moments he stood, reached up to the rack over his head, and pulled down a heavy army overcoat. He came across the aisle with the coat, leaned over me and whispered, "Lift the kid a little, and I'll wrap the coat around him. We're going through Wyoming, and it's cold out there." Tears blurred my eyes as I looked up to thank him, but he just smiled back.

Some time later an inebriated young sailor came through the car looking for someone to tell him the meaning of a painted sign in Japanese that he had removed from the entrance of a café in Tokyo. He woke Father up, who translated the ideograph as meaning "closed," and then he stopped at my seat, wanting to start a conversation. The major interrupted, "Sailor, shove off. If you don't we'll put you off the train." As the sailor staggered off and it became quiet, I leaned my head back gratefully. There was talk going on behind me, but very softly. The boys were talking of home, mothers and fathers, pranks out of their school days, sisters and brothers. I thought, we are alike; families came first and were our reason for being. They were from another tree.

When it was morning, the soldiers returned to their seat. I thanked them for their kindness and turned to go back to the restroom to see how Mother was. As I was leaving, the soldier who had offered us his seat called after me, "What about food for the kid?" I said that I did not want to walk through all the cars to the dining car. I had tried when we first boarded the train and found it too difficult to make my way. At noon, the soldier came for a drink of water, and when he saw me, he gave me wrapped sandwiches and a small carton of milk "for the kid." He said that he had three small children at home that he was looking forward to seeing.

We detrained in Chicago, where Roy was waiting for us. As we were leaving the train, I glimpsed the soldier heading out. He turned to look back at the train, and when he saw us he lifted one hand in a civilian salute and disappeared into the crowd. Roy was in uniform too, and Kay looked up proudly at him. We went to a Chinese restaurant for dinner, but Kay was too interested in the people around him to eat. Then came time to take the next train to Cincinnati. Roy took us back to the station and waited to see us off. On the train to Cincinnati, we had seats for each one of us, and Kay fell asleep on my lap once again. I looked down at that sleeping face and thought: Sweet dreams enfold you. When you wake up, we will be in Cincinnati, where we are to stay.

SPRING'S RETURN

Nothing can break me now,
    For you have given me
Belief in spring's return:
    That I shall see

The quince take flame anew;
    Although the frost should come
By stealth, the flower will bloom
    And not be lost.

AFTERWORD

In her essay "Camp Memories: Rough and Broken Shards," Toyo Suyemoto introduced the following poem in this way: "Conjecture and wonderment remained long after my family had moved to Cincinnati, and still more time had to pass before I could write farewell to our internment camp" (qtd. in Daniels, Taylor, and Kitano 1991, 29):

Topaz, Utah

The desert must have claimed its own
Now that the wayfarers are gone,
And silence has replaced voices
Except for intermittent noises,
Like windy footsteps through the dust,
Or gliding of a snake that must
Escape the sun, or sage rustling,
Or soft brush of a quickened wing
Against the air.—Stillness is change
For this abandoned place, where strange
And foreign tongues had routed peace
Until the refugees' release
Restored calm to the wilderness.
The land now sleeps in quietness,
And prairie dogs no longer fear
When shadows shift and disappear.
The crows fly straight through settling dusk,
The desert like an empty husk
Holding the small swift sounds that run
To cover when the day is done.
(May 1947)

REFERENCES

Arkin, Marian, and Barbara Shollar, eds. 1989. *Longman Anthology of World Literature by Women, 1875–1975*. New York: Longman.

Arrington, Leonard J. 1997. *The Price of Prejudice: The Japanese-American Relocation Center in Utah during World War II*. Delta, Utah: Topaz Museum.

Brittain, Vera. 1943. *Humiliation with Honor*. New York: Fellowship Publications.

Chang, Juliana, ed. 1996. *Quiet Fire: A Historical Anthology of Asian American Poetry, 1892–1970*. New York: Asian American Writers' Workshop.

Daniels, Roger, Sandra C. Taylor, and Harry H. L. Kitano, eds. 1991. *Japanese Americans: From Relocation to Redress.* Rev. ed. Seattle: University of Washington Press.

Faderman, Lillian, and Barbara Bradshaw, eds. 1969. *Speaking for Ourselves: American Ethnic Writing*. Glenview, Ill.: Scott, Foresman.

Harth, Erica, ed. 2001. *Last Witnesses: Reflections on the Wartime Internment of Japanese Americans*. New York: Palgrave (St. Martin's Press).

Hass, Robert, and Jessica Fisher, eds. 2004. *The Addison Street Anthology: Berkeley's Poetry Walk*. Berkeley, Calif.: Heyday Books.

Hosokawa, Bill. 1998. *Out of the Frying Pan: Reflections of a Japanese American*. Niwot: University Press of Colorado.

Inada, Lawson Fusao. 1995. "Ghostly Camps, Alien Nation." Books and the Arts Section. *Nation*, August 28–September 4, 204–211.

Inada, Lawson Fusao, ed. 2000. *Only What We Could Carry: The Japanese American Internment Experience*. Berkeley, Calif.: Heyday Books.

Kawakami, Toyo Suyemoto. 1991. "Camp Memories: Rough and Broken Shards." In *Japanese Americans: From Relocation to Redress,* rev. ed., eds. Roger Daniels, Sandra C. Taylor, and Harry H. L. Kitano, 27–30. Seattle: University of Washington Press.

Matsumoto, Valerie. 1991. "Desperately Seeking 'Deirdre': Gender Roles, Multicultural Relations, and Nisei Women Writers of the 1930s." *Frontiers* 12, no. 1: 19–32.

Personal Justice Denied: The Report of the Commission on Wartime Relocation and Internment of Civilians. 1992. Hon. George Miller, Chairman. Washington, D.C.: U.S. Government Printing Office. March. 102nd Congress, 2nd Session.

Rukeyser, Muriel. 1949. *The Life of Poetry.* New York: A. A. Wyn, Current Books.

Schweik, Susan. 1989. "The 'Pre-Poetics' of Internment: The Example of Toyo Suyemoto." *American Literary History* (spring): 89–109.

Stoneburner, Tony, ed. 1964. *Crux* 1, no. 2 (Easter). Ecumenical Campus Staff, University of Michigan.

Streamas, John. 2005. "Toyo Suyemoto, Ansel Adams, and the Landscape of Justice." In *Recovered Legacies: Authority and Identity in Early Asian American Literature,* ed. Keith Lawrence and Floyd Cheung, 141–157. Philadelphia: Temple University Press.

Suyemoto, Toyo. 1934–1935. Scrapbook of West Coast Japanese American newspaper clippings of Nisei writing. In the Suyemoto Special Collection, Ohio State University Libraries, Columbus, Ohio.

———. 1983. "Writing of Poetry." *Amerasia* 10, no. 1: 73–79.

———. 2001. "Another Spring." In *Last Witnesses: Reflections on the Wartime Internment of Japanese Americans,* ed. Erica Harth, 21–34. New York: Palgrave (St. Martin's Press).

———. N.d. "Sidelights: for Contemporary Authors, 33–36 revision." Typewritten sheet in the Suyemoto Special Collection, Ohio State University Libraries, Columbus, Ohio.

Uchida, Yoshiko. 1971. *Journey to Topaz: A Story of the Japanese-American Evacuation.* Berkeley, Calif.: Heyday Books.

U.S. Congress. Civil Liberties Act of 1988. 1988. Public Law No. 100-383, August 10. 102 Stat. 904, 50a.

Whitman, Walt. 1973. *Leaves of Grass.* A Norton Critical Edition. Eds. Sculley Bradley and Harold W. Blodgett. New York: W. W. Norton.

Yamamoto, Hisaye. 1988. "The Legend of Miss Sasagawara." In *Seventeen Syllables and Other Stories,* by Hisaye Yamamoto, 20–33. Latham, N.Y.: Kitchen Table, Women of Color Press.

Yogi, Stan. 1996. "Voices from a Generation Found: The Literary Legacy of Nisei Writers." *Forkroads: A Journal of Ethnic-American Literature* 5 (fall): 64–73.

About the Editor

Susan B. Richardson has taught English literature and English as a second language in several states in the United States and in Istanbul, Turkey. Her special interests include ethnic literature and cross-cultural studies. At Otterbein College in Westerville, Ohio, Professor Richardson directed an English language program for the college's foreign students. Most recently, she was a member of the English Department at Denison University in Granville, Ohio, where she taught courses in Native American literature and Asian American literature. Now retired, she lives in Granville with her husband, Dominick Consolo.